Intelligence and Human Rights in the Era of Global Terrorism

INTELLIGENCE AND HUMAN RIGHTS IN THE ERA OF GLOBAL TERRORISM

Edited by Steve Tsang

STANFORD SECURITY STUDIES
an imprint of Stanford University Press
Stanford, California
2008

Stanford University Press
Stanford, California

First published in paperback in 2008.

Intelligence and Human Rights in the Era of Global Terrorism by Steve Tsang, was
originally published in hardcover by Praeger, an imprint of Greenwood Publishing
Group, Inc., Westport, CT. © 2006 by Steve Tsang. This paperback edition by
arrangement with Greenwood Publishing Group, Inc. All rights reserved.

Library of Congress Cataloging-in-Publication Data

Intelligence and human rights in the era of global terrorism / edited by Steve
Tsang.

p.   cm.

Includes bibliographical references and index.

ISBN 0–275–99251–9 (cl : alk. paper)

ISBN 978-0-8047-5969-4 (pbk : alk. paper)

1. Intelligence service—Moral and ethical aspects.   2. Human rights.
3. Terrorism—Prevention.   I. Tsang, Steve Yui-Sang, 1959– .

JF1525.I6I572   2007

327.12—dc22   2006028572

To Eric Hotung

Contents

Preface and Acknowledgments

When 19 suicide bombers hijacked heavily fueled airliners and flew them into the World Trade Center and the Pentagon on the clear autumn day of September 11, 2001, they ushered in a new era—that of global terrorism. Much has happened since that fateful day. There is a general recognition that the "global war on terror" that American President George W. Bush declared in response to the atrocities should now be seen as a long-term struggle to rid the world of this new curse. In the five-year interval the United States and its allies have twice employed war as an instrument to destroy modern global terrorism. The Iraq War proved at best ineffective or irrelevant and at worst counterproductive for this purpose, though the Afghanistan War managed to reduce significantly al Qaeda's capacity to function as the chief organizer of global terrorism. In light of such experience it is reasonable to conclude that war is not the most effective or suitable instrument to counter global terrorism, particularly in the long-term.

To win the global war on terror the world and the United States in particular need to look elsewhere. They have to rely on good and timely intelligence and on winning hearts and minds generally. Good intelligence will indeed be essential if fresh terrorist attacks are to be preempted and the terrorist organizations—not just al Qaeda but its offshoots and imitators—are to be destroyed on a long-term basis.

Winning the hearts and minds in this context will require considerable effort committed over a long time. The capacity of al Qaeda to take advantage of extremist and fanatical interpretations of certain elements of the Qur'an is predicated on the existence of serious mistrust and misgivings part of the Islamic community in the world has toward the West and the United States. Whatever motivation al Qaeda as an organization had in launching the 2001 attacks, its postattack strategy suggests that it is seeking to induce the Islamic and the non-Islamic worlds to look at their differences in a kind of "clash of civilizations" paradigm. Should democracies respond to the so-called "jihad" by waging a "holy war" against al Qaeda and its like, they will fall straight into the trap al Qaeda laid for them.

The only way that the Western and the democratic world can effectively meet this new challenge is to prove that the modern and democratic way of life does not pit the West or the democracies against people of the Islamic or, for that matter, any other faith. Tolerance, respect for rights and dignity, as well as scope for development of the individual are the hallmarks of secular modern democracy, even though this modern liberal democratic way of life began in Christendom. If this message can reach the potential recruits and supporters of al Qaeda, it may eventually persuade them to shun the appeal of al Qaeda and its imitators. But to do so successfully, democracies must live up to the high standards of their own liberal rhetoric—uphold the ideas of democracy, liberty, and human rights universally rather than selectively and at a time when tightening up on security is necessary. The starting point is for democracies to respect the human rights of persons of the Islamic faith in the same way as they do that of their own citizens.

Trying to find a balance between the need to preempt terrorist attacks of the type staged by al Qaeda and protecting the individual rights of everyone, including terrorist suspects, is a highly delicate matter. To find a way forward that will enable intelligence services to strengthen their capacity to deal with the sectarian-based terrorist threats on the one hand and to enable the Western world to eliminate the appeal of al Qaeda and its message on the other requires a wide range of expertise and knowledge. To address the many intricate issues involved, one would need a real understanding of how intelligence services work, how they can be changed to adapt to meet the new demands more effectively, how they can be kept under political supervision, and how this can be achieved without undermining the rule of law and human rights. The range of specialist knowledge required goes beyond what one scholar or policy maker or experienced intelligence officer can provide.

It was out of this recognition that I have gathered a team of specialists who either have had first-hand experience or have long studied the many different dimensions of relevant issues to work together to produce this book. I was able to put together such a team because of the support of the Pluscarden Program for the Study of Global Terrorism and Intelligence at St Antony's College, Oxford University.

The Program was inaugurated in January 2005, and it granted me the privilege to use its first international conference as a major vehicle to produce this book. This conference, which took place at St Antony's College, Oxford, in December 2005 also received generous support from NATO.

Indeed, the event was officially designated a NATO Advanced Research Workshop. This volume is largely but not exclusively a product of the intellectual discourse that started intensively at the workshop. It is not really a collection of conference papers, excellent as they are, since about a third of the presentations at the workshop are not included in this volume. Indeed, three chapters in this book were commissioned after the workshop to address some vitally important issues that came up in the conference but not adequately addressed there. Nevertheless, contributors who were present at the workshop took advantage of the brainstorming to reflect on their insights before they revised and, in a number of cases, rewrote their papers to produce a coherent and cohesive collaborative book.

As the editor I am most grateful to my colleagues for their good humor, cooperative spirit, and forbearance when they were asked to meet the very tight deadline while fulfilling their many obligations in academic or other professional work as well as other demands on their time in private life. I am not listing their names here as you already know who they are. Without their understanding and cooperation it would have taken much longer for this work to be ready for publication.

In organizing the NATO workshop at Oxford, I am deeply indebted not only to those presenters of papers who are now contributors to this volume but also to all the friends and colleagues who gave presentations, served as discussants, chaired sessions, and more generally shared their insights in two days of intensive intellectual discourse and debate. In this connection I am grateful to Yaacov Amidror, Sokol Axhemi, Ihsan Bal, Sir Roger Bannister, Hans-Josef Beth, William Birtles, Liess Boukra, Andrew Boyd, Harold Carter, Nigel Churton, Thomas Crompton, Michael Cronin, Antonia Diaz, Angela Gendron, Steve Gibson, Roy Giles, Linda Goldthorp, Michael Goodman, Sir Jeremy Greenstock, Sandy Hardie, Nicole Jackson, Peter Jay, Michael Kaser, Janis Kazocins, Jane Knight, Daniel Lafayeedney, Ann Lane, Saideh Lotfian, Fiona MacLeod, Sir Colin McColl, Kaveh Moussavi, Henry Plater-Zyberk, Chris Parry, Fernando Reinares, Harold Shukman, Mohammed Shaker, Richard Skaife, Brian Stewart, Helen Szamuely, Aigerim Toktomatova, Michael Willis, and Sappho Xenakis. I would also like to thank Hassan Aourid, my original co-director for the NATO workshop, for his input and cooperation, though an unexpected call of duty by his King in Morocco meant he could not himself take part in the workshop. Laura James and Mary Sharpe deserve a special note of gratitude as they both gave sterling help and advice in organizing the event at different stages. Without Mary's input this event would not have taken the form of a NATO Advanced Research Workshop. Without Laura the logistics and organization would not have been as smooth and uneventful despite the need to make considerable last-minute changes. In addition, through their work on the Advisory Committee of the Pluscarden Programme, David Johnson,

Alex Pravda, Philip Robins, Robert Service, and Jennifer Welsh offered kind advice and support in preparations for the workshop. Jennifer Griffiths and the staff of St Antony's College provided, as usual, excellent administrative assistance and practical support.

Steve Tsang
Summer 2006

Abbreviations

AIDS	Acquired Immunodeficiency Syndrome
BfV	Bundesamt für Verfassungsschutz (Federal Office for the Protection of the Constitution, Germany)
BND	Bundesnachrichtendienst (Federal Intelligence Service, Germany)
BSE	Bovine Spongiform Encephalopathy
C3I	Command, control, communication, and intelligence
CAT	Convention Against Torture
CFSP	Common Foreign and Security Policy (EU)
CIA	Central Intelligence Agency
DCI	Director of Central Intelligence
D/CIA	Director, Central Intelligence Agency
DNI	Director of National Intelligence
DGSE	Direction Générale de la Sécurité Extérieure (France)
DI	Directorate for Intelligence
DIS	Defence Intelligence Staff (UK)
DG	Director General
DoD	Department of Defense
ETA	Euskadi Ta Askatasuna (Basque)
FARC	Fuerzas Armadas Revolucionarias de Colombia
FBI	Federal Bureau of Investigation
FBIS	Foreign Broadcast Information Service
FISA	Foreign Intelligence Surveillance Act

GCHQ	Government Communications Headquarters (UK)
GTMO/Gitmo	Guantánamo
GLOT	Global Law on Terror
GWOT	Global War on Terror
GTAC	Global Threat Analysis Center
HPSCI	House Permanent Select Committee on Intelligence
HUMINT	Human intelligence
IG	Inspector General
IMINT	Imagery intelligence
IOB	Intelligence Oversight Board
ISC	Intelligence and Security Committee (UK)
ISID	Inter-Services Intelligence Directorate (Pakistan)
JIC	Joint Intelligence Committee (UK)
JARIC	Joint Air Reconnaissance Intelligence Centre (UK)
Jstars	Joint Surveillance Target Attack Radar Systems
JTAC	Joint Terrorism Analysis Centre (UK)
MAD	Militärischer Abschirmdienst" (Military Counterintelligence Service)
MI	Military Intelligence
MI5	The Security Service (UK)
MREs	Meals Ready to Eat
MWD	Military working dog
NGO	Nongovernment organization
NICs	National Intelligence Cells
NIC	National Intelligence Council
NIE	National Intelligence Estimate
NPT	Nonproliferation Treaty
NSC	National Security Council
OGA	Other Government Agency
OSS	Office of Strategic Services
PGM	Precision-guided munitions
PLA	Palestinian Authority
POW	Prisoner of War
PUC	Person Under Control
SARS	Severe Acute Respiratory Syndrome

SAVE	Struggle Against Violent Extremism
SIGINT	Signals Intelligence
SIS	Secret Intelligence Service (UK)
SitCen	Joint Situation Center (EU)
SitCen/CIC	Joint Situation Center/Civilian Intelligence Cell
SSCI	Senate Select Committee on Intelligence
TECH-INT	Technical Intelligence
U21	Universitas 21
UBL	Usama bin Laden
WMD	Weapons of mass destruction
WUN	World-wide Universities Network

1

Stopping Global Terrorism and Protecting Rights

Steve Tsang

Facing the threats posed by dedicated suicide bombers who intend to cause maximum human suffering and casualties in the most eye-catching way, democratic governments have hard choices to make. On the one hand, they must uphold the basic values of democratic societies based on due process and human rights. On the other, they need to preempt the kind of destruction inflicted upon New York, Madrid, London, and Bali—to name only the best-known recent terrorist attacks. These two requirements appear to conflict with each other, as due process requires presumption of innocence with a high standard of proofs being produced before anyone is convicted of a crime, whereas preemption implies acting to foil an attack before it happens or acting against an individual or a group of people before a heinous crime is committed. Striking a balance between these conflicting imperatives is not easy but not impossible, and it is indeed essential if the democratic way of life so highly cherished in Europe, America, and other emerging democratic societies is to be sustained.

SECURITY AND HUMAN RIGHTS

There is an important distinction between common crimes, however heinous they may be, and acts of terrorism, particularly those modeled after the al Qaeda approach (see Chapter 7 by Stearns). Common criminals are driven by a motive to benefit from their exploits and, as a result, can be stopped and arrested in the act or be persuaded to surrender. Suicide bombers dedicated to cause maximum mayhem and casualties indiscriminately can still achieve a large part of their objectives by triggering explosions before getting to their targets and are therefore substantially less susceptible to persuasion. From the perspective of the police or security services, using minimum force to arrest a common criminal in the act of committing an offense is a sensible and responsible way to proceed, but it is not always an option when faced with suicide bombers in the course of carrying out their missions.

The gruesome reality facing government agencies responsible for preempting or stopping horrendous attacks by suicide bombers accounts for the adoption of some methods that affront defenders of human rights. As there is no other way to prevent a wounded suicide bomber from detonating the bomb but to disable him instantly and completely by killing him, a shoot-to-kill policy has been developed and sometimes adopted. While using such a method may indeed preempt major attacks, any mistake that results in the killing of the wrong person, necessarily an innocent one in such a context, cannot but provoke a huge public outcry, as happened in the shooting of the Brazilian Jean Charles de Menezes in London after the July 2005 bombings. What is at issue is more than the protection of human rights, fundamentally important as it is as a matter of principle.

There is a practical dimension that must be given due consideration as well. An accidental shooting of an innocent person in a preemptive operation that went wrong costs the intelligence and security services dearly in terms of credibility and support from the general public. Its long-term cost may outweigh its short-term benefits. Public interest requires a balance being maintained between the imperative of protecting the security of the general public from suicide bombers and the accidental use of lethal force on suspects who turn out to be innocent.

In devising effective countermeasures against terrorism one must not lose sight of what terrorism is about. It is indiscriminate murder on a major scale intended above all to provoke panic and other reactions that can be harnessed to serve the purposes of the perpetuators and/or the masterminds behind the attack. Whether it is panic or other forms of reaction, it is but a means to an end. In the case of al Qaeda its objectives include starting and sustaining a "jihad" against the West led by the United States, for which inflaming public opinions in the Islamic world against the West is essential. Thus, a Western democracy that overreacts to the threats of global terrorism to the extent of breaching the rights of the individuals, willfully or unwittingly, furthers the cause of al Qaeda (see Chapter 8 by Danchev).

In putting this book together my colleagues and I set out to examine and explain critically the problems complicating changes that democratic governments and their intelligence agencies must tackle in order to confront effectively the challenges posed by global terrorism ushered in by the attacks on September 11, 2001. We also seek to put them in the wider context of history and the different political environments that prevail in various democratic countries in how they respond (see Chapters 4, 5, and 6 by Morrison, Johnson, and Heyer, respectively).

The starting premise of this book is that for intelligence organizations to meet the challenges of global terrorism, they must utilize all of their resources effectively and creatively as well as "think outside the box" (see Chapters 10, 11, 12, and 13 by Maior and Huluban, Ben-Israel, Glees, and Aldrich, respectively). These two requirements may appear to conflict with each other in the eyes of professional intelligence officers, as improving efficiency in intelligence agencies first and foremost requires perfecting the tradecraft. Whatever long-term benefits reforms may bring, making changes will almost certainly mean the opposite in the immediate term, as "perfecting the tradecraft" requires fine-tuning techniques developed over a period of time and strict discipline in applying them.

It may be politically expedient for democratically elected politicians to appear to be doing something immediately after a terrorist attack. There is always a temptation for some of them to advocate reforming the intelligence and security services after a catastrophic terrorist attack as such an event appears to imply "intelligence failure" (see Chapters 2 and 3 by Urban and Caravelli, respectively). However, to do so without first examining the implications of any proposed change will reduce the capacity of the services to respond effectively at a time when they need the greatest latitude to respond flexibly and make the most of their tradecraft. It should be recognized that however good the intelligence community may be, it is impossible to preempt all terrorist attacks, as the security services need to be unlucky only on one occasion and the terrorists can score. A successful terrorist attack should therefore not be seen to represent intelligence failure automatically, though it should of course be studied dispassionately to make sure lessons are learned if mistakes were made.

What is really needed is for intelligence and security services to maintain the highest standards of the tradecraft but also devote sufficient resources to cultivate and sustain a capacity to think outside the box on a continuing basis. In other words, the capacity for intelligence and security services to explore and understand new threats should be provided on a routine basis rather than as additional resources to be allocated after a catastrophic terrorist attack or, worse still, as a new demand being imposed on the already overstretched agencies.

Now that the main thrust of the post–Cold War security threats has crystallized clearly intelligence and security agencies must genuinely think outside the box so that they can not only trace and confront, to borrow from Donald Rumsfeld's terms, "the known unknown," but develop a capacity to anticipate "the unknown unknown" of terrorist threats (see Chapter 9 by Wilson). One of the problems that intelligence agencies faced prior to the September 11 (9/11) attacks was how incredulous the plot might have appeared if the al Qaeda plans were known beforehand. Intelligence and security services analysts are, after all, drawn from the societies in which they serve. We are all limited in our capacity to analyze by our own imagination. Prior to 9/11 how many people in the West took seriously a suggestion that 19 foreign individuals had collectively gone to the United States to commit suicide by working in four teams to hijack four airliners so that they could crash them into major landmarks at roughly the same time? If one should find such a scenario fanciful one would probably not have taken traces of intelligence pointing to such a plot sufficiently seriously to preempt the attacks effectively. What intelligence agencies should do is to build up the human capacity to think the "unthinkable." This may require a fundamental rethink of the current practices and an alternative approach in intelligence analysis (see Chapter 11 by Ben-Israel). It may also mean tapping into the wider communities of scholars, journalists, and others who have been trained to understand the mind-set of the terrorists and their organizations through long periods of study or contact with their cultures and religions in order to assess the likely threats more accurately (see Chapters 12 and 13 by Glees and Aldrich, respectively).

This implies that the intelligence and security agencies must be prepared to go beyond their own community as they think outside the box. By benefiting from insights gained by others, they can acquire a greater capacity to anticipate not only the known unknown but the unknown unknown as well. They can also test their ideas against and accept fresh input from policy makers in other government departments, politicians, journalists, and, above all, academics who have the leisure to take a longer-term perspective and immerse themselves in the study of a highly specialized subject. Stopping and catching terrorists before they strike wins a battle; but to win the war, it is essential to remove the threat of global terrorism as a whole. Such a victory requires more than continuously winning battles on the ground—even if that were possible. It can be achieved only when the intelligence services work in cooperation with others.

Meeting the challenges posed by global terrorism unleashed by al Qaeda requires different responses to conventional conflicts. It ought to be recognized that al Qaeda poses two different threats. One is organized and coordinated by itself and is directed against both the Western world with the United States as its main focus as well as the Middle East with Saudi Arabia as the big prize (see Chapter 7 by Stearns). Countering this is primarily a task for the intelligence and security agencies, but in light of the military forces al Qaeda and its supporters like the Taliban are capable of deploying, they will need to call on the military to help. But the other threat is not any less serious. It is based on the reality that al Qaeda also functions like a "franchise holder" willing to offer free help, advice, and assistance to others resorting to terrorist means to undermine the dominance of the Western democratic and capitalistic way of life. Meeting the latter challenge will need a more imaginative and political response.

To overcome the wider political and terrorist challenges posed by al Qaeda's "free franchising" it is not enough to trace down and arrest the key leaders of al Qaeda and prosecute them in a court of law, however valuable breaking down the organization itself is in limiting its own capacity to attack. As Richard G. Stearns explains (Chapter 7), much of this "franchising" by al Qaeda is conducted for free on the Internet, and variants of this will survive even after the demise of al Qaeda itself.

What is really needed is to secure the peace in this "war on terror" so that there will not be ready takers for the "free franchises" offered by al Qaeda. Winning the hearts and minds of the terrorist organizations' pool of potential recruits will be essential to cut off the supply of suicide bombers (see Chapter 8 by Danchev). This means the United States and the democratic world must actively engage the Islamic people of the world including the fundamentalist elements, in the Middle East and Central and South Asia in particular, listen to their grievances, and persuade them that the Islamic and Christian civilizations are not set on a collision course. Copycat attacks based on al Qaeda ideas, instigation, or methods cannot be stopped unless and until the potential recruits of suicide bombers can be convinced that there really is no point in their sacrifice or that there are alternative channels for them to seek redress of their grievances—and more effectively.

In the world of global terrorism inspired by al Qaeda the issues of enhancing security through better intelligence and protecting human rights everywhere are not mutually exclusive. On the contrary, they must be made to complement each other. The strengthening of the capacity of the intelligence and security agencies to deal with immediate threats is indeed essential in the short-term. However, winning the arguments against extremists, at the moment primarily among people of the Islamic faith, can be achieved only if the potential recruits for suicide bombing missions realize that the governments of their target countries respect their rights and dignity as individuals as much as that of their own citizens. Such an approach will be exploited by the determined terrorists in the short-term, but winning the war on terror requires above all stopping a new generation from feeling it has a cause for which its members would be willing to give up their lives. In operational terms it means that responses against terrorist attacks or planned attacks must be carefully thought through beforehand, and the security services and police tasked to respond must be trained and indoctrinated to respect human rights as they carry out their duties and make hard decisions in the most stressful conditions. Otherwise, winning battles against terrorist attacks will not produce a long-lasting victory in the war against the al Qaeda brand of global terrorism.

The support and cooperation of the people in countries that fall victim to terrorist attacks must also be sustained by ensuring they have confidence in the government and intelligence services. This is no less a delicate issue than engaging ordinary people in the Middle East, Central Asia, and certain parts of Africa. A particularly difficult challenge presented by the London bombings of July 2005 is their potential to provoke sectarian responses from the majority population against their fellow citizens of the Islamic faith, a tiny number of whom had become suicide bombers. Whether this was the original intention of the bombers or of their al Qaeda inspirer, such a response from the general public could easily start a vicious circle of escalating mutual hatred and violence. In 2005 the British public as a whole reacted in their best liberal tradition and generally avoided sectarian responses. But some individual sectarian reactions did happen, and the prospect of a more general sectarian backlash cannot be ruled out and must be prevented. To do so, the government and its intelligence services must not become so focused on preempting terrorist attacks that they infringe upon the rights of some of their citizens and encroach on the democratic norms, and they must also reassure the general public that the presence of a handful of suicide bombers does not mean Britons of the Islamic faith cannot be trusted.

This book therefore addresses not only the question of how intelligence organizations can improve their efficacy in preempting terrorist outrages, but also the wider issue of removing the forces that sustain global terrorism as a scourge of the twenty-first century. In the latter effort, intelligence organizations must work with their governments to address two parallel political priorities. The first is to remove the wider social, religious, economic, and ethnic conditions that enable groups like al Qaeda, its offshoots, and imitators to entrench or regenerate themselves by recruiting new generations of leaders, agents, and suicide bombers. As the July 2005 bombings in London confirm, the problem extends beyond the various Middle Eastern countries and failed states traditionally seen as recruiting grounds for global terrorists. Young people born or brought up in the democratic and affluent West are also susceptible. This problem is closely linked to the second priority: namely, the need for democratic governments and their intelligence communities to ensure that, in tackling the threats from global terrorists, they do not lose credibility and confidence among their own citizens.

In the end, in order to prevail over global terrorism, police and intelligence services must enhance their capabilities to deal with the immediate security challenges. The general public in the target countries and recruiting grounds must also be persuaded that—despite their rhetoric—the terrorists are not engaged in a holy war. Ultimately, the brand of global terrorism promoted by Osama bin Laden and his associates is meant to satisfy their own vanity and aspirations toward semidivine status. The organization they have formed for this purpose is above all a global syndicate that commits serious crimes of a particularly heinous nature, which seeks to cause maximum damage by giving free advice, encouragement, and guidance as if it were a franchising operation. Intelligence services of various countries need to find convincing evidence to prove or, should the case be so, disprove this. But it is up to governments, civil society, and the media in different parts of the world to work together if the evidence unearthed by national intelligence services and others is to be accepted by the general public. Unless the emotional and quasireligious appeal of the global terrorists can be removed, the simple arrest of bin Laden and his close associates—or even the destruction of al Qaeda as an organization—will not be sufficient to prevent others rising to replace them.

To eradicate the al Qaeda brand of global terrorism, Western governments must seize and hold the moral high ground. To preempt individuals from becoming recruits or potential recruits for suicide bombing missions, Western governments have to demonstrate convincingly to communities from where such bombers are drawn that they uphold and respect the human rights of the latter to the same standards as that of mainstream Americans and Europeans.

For this purpose the U.S. government must recognize that while its categorization of people captured in Afghanistan and kept at Guantánamo Bay as unlawful combatants may be technically correct under international law (see Chapter 7 by Stearns), its maintenance of the Guantánamo facility weakens its moral case in the fight against terrorism as it widely offends opinions around the world. Even though the detention and debriefing of the unlawful combatants immediately after their capture could be justified on the grounds that as unlawful combatants they were not entitled to enjoy the privileges accorded to prisoners of war, and information thus acquired would be essential to preempt further terrorist attacks, the latter factor no longer applies. In any event their human rights must still be respected. Those who had committed criminal offenses should be brought in front of the criminal justice system. Those who cannot be released because, for example, they declare their commitment to kill Americans randomly if freed should be detained with the real reasons disclosed and on the basis of proper legal provisions—if the proper legal power for meeting the exceptional situation does not exist, it should be duly enacted with built-in limitations to avoid it being abused. Those who were detained by mistake as they happened to be at the wrong place and at the wrong time should be released.

The continued detention of unlawful combatants without an explanation that the rest of the world can understand and accept is counterproductive. Those detainees who have committed crimes as unlawful combatants should be revealed as such and treated as such, but even then their rights as individuals should be respected, in the same way that the human rights of common criminals are upheld. Terrorists and masterminds of terrorism are but particularly callous and pernicious criminals. Treating them in any other way, such as incarceration in conditions open to question, merely provides grounds for people who feel a strong sense of grievance against or mistrust of the United States to choose to see and portray them as POWs wrongly treated, jihadists, or heroes or victims of some description. The West and in particular the United States cannot maintain the moral high ground, unless they can eliminate the basis for al Qaeda to replenish its ranks or to inspire imitators.

POLITICAL CONTEXT FOR THE CHANGING FACE OF INTELLIGENCE

The intelligence communities in the democratic world entered a period of uncertainty and change when the Cold War ended, as the long accepted rationale for their existence and paradigm for their operations were removed. Different countries responded to the end of the Cold War differently, but none felt they could dispense with the service of their intelligence and security services.

As Mark Urban examines in Chapter 2, the British intelligence community went through different stages of change to seek a proper place and role for itself in the post–Cold War context before it found itself at the forefront tackling the new challenges posed by the al Qaeda brand of terrorism. From the transition of the Cold War confrontation in the late 1980s to the catastrophic attacks on the United States mainland in 2001, the British intelligence and security services had greatly improved on transparency, but they had not been sufficiently reoriented to preempt the new threats. In facing what appears like a confrontation between certain extremist segments of the Islamic world and the democratic and materialistic West descended from Christendom, the central issue for the intelligence community has come to reflect the wider political debate of the time. It is one of idealism versus *realpolitik* or human rights versus realism in how to confront the threats posed by transnational terrorism. Urban rightly concludes that recent controversies over alleged failures that involve the intelligence community have made it even more important for the community to continue to move forward toward greater openness than that achieved in the 1990s.

The most dramatic organizational changes in the U.S. intelligence community since the Central Intelligence Agency (CIA) was founded at the onset of the Cold War happened in response to the implied failings of the intelligence community to preempt the 9/11 attacks. While many of these changes are still under way and are highlighted by Jack Caravelli (Chapter 3), whether they are changing the face of American intelligence in the "right" way remains to be tested. Using the Iranian nuclear program as the anchor, Caravelli has shown that the failure to stop the Iranian program in the 1990s was more a political than an intelligence one. In facing the terrorism threats posed by certain Islamic fundamentalists, one should not focus entirely on the al Qaeda brand of terrorism and lose sight of the challenges posed by others, such as the Iranian nuclear program. There may not be a direct link between the two, but one must take into account the reality that the old Cold War concept of Mutually Assured Destruction as a paradigm for peace no longer applies, at least in so far as an extremist Islamic fundamentalist group or government that can lay its hands on nuclear weapons is concerned. The challenges facing the American intelligence community is to provide timely, reliable, and accurate intelligence on all the major potential sources of threats to policy makers and military commanders so that they have the necessary information to ensure security and people's safety.

The ever greater need for the intelligence agencies in the democratic world to improve their capabilities and efficacy means that it is even more important that the appropriate form of political supervision or oversight is put in place. Indeed, one should heed John N.L. Morrison's admonition in Chapter 4 that a robust system of oversight is required not just for the intelligence community but for the political machinery that uses intelligence as well. As the Iraqi Weapons of Mass Destruction (WMD) dossier case reveals, even in the most mature of democracies, where the top political leaders believe passionately in a course of action, it is not beyond them to ensure intelligence and facts are "fixed around the policy" and can be used to provide justification for their preferred policy option, in this case, war to effect a regime change in Iraq. As Morrison reminds everyone, there is as yet no perfect system of political supervision of intelligence services and every country must develop and fine-tune its own system.

Morrison's thoughtful insights based primarily on the British experience are echoed in Loch K. Johnson's majestic survey in Chapter 5 of how Congressional oversight evolved in the United States. The old *laissez faire* approach might have been abandoned as far back as 1975 as CIA abuses came to light, but the essentially reactive nature in the subsequent strengthening of the oversight apparatus still left scope for improvement. By the start of the twenty-first century the United States might already have one of the best systems for legislative oversight of intelligence, but it still fell short on issues of great importance. It did, for example, on the intelligence community's assessment of the Iraqi WMD issue, one that affected the decision to go to war. The limits in Congressional oversight indeed show remarkable parallel to the British experience. Ultimately the effectiveness of legislative oversight depends hugely on how strongly motivated members of Congress are in pursuing this cause. Even if this is assured, in the case of the United States truly comprehensive oversight of the intelligence community will not be achieved until the relevant Congressional committees can cover effectively also the intelligence operations of the Department of Defense, which in fact spends the lion's share of the American intelligence budget.

This makes a contrast to the approach in Germany where the Bundestag's Control Panel on Intelligence has the power and the responsibility, enshrined in the Federal Constitution, for both the civilian and the military intelligence agencies. As Christian Heyer explains succinctly in Chapter 6, Germany has adopted a different approach than Britain and the United States. It is one that puts greater emphasis on the protection of individual rights on the one hand, and it requires the overseers to work closely with the intelligence services on the other. The German approach to striking a balance between security and the protection of rights was to give the parliamentary Control Panel and its offshoot, known as the G10 Commission, constitutionally guaranteed access to confidential information, and the requirement to maintain confidentiality. There is no doubt that both bodies are meant first and foremost to protect rights and to ensure the intelligence services do not abuse their power and permission to operate in secret. However, their commitment to maintaining secrecy in order not to compromise the efficacy of the intelligence agencies is also real. An insider, Heyer is confident that the German system has so far worked well though there is room for improvement. Whether the German system works as well as Heyer suggests, and whether the inherently conflicting demands being put on the oversight bodies can genuinely be reconciled satisfactorily in practice in the long-term, it is something that the British and the Americans can and should study as they reflect on how best to improve their own systems.

The context in which intelligence services in democratic countries must operate in is not just political but judicial as well. It also cannot be divorced from the nature of the threats against which they are required to confront. To understand what would constitute an appropriate legal framework for dealing with terrorists of the al Qaeda brand one must first inquire into the nature of the threats they pose. Thus, in his judicious assessment (Chapter 7), Richard G. Stearns starts off by examining what modern global terrorism means and why the threats al Qaeda poses are different from those of various secessionist terrorist groups like the Irish Republican Army or anarchist groups like Bader-Meinhof, not to say delusional cults like Branch Davidians. To put matters in perspective we need to recognize that the al Qaeda approach to terrorism as directed by bin Laden is not only a decidedly rational and calculating one, but is also practically global in its ambition and intended to cause destruction of such a magnitude that no comparison can be found in history. Indeed, while al Qaeda has so far merely demonstrated the capacity to use conventional technologies creatively in producing their WMD, it is the only nonstate actor that is actively seeking to acquire in the black market nuclear materials that can be used in a "dirty bomb." The gravity of the threats posed by al Qaeda is such that countering it would require an element of preemption but this should not, at least not as a rule, be at the expense of the rule of law. Admittedly, sticking strictly to the rule of law when confronting the al Qaeda threats may not always be possible and has its problems, as revealed in the trial of Zacarias Moussaoui; accepting a long-term retreat of the rule of law must be rejected as an option. What the United States may need to do is to consider the alternative approaches adopted in various European countries for dealing with the trial of terrorists, such as the introduction of the Diplock courts in Northern Ireland.

Putting matters in its widest context, there is no alternative to upholding human rights when confronting the threats from modern global terrorists. Alex Danchev (Chapter 8) finds echoes of Kafka in Guantánamo and Abu Ghraib in the dehumanizing treatment of detainees. In his poignant examination of some of the better-known cases of abuses in order to secure "actionable intelligence," he highlights such degrading practices corrode our own values and are completely counterproductive. Some information obtained under torture might in principle have helped to prevent an attack here or there, but most detainees had little more than out-of-date information. There is no convincing evidence that the information thus obtained actually preempted any major terrorist attacks. In any event the sorry record of Guantánamo and the grotesque abuses at Abu Ghraib caused so much damage to the reputation of the United States that its claim to moral righteousness in the war on terror was gravely compromised if not utterly destroyed. It matters as the United States and its allies are supposed to be an alliance of values, and one that is vastly superior to what al Qaeda and its offshoots represent. By succumbing to the "9/11 syndrome," or resorting to harsh methods or outright torture in interrogation in order to get information to deal with the challenges posed by a despicable and fanatical foe, the Bush administration has gravely undermined the capacity of the United States, and by association much of the rest of the Western world closely allied to it, in the campaign to win over opinion in the Islamic world. The negative worldwide reactions to Abu Ghraib and Guantánamo have the unintended effect of helping al Qaeda expand its influence in Islamic communities worldwide and undermining the U.S. position in the global war on terror.

MEETING THE NEW DEMANDS

The advent of the era of global terrorism might not have been accurately predicted and preempted, but it does not mean the intelligence communities, at least in the mature Western democracies, had not been continuously changing to meet what they saw as new threats after the end of the Cold War. Indeed, as Peter Wilson makes clear in Chapter 9, the contrary is true. Western intelligence agencies started to develop techniques and structures to deal with transnational terrorist and criminal threats that distinguish themselves from the highly centralized challenges posed by the Soviet bloc during the Cold War even before the 9/11 attacks. But the tempo of change quickened dramatically after September 2001. In adapting themselves to counter the new threats, the intelligence services must develop whatever necessary to defeat the al Qaeda brand of terrorism, but they must also keep an eye on what may be the next surprise lurking on the horizon. This requires not only improvements in efficiency, developing wider professional skills, improving accountability, and promoting innovations within the agencies, but also liaising with the outside world. While the work of the intelligence services must be kept secret, its analytical elements can benefit greatly from independent research conducted by academics or other experts outside of the intelligence community on a wide range of issues that may reveal from where the next surprise may come. The last is particularly important if the intelligence services are to deal effectively with the unknown unknown in addition to the known unknown.

The changes that the intelligence community must pursue in the face of new threats inevitably raise the issue of the allocation of resources. In addressing this issue, George Maior and Sebastian Huluban (Chapter 10) remind us that much of this is of course about the use of money, but it is above all about planning. Maior and Huluban in fact take a slightly different view from Wilson on how much the intelligence communities of the West had changed between the end of the Cold War and the 9/11 attacks. However, this reflects more a difference in how they evaluate the varying tempo of changes both before and after 9/11 than what happened on the ground. They see the post-9/11 changes as much greater than Wilson does, which means that it is, for them, even more important that the intelligence community should allocate their resources efficiently and sensibly. With this in mind they stress in particular the importance of developing human resources to the full and the benefits the intelligence community can gain by borrowing methodologies and ideas developed in other disciplines, particularly but not exclusively in the social sciences. They also highlight the value of widening the context when the intelligence community takes on the issue of resource allocation in the fight against global terrorism.

Given the gravity of the threats posed by global terrorism and evidence of some specific and significant failings in intelligence in recent years, the intelligence community is well advised to subject its standard tradecraft to review. A veteran intelligence officer who has moved to academe, Isaac Ben-Israel provides a thought-provoking alternative to the existing approach to intelligence analysis in Chapter 11. Instead of induction and seeking collaborative evidence to support one's hypothesis in analysis, Ben-Israel advocates the search of counterevidence to test and eliminate hypotheses. This should help to minimize, if not remove, the inherent human tendency to find evidences to prove one's pet theory or preconceptions. It may not be foolproof, but it provides a much more reliable basis for analysts to draw conclusions and assess the real threat. He also urges a rethink over the classic separation between the roles of analysts and field operators, as modern terrorists operate in a highly dynamic and rapidly changing environment, and there is usually only a very short span of opportunity for the intelligence or security services to move against a terrorist who has been located. To be effective against modern terrorism, intelligence and security services must build up their capacity to react to or act on intelligence at hand adroitly and swiftly. What Ben-Israel has proposed goes against the long-established practices in the intelligence world, but deserves careful consideration.

Enhancing the general capabilities and capacity of the intelligence community to deal with the new transnational threats involves, needless to say, more than improving or even overhauling the way analysts should work. It requires the intelligence community to explore and, where appropriate, establish effective working relations with their counterparts overseas. In Chapter 12 Anthony Glees focuses on what the British intelligence services, particularly the Security Service or MI5, have done and examined by way of extending cooperation with other European Union agencies since the 9/11 attacks. It has not been a straightforward matter as Britain also cooperates closely with the United States, which is skeptical of sharing intelligence with some of the agencies in other European Union countries. Glees suggests a way out of this tension, which is to strengthen cooperation and increase sharing of intelligence assessments though not raw intelligence or sources. He also echoes an important point already raised by Peter Wilson—the potential value that the intelligence community can get by reaching out to the academic community.

The value for getting academe actively involved is examined in greater details in the thoughtful analysis of Richard J. Aldrich (Chapter 13). He reminds everyone that serious as the threats of modern global terrorism are they will cause less damage, destruction, and casualty than some other threats that come with globalization itself, such as various forms of "bio-risk." No one will benefit if the world should get too focused on modern terrorism and fail to spot and meet effectively the other more lethal challenges. A new pandemic, for example, respects no national borders and can kill far more people than any terrorist attack, and it is a classical global problem that cannot be tackled by any one government alone. Such problems and threats, as well as challenges posed by the al Qaeda brand of terrorism, are created by globalization and need to be monitored and understood beyond what intelligence services on their own can hope to do. What Aldrich thinks is needed is the founding of something like a Global Threat Analysis Center, which can be co-located or even be part of a world-class research university, but should develop a network with universities and other institutions all over the world on the one hand and liaise closely with the intelligence community on the other. Such a center will rely on open sources for information and benefit from dynamic exchanges with the world's best specialists on whatever subjects that can enhance the understanding of an emerging threat whatever its nature. It will maintain its independence in analysis and will not be susceptible to the problem of "groupthink" in the intelligence community as it will not be a part of the intelligence community. Nevertheless, as it will be founded specifically to enhance national and global security and be available as a resource to the intelligence community, it will work with the intelligence community. Together they can acquire a capacity hitherto unavailable to anyone and tremendously improve the world's scope to understand and anticipate the unknown unknown challenges that globalization will bring.

Part I: Identifying and Rectifying Inadequacies

2

The British Quest for Transparency

Mark Urban

All of us like the romance and mystery contained in the notion of a "quest." It hints of an epic odyssey, a real *Lord of the Rings* trilogy full of vicissitudes, hardship, and disappointment. And certainly the struggle by journalists, parliamentarians, or simply interested members of the public to understand the work of our intelligence community has seemed over the past 20 years like a search for a Holy Grail of openness.

The product at the heart of intelligence—be it agent reports or raw signals intelligence—is a mystery into which those outside the secret priesthood can never fully be initiated. From the perspective of journalist or contemporary historian this must be accepted. Some think this essential limitation makes our quest as pointless as a search for El Dorado. Undoubtedly many people inside the agencies think that way, as do conspiracy-addicted bloggers hashing over the week's news in cyberspace. Intelligence though is simply one of many areas of life where the journalist can never know all the facts, just like organized crime, the divorces of Hollywood stars, or even benefit fraud. The mission of journalists must therefore be to undertake the quest in the same spirit for MI5 (the British Security Service) or GCHQ (Government Communications Headquarters, the electronic eavesdropping and security organization) that we would for any other story—with a commitment to trying to unearth the truth and report objectively, and an understanding that these ideals—truth and objectivity—are the nirvana of journalists, a state of enlightenment to be strived for but never fully attained.

In charting the quest in which I and quite a few others have been embarked over the past 20 years, I would say, we have experienced three distinct periods: the Cold War, the absence of war, and the culture wars. The Cold War of course started shortly after the end of the Second World War, but for the purposes of this discussion I am really focusing on the period between 1985 and 1991. The confused period that followed, in which nobody knew where threats might come from or what to do about them, stretched from 1991 to 2001. As for the period of the culture wars, that is the clash of identity, basically religious, that has defined so much ever since. In the best Tolkien style then we have a trilogy, but one which I will attempt to outline in rather fewer pages than were available to that master storyteller.

COLD WAR

The year 1985 is a good point to begin this because it marks the arrival of Mikhail Gorbachev and the beginning of the end. Any debate between intelligence "insiders" and "outsiders" was defined very largely at this time by class politics. The activities of MI6 (the British Secret Intelligence Service) in fighting proxy wars through coups in the Middle East or of MI5 in battling what it defined as subversion at home had poisoned the attitude of broad sections of the left toward those services.

So it was that Roy Hattersley, speaking in the House of Commons in 1988 derided MI5 as "one of the worst and most ridiculed services in the western alliance."[1] When one remembers that he was Shadow Home Secretary at the time, one has an idea of how far we were from any kind of national consensus about what these agencies should do for the country and how open they should be.

Views in those days were very largely colored by fiction. The salient feature of this climate was that both left and right chose to overestimate the reach and effectiveness of our espionage agencies. The left had to think that British spies were busy assassinating people in order to fuel their outrage at such services being out of control and unaccountable. The right, embodied by Margaret Thatcher of course, had to think it was achieving amazing things in secret in order to justify her policy of not saying anything at all about them. We know now that the agencies had successes in the Cold War—but equally that they did not achieve top-level penetrations—for example, in the Central Committee of the Communist Party or eavesdrop electronically on the Politburo's communications network.

Nevertheless, people were desperate to believe that there was more to it than that. The mutual desire of left and right to inflate the importance of intelligence work and mystify its practitioners came together in the battle over the book *Spycatcher,* the story of a far-right reactionary in MI5—Peter Wright—as written by Paul Greengrass, a card-carrying leftie from the

World in Action television team.[2] They had a mutual interest in pushing the idea that some officers within MI5 conspired to ruin the Labor Party leader Harold Wilson's chances in the 1974 election by leaking the allegation that he might be a Soviet spy. It was sensational—too much so to withstand close examination.

These "revelations," together with the rather more prosaic but believable accusations made by Cathy Massiter in her TV documentary about MI5 produced, however, a groundswell for change.[3]

Some far-sighted people at the Security Service—namely Tony Duff and Patrick Walker—were looking beyond Cold War class-based Punch and Judy to redefine their relationship with society. In time an avowal, placing MI5 on a proper legal footing, became a key part of this. Initially though it consisted of discrete briefings to the press. Tony Duff initially did this through his Legal Adviser, but later, for example, three of my colleagues from the newly launched *Independent* newspaper were entertained to lunch by Patrick Walker at Gower Street.

I well remember their flushed excitement as they spilled out of the taxi. The three journalists concerned were all what you might call members of the liberal left, but they had been inspired by the Director General's message that he wanted to turn MI5 into an open, accountable service, with its phone number in the Yellow Pages and a public profile like that of the American Federal Bureau of Investigation.

Inevitably there was a backlash from those who preferred not to lift the mantle of secrecy. *Private Eye* liked to single out certain journalists as the recipients of such briefings and to imply that they were betraying their journalistic integrity. Those of us covering national security issues who felt that our duty to talk to spies was no different from that of education correspondents to talk to teachers had to get used to the newsroom barbs about being "spooks" or being in the pockets of MI5 or MI6.

The taunts of hacks not involved could not stop what was happening. Prime Minister Thatcher, however, could and did. She was reportedly "incandescent" when she found out about MI5's activities and ordered them stopped. Her conviction that nothing should ever be said about the intelligence services led to a series of bruising political battles: the banning of unions at GCHQ, attempts to prevent the publication of *Spycatcher,* and the banning of a BBC program on *ZIRCON,* Britain's proposed spy satellite.

Even so, as the Security Service Act went through Parliament in 1989 first important steps had been taken. The legislation created a limited kind of oversight of MI5. The organization had begun to transform itself, defining terrorism and organized crime as future missions and discretely telling the press what it was doing. In this way, directors general of the Security Service began undermining the old class-based interpretation of intelligence.

Reform though was only in its infancy at the end of the 1980s. The foreign intelligence gathering agencies had not yet begun to overhaul themselves—and because of this, they were vulnerable to cuts because many in Parliament or the wider public associated them with the Cold War.

In Downing Street, the old mentality could not really be buried until Thatcher departed from Downing Street in November 1990 and the August 1991 coup in Moscow finally put an end to Soviet communism, or what was left of it.

ABSENCE OF WAR

It might seem odd to describe the period of Somalia, Bosnia, and Kosovo as one in which there was an absence of war, but the 1990s were nevertheless a time in which the old concept of Cold War had died, and there was an absence of any similar division or confrontation.

The argument "what are intelligence agencies for?" broke out vociferously in America one or two years before it reached Britain. Some advocated the idea that secret intelligence should be used to enhance economic competitiveness. Others looked for a new enemy—was it China or Iran? Was it something transnational, the "war on drugs," or, of course, terrorism?

There was a subtext of course to all this casting around for missions—the threat of budgetary cuts. A few brave souls—and I can remember the Chief of Defense Intelligence making this argument to me—suggested at that time, the uncertainties required more spending on intelligence, not less. The argument held water intellectually, but was politically impossible.

In Britain, the budgetary pressure finally built in 1993, to the point where cuts were made in the intelligence agencies. The time of troubles coincided, surprise, surprise, with an unprecedented period of briefing by MI5 and MI6. The departure of Thatcher meant that the Security Service was free to resume press and parliamentary contacts, lobbying for work on organized crime and, eventually with much greater success, for the leadership of the campaign against Irish Republican Army terrorism in Britain.

As for MI6, its agents stressed that they had become freer to talk because of the forthcoming Intelligence Services Act, legislation that would put their service and GCHQ on a statutory footing in much the same way that had happened four years earlier with MI5. Like its sister service, MI6 stressed its capabilities to help government on a broad range of "global tasks."

Personalities were important in this period, too: Director General (DG) Stella Rimington at MI5 and Chief Colin McColl at MI6 proved articulate, passionate advocates for their services and also believers in greater openness.

The DG began giving public lectures as well as briefing certain outsiders. The Chief of MI6 managed to outdo her when he appeared at a press conference in November 1993 at the Foreign Office. This memorable occasion—the Director of GCHQ was on stage, too—marked the formal launch of the Intelligence Service legislation. Colin McColl conceded the budgetary pressure facing his service, saying, "we are having a difficult time."

The press conference marked in some ways a high-water mark for openness. Certainly I cannot think of an occasion before or since where heads of the British espionage agencies were made available for questioning by the press on the record.

Many in Whitehall were undoubtedly afraid that things would "go too far," and indeed they were right in one particular: the assumption that the refusal of most of those who briefed the press to discuss operational matters would eventually be undermined. This happened in more recent years, but let us not get ahead of ourselves. Looking back to that balmy moment of openness in the Foreign Office press suite back in 1993, it was interesting to recall how the spymasters tried to make their arguments while remaining behind a symbolic curtain of secrecy—for while the discussion took place on the record, there were to be no pictures.

The Chief of MI6 explained that the publication of his photo might send a disastrous message to his sources overseas, and he reassured them, "[W]e are not going to open up our files, we are not going to allow ourselves to be undressed in public." To our editors, and I suspect readers, though we had reached a point where the undressing, if not public, could certainly be glimpsed through a keyhole of openness and the more we saw, the less sexy we found it. That was just fine to some of those intelligence professionals, emerging from the stresses and strains of the Thatcher years. One of MI6's directors remarked to me, as that press conference ended, "[M]y definition of success would be to call a press conference to which you would all be too bored to come."

Personally, I did not have a problem with this, in that I felt a more informed climate of debate about the qualities and limitations of British intelligence was something to be welcomed—certainly it was good to leave behind Cold War paranoia, of left or right, with all the distortions that involved in the reporting of intelligence matters.

The absence of war of the 1990s was, in terms of the argument about transparency, an absence of conflict within our society about the purpose or morality of intelligence work.

In the late 1990s pressure for greater openness had abated somewhat, along with pressure for further cuts in agency budgets. The climate was also influenced by there being different personalities at the head of the agencies.

At MI6 it was apparently decided that too much had been said in the mid-1990s and that, "mystery was good for recruitment." The MI5, meanwhile, was run by a Director General who told me at an academic event that he could not spare officers to answer "Tom Fool questions from journalists."

Oversight was in place in the form of the Parliamentary Intelligence Services Committee, and its early reports were sufficiently anodyne to send many a news editor to sleep. Internally, meanwhile, MI6's Director of Counter Intelligence and Security was redesignated Director of Security and Public Affairs, and MI5 took its external relations people into its "Corporate Affairs" branch.

One interesting measure of how much things had changed was the treatment given to intelligence whistle-blowers by society more widely. During the Cold War, some dissidents within the intelligence services had enjoyed considerable impact. Cathy Massiter's revelations about MI5 bugging brought legal challenges from two of those who had been tapped, events which accelerated considerably the need to bring that organization out of its legal "grey area" and to be put on a proper statutory footing.

During the mid-1990s though, I found, having made a *Panorama* program about David Shayler's allegations, that my friends and family generally expressed little sympathy for him. Indeed, as a former MI5 officer who had gone public, Shayler was successfully prosecuted under the Official Secrets Act, without public outcry.[4]

The seeds though of a change in attitude were germinating throughout the late 1990s. Although intelligence had become less sexy, it was about to become enmeshed in a wider battle within our society—between those who believed human rights and tolerance should take a central place in our struggle for security and those who believed that a "back to the future" world of religious or ethnic hatreds required a return to *realpolitik*.

Battle lines for a new ideological schism were being drawn as early as the mid-1990s. The murder of 7,500 people in Srebrenica in 1995 influenced many who wanted to place human rights and legality at the center of foreign policy.

On the other side of the divide, Samuel Huntingdon had, by 1993, published his "Clash of Civilizations?" thesis, baldly placing age-old religious or cultural differences back at the center of the foreign policy debate.[5]

The relevance to the intelligence debate of these differences in perspective really became apparent only after the 9/11 terrorist attacks.

CULTURE WARS

In discussing the climate for transparency and debate about intelligence work, the emergence of this dynamic is important because it heralded a new cleavage within society about how those agencies were perceived and what should be expected from them. This divide is, in my view, every bit as deeply held as the old left/right schism about espionage and informs much of the current debate about how much we need to know.

The division now is not left and right. It has more resemblance to the old Whig and Tory. It is about idealism versus *realpolitik*. We might call the two tribes "human rightists" and "reality checkists," and certainly some of the idealists are Tories and many of those who say they have taken a "reality check" are Labor Blairites.

Our debate then is now polarized again. The difference between now and the Cold War is that whereas the old left and right tended to overestimate the efficacy and reach of espionage, the new commentators often believe that the agencies are ineffective or suspect.

Human rightists see them as ineffective, producing politically colored assessment and falling in too easily with those who stand to gain from exaggerating the threat to Western societies. To them the Iraq dossier was just spin, the "tanks at Heathrow" terror alert simply a piece of political theater.

Their opponents in the current debate also tend to feel that the intelligence agencies cannot add much to our security, but tend to believe that this is because they have been emasculated. Reality checkists therefore tend to be enthusiastic about extended police antiterrorist powers and would like Britain to adopt tougher tactics—arguing either for French-style detention without trial or the American model of rendition of suspects.

This cleavage came to a head as the United States unleashed its military campaign against the Taliban. One definite symptom of it was the British government decision to publish a paper about Osama bin Laden's responsibility for the attacks.

Such an exercise—the first British government dossier of declassified material—was an early installment of the "realists" trying to convince the public that the skeptics were wrong. It began with a preamble noting "this document does not purport to provide a prosecutable case...intelligence often cannot be used as evidence...but on the basis of all the information available HMG is confident of its conclusions."[6]

As the White House followed its campaign in Afghanistan with a drive to put Iraq in the international dock, the use of intelligence became more comprehensive and controversial. The British government dossier of September 2002 was essentially a Joint Intelligence Committee (JIC) assessment bolted together with some historical background and political messages. It went much further in length and scope than the earlier bin Laden document.

At the same time—between 9/11 and September 2002—when JIC assessments were put out for public consumption, it was also a busy period of briefing by the agencies on terrorism and weapons of mass destruction. I do not intend to break confidences, or be too specific, but I will say that this period was characterized by the emergence of a different type of briefing by the agencies.

Whereas, in the mid to late 1990s they had confined themselves to matters of mission, organization, or budget, in the heated post-9/11 atmosphere they found themselves under great journalistic pressure to give their assessment of various operational factors, and they often yielded.

I cannot say whether the greater specificity about terrorist or weapons of mass destruction threats resulted from some deliberate decision by central government or whether it simply reflected that the stakes—of a massive terrorist attack on London or of invading Iraq—had become much higher. Maybe those willing to talk to us felt frustration at the skepticism or indeed cynicism that underlay much press or public comment on these matters.

In time, we saw, through the Intelligence and Security Committee, Hutton Inquiry, and Butler Commission reports, a massive amount of what was previously secret material released into the public domain. In some matters, such as assessments of the reliability of MI6's human sources in Iraq, this material came very close to the most sacred secrets of that agency, the type of information about how long a source had worked for it or how reliable that person was assessed to be that briefers ten years earlier had assured us would never ever be divulged.

The result of all this self-examination was to deepen the new schism about intelligence—between human rightists and reality checkists. The former has used the lessons of Hutton or Butler to argue that they will not believe anything they are told about Iran or Syria. The hard-liners or neorealists have been convinced that ruthless terrorists should prompt ruthless countermeasures. The average member of the public sits bewildered between these two poles.

It is not yet clear how far the new schism in public attitudes will define the environment for intelligence operations or media reporting of them, but my own feeling is that it could prove as sharp a division as the old class-based one of the Cold War.

The reactions to the July 7, 2005 (7/7), London bombings give us some feel for this polarized debate. In the days after the attacks, senior police officers believed they had seen an opening to push for greater powers and bigger budgets. But they were opposed by many commentators and indeed a big section of the public. Many of those who had previously accused Prime Minister Tony Blair of exaggerating or even inventing the terrorist threat switched effortlessly to attacking him after "7/7" for causing the bombings by joining in the invasion of Iraq.

After the 7/7 bombings these tensions within society played themselves out with calls for a full inquiry into how the bombings happened and an emotive line by line parliamentary battle over the terms of new legislation. The salient point though was that security chiefs did not get the new powers they asked for and that attempts by senior police officers to make the case publicly for such changes led to them being attacked by some in parliament for playing an overtly political role.

The shock of those bombings had many effects, but it is important to record that it did not produce a mood of national consensus about counterterrorism and the intelligence work needed to drive it. One need only to look at the debate in various European legislatures about "extraordinary rendition" of terrorist suspects to see that the new schism about the value and morality of intelligence work is something that goes far wider than the British home debate about civil liberties and could have profound effects on intelligence operations.

CONCLUSION

Those who work in the British espionage system may look at the way polarized public debate about their work and become convinced that now is the time for less transparency rather than more. This would be a great mistake.

Personally, I believe greater transparency could play an important role in checking or even lessening the current schism about intelligence. We need change in several areas:

- It became obvious during the Foreign Affairs Committee's 2003 hearings into the Iraq War that members of Parliament and others were bewildered about the briefing activities of the intelligence agencies, so the system needs to be brought properly into the open. Ideally they would have spokesmen to whom statements could be attributed by post if not by name.

- Since 9/11 we have learned many lessons about the importance of the JIC and its product. The JIC needs its own spokesman, too, to offer occasional briefings. I know Downing Street might be terrorized by the idea of some alternative message escaping JIC, but the truth will come out in key matters of foreign policy, as we have learned from the recent past.

- We need to see the DG of MI5 or Chief of MI6 and indeed the Chairman of JIC on TV or hear them on the radio from time to time, being interviewed. I do not mean that it should be anymore often than the head of the Prison Service or Chief of Defense Staff, but it is essential to public confidence in those organizations.

- Some of what I have been describing has to apply to GCHQ, too. The members of GCHQ have kept their heads down for too long. They cost too much to carry on in such obscurity.

- Finally the business of Parliamentary scrutiny will sooner or later have to evolve into a proper select committee. Special arrangements will have to be in place to allow classified briefings, but the current setup, allowing the Prime Minister to veto material in the current committee's reports deprives the whole venture of credibility or independence.

Today, as in the Cold War era, saying nothing simply leaves the field open to conspiracy theorists or those with an axe to grind. Of course, such people tend to brush off anything with an official imprimatur, but transparency ought to work in favor of the majority or center rather than those on the extremes. It is time for a new push forward in the quest for greater openness.

3

Lessons from the Iranian Case and the Changing Face of American Intelligence

Jack Caravelli

IRAN: AN INTELLIGENCE OR POLICY FAILURE?

The structure and focus of the U.S. intelligence community have undergone significant changes after the successful terrorist attacks on the U.S. mainland in September 2001. While the main force for change was undoubtedly unleashed by the soul-searching and public inquiries conducted as a result of these horrendous attacks and apparent failure of intelligence, the U.S. intelligence community had been experiencing a new set of challenges and priorities since the end of the Cold War in 1991. This chapter sets out to highlight the main changes to the U.S. intelligence community since 2001. In order to put things in perspective, it uses the U.S. government's efforts to monitor and respond to the nuclear and missile programs of Iran since the 1990s as the starting point.

For over a decade a growing body of evidence from both intelligence sources as well as international bodies such as the International Atomic Energy Agency has indicated that under the cover of a civilian nuclear research program Iran has been pursuing the development of nuclear weapons. Under a separate program, the means to deliver them also have been pursued and, in this case, with considerable success. Iran achieved this with the successful flight-test of the Shahab-3 missile in 1998. With a range of over 1,000 kilometers, it has the capability to hit targets throughout the Middle East. Iran thus demonstrated the potential to change profoundly the strategic balance in the Middle East if its nuclear program could produce sufficient fissile material to make nuclear weapons.

As of May 2006 there were signs that the situation was worsening. The International Atomic Energy Agency, which had been attempting to carry out inspections of Iranian nuclear activities with ever-increasing frustration, passed a resolution in early 2006 saying that Iran had violated its obligations under the Nonproliferation Treaty (NPT) by secretly developing a nuclear program. The diplomatic scene then shifted to New York where the United Nations Security Council was negotiating the possibility of a formal declaration against Iran under Chapter 7 of the UN Charter that could pave the way for economic sanctions or military action.

A series of actions and statements emanating from Tehran did little to moderate the West's growing anxiety about Iran's intentions. Reports from the *Washington Times* claimed that Iran's new president, Mahmoud Ahmadinejad, has turned control over Iran's nuclear program to the military, undercutting any Iranian assertion that its program is for civilian purposes despite another assertion from the Iranian president that Islamic law prohibits the acquisition of nuclear weapons. The Iranian president continued making bellicose and reprehensible statements, including "Israel should be wiped off the face of the map." The international community, including U.S. President George W. Bush, Russian President Vladimir Putin, and British Prime Minister Tony Blair, roundly condemned this malicious rhetoric. Perhaps the most troubling of all was the Iranian claim that it had enriched a small quantity of uranium to low levels, which, if true, is a critical step to achieving the enrichment levels required to make an atomic device.

It is not inevitable that Iran will cross the nuclear threshold. Iran could still encounter problems in building and operating the large number of centrifuges, linked together in what are known as cascades, required to produce adequate levels of material suitable for building a bomb. For this and related reasons estimates also vary considerably—ranging from three to ten years—among experts as to when it might be able to do so. Adding confusion to an already tense situation, the Iranian president has said Iran would return to "unconditional negotiations" with little additional elaboration. Nonetheless, should Iran succeed in what has all the markings of a long pursuit of nuclear weapons, U.S., European, and Middle East policy makers would encounter a series of diverse, complex, and often vexing questions that will challenge the conventional capabilities and methods of those institutions that collect and analyze information for those policy communities. For example,

- Israel would confront a threat first described to a senior White House official in 1997 by then Prime Minister Benjamin Netanyahu as "existential." That threat could arise not only from direct military action, but also from Tehran's possible willingness to provide nuclear materials or weapons to terrorist groups. How will Israel respond?

- Will Arab states in the region such as Egypt and Saudi Arabia come under severe pressure to undertake efforts to match the Iranian capabilities, further undermining the already shaky NPT?

- U.S. and Western security policies in the region also would confront the challenge of assessing the intentions of a seemingly implacable foe well insulated from the economic sanctions that Western governments would seek to impose on Tehran, with or without UN concurrence. How would Tehran assess its geostrategic options and relationships if it becomes a nuclear power?

- What changes would likely occur in Western relations with the various Middle East nations that would be within range of Iranian missiles? Would those nations seek closer ties to Washington or, alternatively, pursue more independent policies?

- How would other regional actors such as Russia and Pakistan react to a nuclear capable Iran and how, if at all, should the West consider responding?

In various forms those questions have been lingering not far beneath the policy surface for a number of years as revelations surfaced about Iran's nuclear and long-range missile ambitions. This chapter examines the insights and limitations of various information sources. The approach for doing so is through an assessment of the extent to which those sources have and can be expected to support policy deliberations on the pace and scope of Iran's nuclear and missile programs, as well as the above described set of questions. A concluding section assesses a series of issues for the U.S. intelligence community as it undertakes a series of sweeping reforms brought about by the events of September 11, 2001.

Central to U.S. policy debate on Iran and its nuclear program has been reliance on a set of collection and analytic capabilities developed during and shaped by the Cold War. Throughout that epoch the U.S. intelligence community, supported by several important European allies, deployed and invested heavily in an array of national technical means, the term for sophisticated techniques for monitoring the activities and communications of putative adversaries. In addition, and drawing upon those capabilities, the analytic corps at the Central Intelligence Agency (CIA) and other parts of the intelligence community provided policy makers a constant stream of reports and estimates on topics ranging from Soviet missiles to South American politics. For all of its impressive breadth, the collection and analytic capabilities of the intelligence community would prove to be only partially successful in addressing the most pressing policy questions associated with Iranian nuclear and missile activities during the second Clinton administration.

EARLY AMERICAN RESPONSES

U.S. national security policy, as described in a myriad of scholarly works, reflects an amalgam of political, military, economic, and intelligence influences. In one respect, the Iranian weapons case study was a policy anomaly. Ironically, it was not the U.S. intelligence community, any domestic political debate, or any other Western intelligence service reporting that triggered the U.S. government's decision to develop a diplomatic strategy of conducting high-level negotiations with the Russian government, the nation most closely identified as providing support to Iran's emerging missile and nuclear programs. Rather, a briefing by senior Israeli diplomatic and intelligence officials to senior White House staff in early 1997 was the catalyst for the aforementioned negotiations. The Israeli briefing painted a stark picture of an Iranian government moving aggressively to develop nuclear weapons and long-range missile technology. In some areas the information provided to U.S. officials overlapped that available through Western intelligence services, but in some critical areas (which, regrettably cannot be made public at the moment) it was sufficiently unique and persuasive to goad the administration into action. Because the U.S. government did not have diplomatic relations with Iran, it was unable to engage Tehran directly. What was deemed by Clinton administration officials as an acceptable substitute was to endeavor to limit or, ideally, sever the external assistance Russia was rendering Iran.

The decision to undertake bilateral negotiations with Russia over its nuclear and missile support to Iran was taken at the highest levels of the U.S. government. In a telephone conversation with Russian President Boris Yeltsin in early 1997, President Bill Clinton stated that it was the position of the U.S. government, supported by extensive sensitive information, that Russian experts were contributing significantly to Iranian progress in both nuclear and missile technology. Predictably, Yeltsin rebuffed the charges, claiming that the Russian government opposed any Iranian attempts to acquire such capabilities. Nonetheless, he conceded that there could be "rogue" individuals operating beyond the knowledge of Russian authorities and that it probably was desirable for an exchange of information between the two countries. Yeltsin appointed two Russian interlocutors to address U.S. concerns. They were Yuri Koptev, the respected Director of the Russian Space Agency, who was appointed to lead the Russian discussions on missile technology, and Yevgeny Adamov, Russian Minister of Atomic Energy, to represent Russia in discussions on nuclear cooperation issues. To underscore its seriousness of purpose, the U.S. negotiating team was selected by National Security Adviser Sandy Berger, approved by President Clinton, and led by one of America's most senior diplomats, Frank Wisner. I accompanied Wisner on the delegation and reported directly to Berger.

The extent and manner in which sensitive intelligence would be shared with the Russians was the subject of considerable, and sometimes uneasy, debate within the U.S. policy and intelligence communities. Both elements of the U.S. government were faced with a dilemma that repeats itself in many national security questions. It was widely recognized that without the use of some reasonably specific and accurate information almost exclusively derived from sensitive sources that the negotiating team would have an exceptionally weak case to persuade the Russian government to move aggressively against those Russian entities assisting Iran, the ultimate objective of the negotiations. Within the intelligence community suspicion of the Russians ran high, partially as a vestige of years of enmity between the two nations and their respective intelligence services and partially because of the conviction held in some quarters that the Russian government had made a policy decision to, at a minimum, turn a blind eye to the type of cooperation with Iran that Yeltsin claimed he had prohibited. After protracted internal debate, the resulting accommodation provided U.S. negotiators with adequate information to press their case without revealing sensitive sources and methods.

There were also established and in some cases significant limits on the information cleared for use with the Russians. Part of the evidentiary base against Russia was deemed so sensitive that it was never approved for use in any form. That judgment, reached concurrently by former Director of Central Intelligence George Tenet and National Security Adviser Sandy Berger, would in at least one critical case prohibit the negotiators from confronting the Russian government with unambiguous evidence of Russian-Iranian collaboration on a specific element of missile technology, that, if brought to a halt, could have slowed Iran's development of the Shahab-3 missile. This was a case of "actionable intelligence" not being put into action. The use of intelligence, balanced against its protection, would remain a continuing source of friction between the policy and intelligence communities as the U.S. government endeavored to reorganize itself to respond to the set of challenges posed by transnational terrorism.

Because of the sensitivity of the negotiations, the U.S. negotiators deemed it important to develop with their Russian interlocutors in advance a series of ground rules. It was mutually recognized that the negotiations would have little or no chance of success if the process or results were leaked to the media in an attempt to score political points at the expense of the other. The Clinton administration, committed to strengthening its overall relationship with the Yeltsin government and committed to supporting Russia's fledgling democracy, deemed any unauthorized disclosure of the purpose of the negotiations or their contents a highly undesirable possible embarrassment for the Russian government. Senior policy officials also judged that Russian cooperation was unlikely to be forthcoming in an atmosphere of accusations and recriminations. Throughout nearly three years of negotiating sessions both sides adhered to this goal, usually issuing only perfunctory and mutually agreed upon statements during summit meetings or other high-level exchanges.

Beyond the bilateral commitment to confidentiality, there were, however, other parties keenly interested in the negotiations; this interest greatly complicated the administration's diplomatic strategy. For the Clinton administration, the Israeli government and the U.S. Congress, controlled by the Republican Party, were the most significant entities—and more than occasional critics—of the White House's approach. The government of Israel at the highest levels formally supported the administration's efforts. In turn, the U.S. negotiating team expended considerable effort in Jerusalem, Tel Aviv, and Washington, D.C., providing extensive debriefs for senior and highly knowledgeable representatives of the Israeli government. Reflecting the keen interest of the Netanyahu government, Israeli diplomats routinely pressed their American counterparts not only for all relevant information from the negotiations, but also offered what in many cases were highly useful insights into the negotiating process. Those diplomats also were not reluctant to critique in various forums the progress being made by the negotiators.

By the middle of the second Clinton term, the White House's relations with a Republican-controlled Congress could best be described as tumultuous. The administration was being buffeted by political scandals and the opposition party saw the progress of Iran's nuclear and missile programs as another indicator of the White House's alleged "softness" on national security threats. This critique notwithstanding, briefings at the start of the negotiations by the U.S. ambassador and myself resulted in Congressional agreement to closely monitor but not immediately interfere in the negotiations through such means as legislation or media leaks. This agreement was honored for an extended period of time as the negotiations proceeded, but it did not last.

LIMITS OF DIPLOMACY AND INTELLIGENCE

The first year of negotiations with both Adamov and Koptev, all held in Moscow, yielded few substantive results, but they provided considerable insight into what would be the persistent Russian response to virtually every issue or source of concern raised by the U.S. team. This response is best summarized by one word, denial. It became apparent quickly to the U.S. negotiators that their interlocutors were not prepared, or perhaps not authorized, to acknowledge transgressions of Russia's declared policy of no cooperation with Iran on nuclear and missile technologies. These denials came to be understood in Washington as an admixture of Moscow's desire to avoid embarrassment, to avoid the possible imposition of U.S. sanctions that some critics in Washington and Jerusalem were advocating, and to preserve its relationship with Iran—including the ongoing and much delayed construction of a U.S.$800-million power plant at Bushehr. Whatever the Russian motivations, the results were the same. After a year of negotiations and countless hours of exchanges, there was only the most rudimentary agreement by the teams as to a set of facts that could serve as the basis for possible action by the Russian government.

This unambiguous lack of progress triggered clamoring in the Congress, Israel, the U.S. intelligence community, and even parts of the administration for the cessation of negotiations and the development of a more confrontational policy with the Yeltsin government. Again, the administration chose to persist with its established strategy. The tipping point for that decision was the continuing flow of sensitive information indicating that Russia's cooperation with Iran in both areas of concern probably was increasing, not decreasing. It was judged that under these circumstances diplomacy had to be given another chance to disrupt this trend.

The resumption of negotiations in late 1998 served only to confirm what the first round of negotiations had demonstrated. Adamov—whose negotiating approach is best described as brusque—and Koptev, a more polished interlocutor, continued their now established pattern of listening for hours to U.S. concerns and, in turn, offering little more than usually unmet promises to investigate them and take appropriate actions.

Against this backdrop, political pressure on the administration rose precipitously, fueled, deliberately or not, by briefings by senior intelligence officers to Congress. Relations between policy officials and the intelligence community often soured over the perception—in some historical cases accurate and in others less so—that intelligence officers would attempt to influence and engage indirectly in the policy process (a generally proscribed activity in the U.S. system) via briefings to the Congress or through unauthorized leaks to the media. This dynamic—far too complex for exhaustive treatment here—surfaced again in 1998. Fueled by a mixture of palpable frustration with the lack of progress and political opportunity, several congressional committees, notably the House International Relations Committee and the Senate Armed Services Committee turned to the intelligence community for insights into the state of negotiations. For their part, some senior intelligence officers, disgruntled by the use of intelligence for no apparent policy gain, appeared from the White House vantage point enthusiastic to detail the negotiations' shortfalls, including through leaks to the media, even as White House officials were conveying a more nuanced message that acknowledged lack of progress while arguing that even limited progress could not be made in the absence of continuing dialogue.

The negotiating team had its own set of frustrations with the intelligence community. In its attempts to establish a negotiating framework the team sought insights into Russian and Iranian policies reflected in the questions presented at the outset of this chapter. Those questions, as noted, were most likely to be answered most fully by human intelligence. As would come to be understood and described by the Commission that investigated the attacks against the United States on September 11, 2001, the U.S. intelligence community, by the late 1990s, was beset by a series of limitations on its ability to collect such information. As a result, many of the most fundamental and policy-relevant questions surrounding Russian assistance to Iran's nuclear and missile programs were never answered fully. Similarly, Tehran's plans and strategic objectives were the subject of intense assessment, but supported only by a circumscribed evidentiary base.

It was well understood that the status quo was unacceptable in policy terms. Albeit reluctantly, the Clinton administration yielded to rising pressures from Congress by imposing economic sanctions against several Russian entities alleged to have cooperated with Iran. While the financial effects of the sanctions were modest, the political repercussions and symbolism were considerable. Predictably, the bilateral relationship suffered a serious but not fatal setback as the Russian government reacted with considerable vigor to the implication that it could not or would not stop Russian entities from working with Iran.

The imposition of sanctions drew to a close a chapter in U.S.–Russian engagement over Iran. A new approach awaited the arrival of the Bush administration, and the results of those efforts are yet to be known. A Russian government led by a sober-minded president appears capable of addressing U.S. concerns, should it choose to do so. What can be assessed in more detail for the purposes of this chapter are the lessons learned for the "changing face of intelligence." In hindsight, a number of conclusions can be drawn from the case study of the Clinton administration's efforts to negotiate with Russia on the Iranian problem.

THE CHANGING FACE OF INTELLIGENCE

Perhaps the most important lesson for the negotiators—and one that became a fact of daily life for them—was the uneven quality of the available intelligence. In some areas it was excellent, providing critical details on Iranian and Russian activities. In other areas, including the requirement for insight into Russian and Iranian motives and plans, the intelligence stood largely silent. It is perhaps harsh to term this lack of intelligence a failure given the considerable efforts expended by dedicated professionals to answering these questions. Nonetheless, this inability to divine the strategic plans and intentions of an adversary would return to haunt the intelligence community, the American public, and its government in September 2001.

In one fundamental respect, therefore, the face of intelligence has hardly changed in that there remain shortfalls of credible, timely, and accurate human intelligence on the broad strategic issues—whether they are nonproliferation or terrorism—in the Middle East. President Bush identified this intelligence gap as perhaps the highest priority for former CIA Director Porter Goss, directing Goss to expand greatly the personnel in the CIA's clandestine service. Goss had made considerable strides in this area before being forced from his position in May 2006. Accomplishing this goal will take years, however, given the length of the recruitment process and the disrepair wrought on the clandestine service. Through much of the 1990s its ranks were thinned by budgetary cuts arising from the perception that, after the breakup of the Soviet Union, there would be a "peace dividend" for the American public as well as the misguided judgment that national technical means could largely compensate from a reduced physical presence in troubled areas of the world.

In turn, the intelligence community's diminished capabilities resulted in a frequent reliance on liaison reporting. Liaison reporting proved highly useful to the Clinton administration at the start of its efforts to negotiate with the Russian government and remains a staple of the information sources used by the intelligence community. That source in many cases should and must remain a critical source of insight into some of America's most intractable security concerns. Nonetheless, and on a case-by-case basis, the lessons of the war on terrorism, unlike the case study presented here, demonstrate that too heavy a reliance on reporting by other nations that always are subject to various forms of manipulation can lead to highly undesirable intelligence and policy outcomes. There would appear to be no organizational "fix," along the lines described below, that remedy this dilemma. Albeit painful to some individuals and resisted by others, what CIA Director Porter Goss attempted to do during his tenure was to undertake a series of personnel changes designed to infuse a new cadre of leadership for the operational and analytic sides of the organization.

Beyond the widely acknowledged need for reform in the clandestine service and the way in which it uses liaison reporting, in the wake of the September 11, 2001, terrorist attacks, sweeping reforms have been enacted throughout the U.S. intelligence community. These reforms, the most sweeping since the 1947 National Security Act established the Central Intelligence Agency, the National Security Council, and other parts of the U.S. national security establishment, resulted primarily from the findings of the 9/11 Commission chaired by former New Jersey Governor Thomas Kean, supported by a groundswell of public opinion clamoring for change in the organization and operations of the U.S. government. After considerable congressional debate and initial White House skepticism on the scope and nature of needed change, the U.S. Congress passed and President Bush signed into law a major restructuring of the intelligence community in December 2004, titled the Intelligence Reform and Terrorism Prevention Act.

The most visible change centered on the creation of a Director of National Intelligence (DNI). Under the previous organizational model, the Director of Central Intelligence (DCI) carried out three distinct functions: serving as director of the CIA, serving as at least the nominal coordinator of intelligence activities throughout the U.S. government, and serving as the president's intelligence adviser. The scope of these duties virtually guaranteed that no DCI could carry out each of the three roles vigorously and effectively. The creation of a Director of National Intelligence was the congressional response to this situation. Under the new legislation the first DNI, veteran diplomat John Negroponte, assumed two of the previous functions carried out by the DCI. Negroponte now serves as the president's daily intelligence adviser and briefer while also exercising authority over perhaps the most critical function of any senior executive, the budgetary process. Negroponte already has demonstrated a willingness to engage forcefully in this budgetary process, scaling back previous plans for a highly sophisticated but expensive collection platform. Albeit very early in the reshaping of the intelligence process, it appears that the face of U.S. intelligence is changing in terms of budget formation. How this process plays out over the next few years will go a long way to judging the actual influence the DNI will exercise over the intelligence community.

The other standard by which to judge the changing face of intelligence will be in the process and product of the analytic cadre. In its 400-page report, the 9/11 Commission uncovered a myriad of failures of various elements of the U.S. government, not just the intelligence and security agencies. For example, harsh judgment was rendered on the failure of the Department of Energy and its political and senior career officers to build on the progress made in 2000–2002 to secure with the Russian government's cooperation the vast stocks of often poorly secured Russian fissile materials. Corrupt and inept management at senior levels, tolerated by the political appointees, resulted in the mass defection of dedicated and capable officers who were moving the program forward. That judgment, shared by many informed observers in and out of the U.S. government, underscores long-standing national security vulnerability. It is well understood that securing dangerous materials far from U.S. borders offers the best chance to protect the American public given the ongoing challenges of interdicting illicit smuggling of almost any type at U.S. borders.

Nonetheless, the most damning Commission judgment was reflected in the phrase that the U.S. government, beginning with the intelligence community, had suffered from a "lack of imagination" in failing to recognize that the threats America and the West confronted for several generations during the Cold War had changed dramatically. It was not that the U.S. government had not been warned, both by its own employees, including those who served in various law enforcement and policy positions during both the Clinton and Bush administrations, as well as by previous attacks against U.S. assets and interests in the Middle East, Africa, and elsewhere.

A lack of imagination is an analytic failing. No other organizations in the Commission's critique came under more direct and indirect scrutiny than the CIA Directorate for Intelligence (DI) and the National Intelligence Council (NIC), the organization charged with producing National Intelligence Estimates, the most complete assessment of a subject by the intelligence community. For at least several decades the DI and the NIC, both located at CIA headquarters, operated largely in tandem. The NIC maintains a small permanent staff of mostly senior, and in most cases, highly capable officers. The pace and scope of its work usually requires the NIC to draw on external personnel resources to carry out its mission. In most cases these resources came from the CIA's Directorate of Intelligence, in part because of the co-location of the two organizations and in part because of the considerable size of the analytic cadre in the DI.

The senior leadership of these organizations was criticized by the Commission for failing to create a culture of information sharing between intelligence organizations and the FBI, a problem for which the Bureau's senior leadership also was castigated. Most informed observers shared the Commission's assessment and commended CIA Director Goss for undertaking several personnel changes in response to this problem, including removing the former Deputy Director of Intelligence, described by one senior intelligence official as "being in over her head." In this respect another element of the changing face of intelligence has surfaced: the expectation of senior officials that a greater degree of accountability is required in the intelligence community.

The analytic work of the intelligence community also is undergoing another change. The once symbiotic relationship between the CIA analytic cadre and the National Intelligence Council is being changed, at least physically, with the departure of the NIC from Langley Air Force Base to a new location in the Washington area. Perhaps more importantly, the NIC becomes an asset under the direct authority of DNI Negroponte, as it ended its previous reporting relationship with the DCI. The extent to which Negroponte and his staff seek to expand the analytic support to the NIC will go a long way in judging whether the intelligence community's products take a fundamentally different shape.

CHANGING IN THE RIGHT WAY?

The face of intelligence is changing in the United States. Changes are discernible in the budgetary process, in the personnel process, in the clandestine service, and in key components of the intelligence community's analytic assets. In the aggregate, these changes are revolutionary. They also are judged essential by most informed observers. What is far less certain is whether they are a sufficient response to a set of national security problems that look little like those past problems that shaped nearly half a century of approach to intelligence. Within the American government there is a long history of making organizational changes in response to various crises. Subsequent events often demonstrated that organizational changes alone do not necessarily confer enhanced governmental efficiency or demonstrably better policy results. In confronting radical Islamic fundamentalists, the theocratic regime in Iran, and other vexing problems the litmus test for intelligence will center on its ability to provide timely, reliable, and accurate intelligence to policy makers and military commanders. While that standard also was the norm during the West's competition during the Cold War, radical Islam poses not only a different strategic challenge but also a different analytic challenge.

That challenge can be summarized in the phrase "asymmetric warfare." This term, often employed by British experts to depict the changing strategic environment, reflects both the relative lack of resources at the disposal of Islamic fundamentalists compared to those of the United States and the West as well as the capacity of the Islamic fundamentalists, even with limited resources, to inflict substantial physical and economic damage on the West.

For the U.S. intelligence community, understanding the nature of asymmetric warfare and developing the analytic tools requisite for providing insights into it represents its most pressing challenge in the first part of the twenty-first century. What remains to be answered is the extent to which the above-described organizational changes will enhance the capabilities of the intelligence community to meet that challenge.

Throughout the Cold War the underlying analytic framework employed for assessing Soviet motives and actions was derived largely from the tenets of game theory, an economic and mathematical model developed and refined by Nobel Prize winners John Nash, Reinhard Selten, Thomas Schelling, and Robert Aumann. Schelling's seminal 1960 work, *The Strategy of Conflict,* was an attempt to apply game theory to international politics. Schelling's work focused on ways in which two bitter and heavily armed rivals, the United States and the Soviet Union, could preserve the peace. Schelling judged that there would be an underlying rationality in the actions of the antagonists and that neither side would undertake actions without first calculating the response of the other side. In turn, this fostered the idea propagated by Schelling and other theorists that it was more desirable for each nation to demonstrate that it could withstand an attack and retaliate with overwhelming force than to demonstrate that it could protect its citizens.

In the face of asymmetric warfare, this analytic paradigm that underpinned U.S. national security deliberations for several generations has greatly reduced utility. Islamic fundamentalists have shown little, if any, inclination to be deterred by U.S. or Western conventional military power, notwithstanding the fact that military operations in Iraq have killed thousands of terrorists and various intelligence and law enforcement operations have interdicted various plots against Western interests. Albeit speculative, Islamic fundamentalists may have calculated that their use of a nuclear, radiological, or biological weapon against a city or major economic target probably could not trigger a proportional Western response since it would be unlikely that the West could identify an appropriate target and, even if it could, would be loath to inflict tens of thousands of casualties on innocent civilians. In an age of terror the fundamental calculus has changed. In the past, the Soviet Union had the means to destroy much of the United States and the West but was self-deterred. The lessons of the Cuban missile crisis were learned by both superpower rivals who continued to bitterly compete, but mostly through proxy wars in fringe areas such as Angola and Afghanistan. Today, Islamic fundamentalists apparently do not yet have the means to employ weapons of mass destruction against the West, but there is little reason to judge that, if in possession of such capabilities, they would be self-deterred from using them. That reality underscores one of the most compelling reasons for supporting the Bush administration's efforts to stop the Iranian nuclear weapons program.

From this perspective the Iran case study represents an analytic bridge between the world of those who would and those who would not be deterred. At first sight Iranian efforts to develop long-range missile and nuclear capabilities are another manifestation of the global fight against nuclear proliferation. Nonetheless, there remain a series of disturbing data points indicating that the Iranian leadership may not prove to be self-deterred if it crosses the nuclear threshold or that it is prepared to materially support Islamic fundamentalist groups who also show little inclination to self-deterrence.

For those responsible for reforming intelligence, the organizational changes put in place at enormous political cost and time are unlikely, in themselves, to fully inform and prepare Western leaders for the challenges they will confront, beginning with that posed by Islamic fundamentalism. The ultimate test of whether the often painful lessons of the past several years have been absorbed will best be answered in the development of the imagination and creative insight intelligence professionals and policy makers alike bring to the foremost security challenges of a new century.

Part II: The Wider Political Context

4

Political Supervision of Intelligence Services in the United Kingdom

John N. L. Morrison

INTRODUCTION

In mature democracies it is generally—though not universally—accepted that the activities of intelligence and security agencies should be controlled and limited by some form of "political" supervision which will ensure that they are answerable as appropriate to the government, legislature, and judiciary. This supervision may take several forms, as will be seen, and is usually embodied in statute law. There is an implicit assumption that a balance must be struck, with intelligence organizations—individually or collectively—operating on one scale of the balance and external "supervision" of their operations on the other. While this crude distinction is essentially valid, we are dealing, as is generally the case in the area of intelligence, with considerable complexity on both sides of any "balance," and it is necessary to consider the composition of each in some detail. This chapter argues, drawing mainly on the U.K. experience, that there is a complex web of relationships between various elements of "intelligence supervision" and a range of "intelligence organizations." It does not seek a precise definition of "intelligence," a task that has been attempted by many to the satisfaction of few (except of course, the authors of the various definitions). It should be noted, though, that there are different cultural approaches to the concept of intelligence, notably between the United States and the United Kingdom, as Philip Davies has argued:

> Bluntly put, "intelligence" does not mean the same thing on opposite sides of the Atlantic. Intelligence in United States government circles is a very broad concept, subsuming both the collection of information and its analysis; in the British system the idea is narrower.... "Intelligence" in the UK refers only to a particular kind of information gathered from indirect or clandestine sources.[1]

Rather than choose between the U.S. and U.K. concepts, this chapter considers both to be valid in appropriate contexts.

To begin, take the intelligence organizations: these undertake a variety of functions which may or may not be exclusive to each—intelligence agencies may have their fingers in several pies. In broad terms, we are considering the following areas of activity in which they are involved, and which often overlap in practice:

Intelligence Collection

"Secret information secretly obtained" is how intelligence has been described. Governments and military forces require this intelligence for a variety of reasons. The simplest is that the more information they have the better placed they are to ensure that they are alert to actual and potential threats and that their policies are implemented effectively. They also need to be warned about current and future developments that could impact on those policies, require them to be changed, or require a new policy to be developed, on the grounds that "what you don't know can hurt you." This is seen perhaps most clearly in the military arena, where the things a commander most needs to know are those the enemy is most concerned to keep secret.

It is probably safe to say that every country has some form of intelligence collection capability, in larger ones divided among different agencies along more-or-less functional lines. This is particularly so in Britain, where the Secret Intelligence Service (SIS) concentrates on intelligence from human sources and the Government Communications Headquarters (GCHQ) majors in electronic interception. But even in the United Kingdom the demarcation lines are fuzzy and shifting, while other countries draw them differently. In mainland Europe military intelligence typically runs the national signals intelligence capability and may have reconnaissance troops under direct command.

Collection must of course be directed, in the interests of both effectiveness and efficiency, hence the need for externally imposed requirements and priorities, either generated centrally at the national level (as in the United Kingdom) or by individual departments of state (as in France).

Threat Countering

Governments need to be aware of external and internal threats to their citizens and institutions, preferably in time to counter them and render them ineffective. Thus we have threat-countering agencies such as the Security Service in the United Kingdom, the BfV (Bundesamt für Verfassungsschutz) in Germany, and the FBI in America. As the British Security Service never tires of pointing out, it is not a collection agency responding to national intelligence requirements; rather it identifies threats to the nation and collects intelligence on a self-tasking basis. It could be argued that this is more demanding than "pure" intelligence collection, since threat-countering agencies are in effect responsible for the whole intelligence cycle—requirements setting, collection, analysis, and dissemination—as well as support to the law enforcement agencies. They are also particularly open to criticism if they fail to identify future threats and take the necessary action to avert them.

Covert Action

The existence of collection and threat-countering agencies provides the opportunity to use them proactively and behind the scenes. Such use can range from the diplomatic arena—"back channels"—to what amounts in effect to clandestine military action. It goes without saying that this is a particularly sensitive area of activity that requires effective political supervision.

Intelligence Analysis

Raw intelligence may be of great value at the "tactical" level (e.g., in day-to-day support of negotiations), but in general it must be analyzed and assessed[2] by experts, together with other intelligence and overt information, to produce an "all-source assessment" for the policy maker. The process of analysis may be hierarchical and unified, as in the United Kingdom, with the Joint Intelligence Committee (JIC) providing a single top-level analysis body. Or it may be fragmented, as notably in France but also to a degree in the United States, where even the National Intelligence Estimates have in the past allowed dissenting footnotes. Traditionally, intelligence analysis has been subject to internal quality controls, with the customer assuming those controls ensure that it is of the highest possible quality. However, the sorry history of the JIC's incorrect assessments of Iraq's weapons of mass destruction (WMD) capabilities has ensured that, in the United Kingdom at least, this can no longer be taken for granted.

Intelligence Support to Military Operations

It could be argued that this is not a separate category, and in one sense this is correct. It does not have unique elements not included in the previous four. But it does operate in a different environment, where the time pressures can be great and the penalties for failure death rather than political embarrassment. The commander and his military intelligence staffs may be required to act autonomously, and the pressure to achieve results may push them to individual and collective excesses. Supervision here (as elsewhere, though to a greater degree) requires that the requirements of proportionality are observed and that human rights are not abused.

TYPES OF POLITICAL SUPERVISION

There are countries where intelligence agencies are political players in their own right; it is generally assumed that Pakistan's Inter-Services Intelligence Directorate has on occasion operated according to its own undemocratic agenda, and the same applies in a number of other countries. But in mature democracies it is generally felt that intelligence organizations should be politically neutral, this being defined as "not acting according to an agenda of their own." That said, there is a sense in which they cannot and will not be politically neutral, since they all—including military intelligence—ultimately exist to serve political ends and assist in their achievement. As administrations change, so will their policies and the directions they give to the intelligence community, which will change tack accordingly.

There have long been fears in the United States (and, to a lesser extent, in the United Kingdom) that intelligence agencies, left to their own devices, will behave like "rogue elephants," as the late U.S. Senator Frank Church memorably described them:

> The image of this creature took shape because of press reports about illegal activities of the Central Intelligence Agency (CIA) within the US or against American citizens, and the now notorious excesses of the Federal Bureau of Investigation (FBI) against civil rights and anti-war activists (and, indeed, almost anybody who incurred the wrath of its director J. Edgar Hoover) during the early 1970s.[3]

In fact, where intelligence agencies in liberal democracies have behaved illegally or unethically, it has usually been at the behest of their political masters, frustrated at the constitutional or legislative limitations on their powers.

Turning now to "political supervision," it is immediately apparent that this can take three forms. The first is effective governmental control of the agencies' activities by the responsible Minister, who provides approval for sensitive operations either as a matter of custom or within a legislative framework for intelligence. Thus in the United Kingdom there is a complex system of "warranting" intelligence operations, with clearance being formally sought at various levels according to the sensitivity of the operation, the most critical going to the relevant Secretary of State[4] for approval. Woe betides a U.K. agency head who drops his or her Minister in the political mire by failing to obtain his or her blessing for an operation, leading to public embarrassment.

This of course allows the abuse of political supervision on a top-down basis, with the possibility that intelligence agencies will be directed by their political masters to operate illegally or unethically. Such behavior is more likely in nondemocratic societies, but, even in countries where intelligence agencies are supposed to behave themselves, the combination of an unscrupulous political leader and "gung-ho" subordinates can lead to agencies being drawn into unacceptable activities, as with the Iran-Contra affair in the United States or the "Rainbow Warrior" bombing in New Zealand by the French Direction Générale de la Sécurité Extérieure. So while political supervision by members of the government is necessary, it is not a sufficient protection against misuse of a nation's intelligence resources.

The next type of political supervision that can guard against such misuse is the provision of "Inspectors General," either embedded within the intelligence and security agencies, as in the United States, or external to them, as in Australia and New Zealand. The inspector-general (IG) system is most highly developed in the United States, with 58 IGs having responsibilities for federal bodies, ranging from the CIA to the Railroad Retirement Board, and making up their own IG community—www.ignet.gov—which, in their words, "continues to be a positive force in the Federal government for recommending improvements and detecting fraud, waste and abuse."[5] IGs in the United States have a dual responsibility to the head of the agency they cover and to Congress; they therefore provide an "aid to management" service as well as acting as surrogates of the legislature.

Indeed, both Ministers and IGs ultimately answer to the legislature, which provides the third—and most critical—formal element of political supervision (it will be suggested later that there is a further informal "fourth sanction"). And because intelligence is a recondite and specialized subject, many countries have felt a need to set up specialist parliamentary committees that can police the politicians as well as the intelligence agencies and ensure that the proprieties are observed. This is generally known as "oversight"—an individual or body of individuals who are privy to most or all of the secrets of the agencies and can assure the government, legislature, and public at large that all is well (or not, as the case may be). Oversight takes many forms around the world: there may be standing committees of the legislature, as in the United States,[6] or there may be unique solutions such as the Intelligence and Security Committee (ISC) in the United Kingdom. And, of course, it is quite likely that there are hybrid combinations:

in the United Kingdom we have not only the quasiparliamentary ISC, but also quasijudicial oversight in the form of the Interception of Communications Commissioner, an Intelligence Services Commissioner, and an Investigatory Powers Tribunal.

But whatever form oversight takes, it faces a fundamental problem: how to convince the public at large (including the legislature and the media) that the responsible body has been given the access it requires to do its job, has carried that job out effectively, and is reporting fully and frankly. The peculiar difficulty of intelligence oversight is that those who exercise it must operate within what has become known as "the ring of secrecy" if they are to be effective; yet they must ultimately produce unclassified reports for public consumption. In principle this can be a single-step process; thus the Butler Report on Iraqi WMD[7] was issued without any deletions. However, the general pattern is for oversight bodies to start by producing classified reports that are then sanitized for public release. This is the practice of the British ISC, which replaces sensitive text in its reports with asterisks—a practice that inevitably results in media complaints and even derision and has been described as the Prime Minister exercising his "veto" over what should be published. The latter allegation is unfounded. The redactions to the ISC's published report are required purely for security reasons, and there is no evidence that the Prime Minister plays any part in the sanitization process. Whether so many deletions are actually necessary is another matter, not explored here.[8]

As already noted, the British ISC is a unique committee, largely because of the problems involved in reporting its findings. It was realized from the outset that if an oversight body was to be effective in carrying out its statutory obligations,[9] it must clearly be able to report on the most sensitive subjects. One of the ISC's early reports was so sensitive that not even the subject has ever been revealed. But to whom should it report on such delicate matters—clearly not to the House of Commons as a whole, as a Select Committee would? Perhaps to a group of security-cleared Privy Counsellors who would then report back to the House? But that would just push the problem back a step—why should the Privy Counsellors be more worthy of trust than the body reporting to them? The British solution was for the Prime Minister to appoint to the ISC nine parliamentarians not holding public office, who would then report candidly to him in the first instance and lay redacted versions of their annual reports and, as security permitted, special reports before Parliament.

The key elements of the Intelligence Services Act 1994 (ISA 94), which established the ISC and legitimized the Agencies[10] were as follows:

- The ISC was to be a unique committee of parliamentarians operating under statute and reporting to the Prime Minister. As such, it did not need to follow the conventions governing Standing and Select Committees of Parliament.

- It would operate within the ring of secrecy, with members cleared to see the most sensitive information, though not entitled to see all such information.
- It was required to provide an annual report to the Prime Minister.
- It could provide additional reports on any matter relating to the discharge of its functions.
- Sanitized versions of its annual reports would be laid before Parliament.[11]
- Its remit was to examine the "expenditure, administration and policy" of the SIS, the Security Service, and the GCHQ; it had no authority to obtain "sensitive information" as defined in the Act.
- However, Agency Heads were free to disclose sensitive information if they felt it safe to do so.

The provisions of the Act and the subsequent development of the ISC provide an illustration of two main problems affecting the parliamentary oversight element of political supervision: limited responsibilities and limited access. The ISC was set up to look only at the three U.K. intelligence and security agencies; it had no remit to examine the Defence Intelligence Staff (DIS) or other military intelligence organizations, nor the central JIC intelligence assessment machinery, nor the intelligence elements of departments such as Customs and Excise.[12] It was therefore looking at only some of the core members of the U.K. Intelligence Community, let alone its intelligence hinterland. And even its examination of the three U.K. Agencies was limited by the ability of the Agency Heads, as spelled out in ISA 94, to withhold sensitive information. In some countries parliamentary oversight committees have the right of access to all information, no matter how sensitive—not so in the United Kingdom.

In practice, though, matters turned out somewhat differently. The first ISC,[13] chaired by Tom (now Lord) King gradually but steadily extended the scope of its activities, first by asking the Agencies' customers, including the DIS and JIC, about the value of Agency products, then by asking to visit these same customers to learn more about the way they worked. In this way, by the start of the twenty-first century the ISC had *de facto*, if not *de jure* oversight of the whole U.K. Intelligence Community. That still left the problem that it lacked access to sensitive information, but here too the Committee proceeded by stealth. It established a relationship of trust with the Agencies, whose heads began to feel they could have confidence in the ISC's ability to preserve their secrets (it is perhaps remarkable that for over a decade there was never a leak of classified information from the ISC)[14] and thus to reveal more than they strictly needed to under the Act. It should be noted, however, that while the estimable record of not leaking ISC findings in advance was maintained by the first three Committees under Tom King and Ann Taylor, the main conclusions of the report by the fourth Committee into the July 7, 2005, London bombings were leaked to the BBC[15] the day its Chairman, Paul Murphy, submitted it to the Prime Minister and some six weeks before the sanitized version[16] was published.

But the establishment of a relationship of trust, however valuable it may be in some respects, leads to another problematical aspect of political supervision, whether exercised by Ministers, Inspectors General, or parliamentary oversight bodies: that they may become too close to, and too uncritical of, the agencies they are supposed to be supervising. It should be borne in mind that intelligence and security agencies are in the business of surreptitiously acquiring the secrets of others while maintaining their own, and this makes them deft manipulators of their interlocutors. The sanction against them seducing their overseers is that they may be found out, with dire results; but one ex-Agency Head (Sir David Omand) has maintained that if an agency does not want to tell you something, you will never find out about it (he was, though, referring to an agency's ability to withhold information the oversight body is not entitled to obtain).[17] In principle, an oversight body with total rights of access should be impossible to hoodwink, but in practice such a deception would be simple to accomplish for any experienced intelligence organization—at least until one of the staff decided to turn whistle-blower and inform the oversight body that information was being improperly withheld from it.

THE LIMITS OF POLITICAL SUPERVISION

So far this chapter has described the elements that make up each side of the supposed balance without stating explicitly that such a balance is necessary or even desirable. It could be argued that only governmental control is an absolute requirement. No administration would want its intelligence and security agencies to be out of control and operating against the national interests (as it defines them) rather than in support of them. Any country's government will therefore do its best to ensure that the agencies are kept under as tight a control as the political system allows and—given that intelligence can be a very expensive business—that they provide value for money. As I and my co-authors argue in a forthcoming book,[18] "the most effective control architecture for intelligence" must consist of three main elements:

- Requirements: A comprehensive set of national intelligence requirements and priorities, under which the intelligence goods and services being paid for by the public purse are set out as explicitly as possible.
- Budgets and Resourcing: Although desirable, line-item budgeting is difficult to apply strictly to intelligence where expenditures cannot be planned in advance because targets and sources of opportunity may come out of the blue. However, tying expenditure strictly to activities directed towards national requirements is essential, and maximizes the opportunity cost constraints on agency activity.

- Authorisation and Approval: Operational approval may indeed have to take into account questions such as risk and consistency with national policy, but really effective control comes from testing any proposed operation against the national requirements it is supposed to fulfil. If operational expenses are tied to an approval process that takes as its first criterion the ability of an operation to fulfil one or more national requirements, then it is intensely difficult to undertake "free enterprise" simply because the moneys needed to undertake it will not be forthcoming.

A system like that described both provides maximum control in principle and has been used in practice in the SIS for decades.[19]

Certainly Inspectors General are not an essential component of political supervision (many countries, including the United Kingdom, do not have them),[20] while the lack of parliamentary oversight of a country's intelligence and security agencies, as in France and Russia, does not appear to have damaged those agencies' operational capabilities. But there are two main factors that necessitate an oversight mechanism above and beyond the three basic administrative controls set out above.

First, as already noted, there is the possibility that intelligence agencies may, under ministerial direction, engage in illegal or unethical activities that the government would not be able to defend in public. However efficiently the agencies may commit such misdeeds, there is a consensus in most modern liberal democracies[21] that there should be some nongovernmental mechanism to ensure that intelligence organizations do not overstep the mark. The suspicion that the intelligence community is "up to no good" is a common one, often fostered by the media, even if in most cases it is unjustified. And it would be hard to argue that such a sensitive area as intelligence should be free of any nongovernmental ethical audit.

Second, parliament (and to a much lesser extent the public) wants to be assured that the intelligence and security agencies, both individually and collectively, are effective and efficient. The human beings who make up the agencies are as capable as anyone of making mistakes, so their work can prove suboptimal. Perhaps of more concern is the fact that even if each individual agency were to do its work as well as humanly possible, they might not cooperate properly as a whole. As the joint congressional inquiry into 9/11 noted in beginning its factual findings,

> In short, for a variety of reasons, the Intelligence Community failed to capitalize on both the individual and collective significance of available information that appears relevant to the events of September 11. As a result, the Community missed opportunities to disrupt the September 11th plot by denying entry to or detaining would-be hijackers; to at least try to unravel the plot through surveillance and other investigative work within the United States; and, finally, to generate a heightened state of alert and thus harden the homeland against attack.

No one will ever know what might have happened had more connections been drawn between these disparate pieces of information. We will never definitively know to what extent the Community would have been able and willing to exploit fully all the opportunities that may have emerged. The important point is that the Intelligence Community, for a variety of reasons, did not bring together and fully appreciate a range of information that could have greatly enhanced its chances of uncovering and preventing Usama Bin Ladin's plan to attack these United States on September 11, 2001.[22]

However well a minister may supervise the agencies for which he or she is responsible, and however efficiently those agencies may conduct their operations, there will need to be some governmental or bureaucratic mechanism to ensure that they work together effectively and that the pursuit of their individual goals does not lead to a collectively suboptimal outcome.

So far this analysis of relationships between political supervision and intelligence organizations has largely ignored the important dynamic element—the impact of crises (real or presumed), which can lead to the misuse of intelligence to serve political ends. At its worst this can result in policy makers refusing to accept intelligence analyses that do not fit their preconceptions, as was famously the case in Joseph Stalin's conviction that Adolf Hitler would not attack the Soviet Union—his intelligence advisors knew better than to argue against him.

More recently, there have been allegations that the U.S. administration "cherry-picked" intelligence to make a case for the invasion of Iraq. This of course begs the question of whether intelligence was in fact a driver for the invasion. In the United Kingdom Prime Minister Tony Blair based his passionately presented case for the invasion on supposed intelligence (much of which is now admitted to be incorrect) that Iraq possessed weapons of mass destruction and thus posed a threat to British interests which must be nullified.[23] However, despite Blair's repeated assertions in late 2002 and early 2003 that military action was not inevitable, it appears that the United States had already decided to overthrow Saddam come what may, as Sir Richard Dearlove, the Chief of SIS, ("C"), reported in the notorious "Downing Street Memo" of July 23, 2002:

> C reported on his recent talks in Washington. There was a perceptible shift in attitude. Military action was now seen as inevitable. Bush wanted to remove Saddam, through military action, justified by the conjunction of terrorism and WMD. But the intelligence and facts were being fixed around the policy.[24]

This chapter does not attempt to pass judgment on the sincerity of U.K. and U.S. decision makers prior to the invasion of Iraq, though it seems unlikely that history will treat them kindly.[25] But it is clear that both publics were severely misled about the necessity to invade Iraq—to put it mildly, the rhetoric went far further than the intelligence justified. Under certain circumstances there will always be the temptation to misuse or abuse intelligence in the furtherance of political imperatives. External supervision will be unlikely to prevent this happening at the time, though it may expose it later. However, recent experience in both the United Kingdom and the United States shows how difficult it can be to mount an impartial and effective examination of politicians' use of intelligence—in effect, to answer the question, "Were they lying?"

The postmortem on the intelligence dimension to the invasion of Iraq shows both the need for external supervision and its limitations. The Hutton and Butler inquiries in the United Kingdom and the Senate Intelligence Committee's "Report on the US Intelligence Community's Prewar Intelligence Assessments on Iraq"[26] have thrown unprecedented light on the weaknesses of intelligence and intelligence assessments (though Butler also distributed a few bouquets), but did not pursue their inquiries to the top. Indeed the Senate Committee's first conclusion put the blame squarely on the U.S. Intelligence Community:

> Most of the major key judgments in the Intelligence Community's October 2002 National Intelligence Estimate (NIE), Iraq's Continuing Programs for Weapons of Mass Destruction, either overstated, or were not supported by, the underlying intelligence reporting. A series of failures, particularly in analytic trade craft, led to the mischaracterization of the intelligence.

Intelligence oversight is ultimately limited by an administration's ability to ignore adverse findings unless they demonstrate culpable illegality—and even then there may well be loopholes that politicians can exploit to avoid being brought to trial. And, as shown by the Senate inquiry's failure so far to move to its second stage—consideration of whether the U.S. administration consciously manipulated and misrepresented intelligence—the majority party can use its political clout to delay unwelcome attention to its actions.

Most mature democracies accept that intelligence agencies are needed to inform and support national policy objectives, but that their activities must be monitored by some nonadministration mechanism that can report back to the legislature and public in order to ensure that they observe legal and ethical standards, and that they operate effectively and efficiently in the interests of the nation. Differing constitutional frameworks mean there can be no ideal or "one size fits all" model for supervision, but there appears to be a general consensus that the various supervisory mechanisms that have developed over the past two decades go a long way toward striking an appropriate balance between these two imperatives. This however leads to a not unimportant question: Can and should supervision be developed further (and, if so, where and how?) to provide more effective oversight of intelligence, or would this tip the balance too far in that direction, unnecessarily limiting the ability of the intelligence agencies to perform their tasks in support of national objectives?

But such questions are essentially about effectiveness and efficiency; in the wake of Iraq a much more important question (certainly for the United Kingdom and the United States) is how oversight can discover, and ideally prevent, the misuse and abuse of intelligence by the administration of the day. This is where most if not all supervisory systems have fallen down, failing to follow the trail all the way into the darkness at the back of the cave. But if oversight is to be wholly effective it must take those final steps, so that legislature and public can see whether politicians' actions were properly informed by the intelligence they received, or whether intelligence was manipulated for propaganda purposes, being used as a pretext for actions with quite different motivations. Yet it would be a remarkably noble and selfless administration that would set up a mechanism holding it formally and strictly to account in such a sensitive area.

For anyone who has spent a career in intelligence, trained to keep secrets secret in order to protect intelligence sources and methods, leaks of classified information to the media are anathema. Yet had it not been for the leaking of key 2002 U.K. minutes we would not know how early the British government was committed to supporting a U.S. invasion of Iraq, or how desperate was their subsequent search for a legitimate *casus belli* based on intelligence. So it may be that the ultimate sanction against an administration's misuse or abuse of intelligence lies not in any of the formal systems and structures of oversight considered in this chapter, but in the unauthorized and possibly illegal activities of whistle-blowing insiders and their allies in the media—a fourth sanction in addition to the three already described.

This is not a comfortable conclusion to reach, and many will instinctively reject it. In fact, whistle-blowers may be unreliable sources for various reasons. They may be junior personnel who have seen only part of the bigger picture and reached a false conclusion that there has been misdoing. They may be leaking selectively according to their own agenda. Indeed (if they provide documentary evidence) they may be forgers out to make mischief or a profit. The suggestion that whistle-blowers may provide an ultimate fourth sanction should not be seen as any defense of former insiders nurturing a grudge, such as Peter Wright, Richard Tomlinson, or David Shayler. But those who totally reject whistle-blowing under any circumstances, and whatever government dishonesty it may reveal, should either put forward an alternative way of curbing the ability of governments to misuse intelligence or accept that this is ultimately impossible.

CONCLUSION

It would be pleasant to conclude that in democratic societies around the world there is a vigorous debate about best practice in intelligence oversight. Sadly, this is not the case; it may well be that the last decade of the twentieth century marked the high point of interest in the subject and that oversight mechanisms will become less, rather than more, able to limit excesses. Such debate as there is may arouse little interest beyond the academic community, in which environment it will certainly reach no clear conclusions.

Yet debate is needed. Oversight of intelligence is too important a subject to be the victim of benign neglect. Many countries have oversight systems; unless one assumes that each is perfectly fitted to its constitutional environment and has reached perfection, they must all be capable of improvement. Should this take the form of continuing fine-tuning, or does experience point to a more radical shake-up of a country's oversight arrangements? If each oversight system has its particular strengths and weaknesses, how far is it possible to import elements from other countries' oversight organizations in the interests of best practice? How can the international community persuade countries with weak or nonexistent oversight of intelligence that this is an essential component of a mature democratic state? Such questions ought to be a part of the ongoing political debate, but it would be a triumph of hope over experience to believe that they will be.

5

Intelligence Oversight in the United States

Loch K. Johnson

This chapter[1] has two objectives. The first is to present a historical overview of intelligence oversight or accountability in the United States since the end of the Second World War. This provides the context for understanding the problems involved, and progress made, in the political supervision of the intelligence services. The second is to examine the chief obstacles to effective oversight that still apply today.

HISTORICAL OVERVIEW OF INTELLIGENCE OVERSIGHT

In most nations, intelligence agencies are treated as exceptions from the rest of government. They are cloaked in secrecy, allowed privileged access to policy makers, and given broad leeway to help maintain the nation's security—even if that means breaking laws overseas (almost always the case) and engaging in other unsavory activities that would be deemed inappropriate for regular government agencies. From its earliest days, the United States embraced this *laissez faire* philosophy for intelligence operations. The nation's founders well understood the dangers from abroad faced by the new Republic and were willing to grant broad discretionary powers to America's intelligence officers.[2] As the nation matured and its intelligence services expanded in the aftermath of the Second World War, this hands-off philosophy continued.

In modern times, beginning with the creation of the Central Intelligence Agency (CIA) in 1947, intelligence oversight has gone through five major phases: an Era of Trust (1947–1974), an Era of Uneasy Partnership (1975–1986), an Era of Distrust (1987–1991), an Era of Partisan Advocacy (1992–2001), and an Era of Congressional Ambivalence (2002–now).

Era of Trust (1947-1974)

The philosophy guiding U.S. intelligence during the Cold War was clear: the struggle against the Communist world required a strong intelligence shield. In the nuclear age, a nation might not survive another surprise attack like Pearl Harbor. America's secret agencies would have to be as tough and effective as anything the Soviet Union could field. This is not to say the CIA was without supervision, even in this warlike climate. Most of its activities were approved by the White House and reported, in broad outline at least, to oversight subcommittees in the House of Representatives and the Senate.[3] The approvals were highly discretionary, however, allowing broad leeway to the Director of Central Intelligence (DCI)—the nation's chief spymaster until replaced by a new Director of National Intelligence (DNI) in 2005. The DCI's reports to Congress tended to be sketchy, perfunctory, and often unwanted by lawmakers.

Era of Uneasy Partnership (1975-1986)

In 1975, this philosophy of intelligence exceptionalism underwent a dramatic reversal. The shift resulted not from any sudden sea change in world affairs; that would not happen until the dissolution of the Soviet Empire in 1991. Rather, the stimulus was a series of articles appearing in the *New York Times* in the final months of 1974, charging that the CIA had abused its power by spying inside the United States and seeking to topple a democratic government in Chile. In response, Congress enacted on December 31, 1974, the first major law to institute tighter supervision over the CIA: the Hughes-Ryan Act.[4] This statute strengthened executive and legislative control over covert action, the most aggressive form of intelligence through which the CIA attempts to secretly manipulate events abroad by means of propaganda, political, economic, and paramilitary operations (as occurred in Chile during the Johnson and Nixon administrations).

Turning in January 1975 to the even more worrisome charges of spying at home, government investigators uncovered a startling number of intelligence transgressions in what is now remembered as the "Year of Intelligence." The inquiries uncovered illegal mail openings, wiretaps, and international cable interceptions; intelligence files on over a million American citizens; improper drug experiments and the unlawful sequestering of prohibited chemical and biological materials; a master spy plan to conduct surveillance against Vietnam War dissenters in the United States;

intelligence infiltration of a range of groups in American society, from universities to religious and media organizations; the incitement of violence against African-American groups; and questionable covert actions abroad, including assassination plots against foreign leaders.[5]

A counterintelligence program run by the Federal Bureau of Investigation (FBI), code named "Cointelpro," stunned members of the Senate investigating panel (the Church Committee, led by Frank Church, D-Idaho).[6] Documents revealed that FBI agents had conducted smear campaigns against individuals across the country from 1956–1971, simply because they had expressed opposition to the war in Vietnam or criticized the slow pace of the civil rights movement. The attacks were aimed at people in all walks of life and various political persuasions, an expansive hatred that embraced black leaders, white supremacists, and war dissenters alike. The Ku Klux Klan, the women's liberation movement, socialists, the New Left, and anti-war and civil rights activists all became enemies of the Republic whom the FBI set out to destroy.

The effect on lawmakers of this catalog of improprieties was profound. From 1975 on, America's support for a muscular, unbound intelligence capability would have to compete with another value that had long invested the rest of the government, namely, liberty. It means safeguarding the American people against the power of their own government, not just foreign governments. Officials in Washington began an unprecedented experiment in trying to balance security and liberty with respect to the nation's secret agencies. The Ford administration conducted its own investigation into intelligence (the Rockefeller Commission), leading to the establishment of an Intelligence Oversight Board in the White House and an executive order prohibiting assassination plots both in 1976. In the same year senators created a Senate Select Committee on Intelligence (SSCI), while House members followed suit with a House Permanent Select Committee on Intelligence (HPSCI) in 1977.

The scope of intelligence oversight continued to expand. In 1978, lawmakers brought the judicial branch more directly into the realm of intelligence review by creating, through the Foreign Intelligence Surveillance Act or FISA,[7] a special "FISA Court" to review national security wiretap requests from the executive branch. In 1980, Congress enacted an important Intelligence Oversight Act to tighten supervision over the secret agencies, namely, by requiring *prior notice* to the Congress before implementation, of *all* important intelligence operations (not just covert actions).[8]

The Era of Trust had relied on an attitude of benign neglect by overseers: a "don't ask, don't tell" approach, shattered by the investigative findings of the Church Committee and the Rockefeller Commission. Beginning with implementation of the Hughes-Ryan Act and carrying on until the Iran-Contra exposé in 1987, lawmakers, presidents, and DCIs attempted during the Era of Uneasy Partnership to fashion a workable relationship between democratic openness and effective espionage, between liberty and security.

Each step along the way was riven by debate, intense negotiations, and sometimes bitter quarreling. The creation of SSCI and HPSCI had to overcome strong opposition from the intelligence community, the congressional Armed Services Committees, and key members of Congress. Then the newly established Intelligence Committees had to fight for the fulsome reporting on covert actions envisioned by the Hughes-Ryan Act.[9] An attempt by legislative reformers to enact a 276-page omnibus intelligence charter was rebuffed, leading instead to the two-and-a-half-page Intelligence Oversight Act of 1980. The longest serving DCI during this era, William J. Casey of the Reagan administration, displayed disdain toward the idea of legislative oversight, maintaining that the "business of Congress was to stay the f— out of my business."[10] He even managed to alienate Senator Barry Goldwater (R-Arizona), the chair of SSCI, who himself was ironically an arch-critic of oversight, that is, until Casey misled him by failing to adequately report to SSCI on the existence of aggressive CIA paramilitary operations in Nicaragua (most notably the secret mining of the Corinto port).

Despite occasional setbacks in their efforts to enhance oversight, members of Congress managed to establish the precedent of a serious, ongoing review of intelligence programs and budgets within the hearing rooms of SSCI and HPSCI, as well as within the offices of the two congressional appropriations subcommittees dealing with intelligence. The judiciary committees also got into the act, successfully demanding a continued jurisdiction over the FBI, whereas the armed services committees maintained a choke hold on matters related to tactical military intelligence. Congressional staff experts pored over budgets, organized hearings, and, less formally, met with intelligence officers in an ongoing review of their operations. With various degrees of enthusiasm, lawmakers posed questions during hearings, visited the secret agencies, and traveled abroad to examine operations in the field. As Gregory F. Treverton has noted, the intelligence agencies had become a part of the regular government and now faced a full panoply of oversight procedures.[11]

Even the abbreviated Intelligence Oversight Act of 1980 contained significant language that required more robust reporting to SSCI and HPSCI ("prior notice") than even the Hughes-Ryan Act had posited ("in a timely fashion").[12] Moreover, DCI Admiral Stansfield Turner of the Carter administration enjoyed reasonably good relations on Capitol Hill. Unlike his successor, William J. Casey, the Admiral agreed with the need to establish more meaningful intelligence oversight and labored toward the cultivation of a cordial legislative-executive intelligence partnership.

Beyond Casey's irascible personality, the major irritant to a working partnership during the 1980s was partisan disagreement over the threat posed by a Marxist regime in Nicaragua and whether extreme covert actions ought to be used to dislodge the regime. Hitherto, almost all SSCI and HPSCI decisions had been approached in a spirit of consensus. Nicaragua, in a foreshadowing of what would become more common behavior in the 1990s, split this union apart along party lines in both Committees.

Era of Distrust (1987-1991)

With the Democrats holding a majority in both chambers during the 1980s and determined to curb covert action in Nicaragua (through the Boland Amendments, named after their sponsor, HPSCI Chairman Edward P. Boland, D-Massachusetts), the Reagan administration turned to extraordinary means for achieving its regime-change objectives. Aides on the National Security Council (NSC) secretly created an organization known as "The Enterprise" to conduct privately financed covert actions in Nicaragua, outside the framework of the intelligence community and the constitutionally based congressional appropriations process.

In face-to-face meetings with SSCI and HPSCI leaders, the NSC staff architects of this supersecret operation denied its rumored existence. In 1986, however, a Middle East newspaper disclosed the secret operation and ushered in a major investigation into the Iran-Contra affair, so-named because covert funding by the Reagan administration for the anti-Marxist *contras* in Nicaragua came partly from hidden CIA weapons sales to Iran. Reeling from the rupture of trust that lawmakers had been trying to develop since 1975, oversight became engulfed in the acrimony of public hearings in 1987 and proposals for new laws to tighten accountability. Interbranch comity slid downhill rapidly.

The Iran-Contra scandal was a major setback to the "New Oversight" setup between 1975 and 1984, as the Reagan administration bypassed all of these rules and statutes in its conduct of a covert war in Nicaragua. The scandal led Congress to pass new restrictions, chiefly the Intelligence Oversight Act of 1991, which further tightened intelligence supervision by clarifying reporting requirements. In the aftermath of the Iran-Contra affair, lawmakers also created an Office of Inspector General in the CIA, confirmed by the Senate, and accountable to members of Congress as well as to the DCI (now DNI).

Era of Partisan Advocacy (1992-2001)

In the aftermath of the Iran-Contra scandal, DCIs William H. Webster, followed by Robert M. Gates, attempted to heal the breach between lawmakers and spies. According to one study, Webster "set a new standard in comity between the branches of government...intelligence oversight had reached its full flowering."[13] Moreover, Gates had a close working relationship with SSCI Chair David Boren (D-Oklahoma). The United States, however, was about to enter into an era of pronounced internal political warfare on Capitol Hill, as state-by-state redistricting along party lines and the rise of deeply ideological lawmakers (such as Newt Gingrich, R-Georgia) introduced a heightened level of partisan discord in Congress. In 1995, the Republican Party (GOP) achieved its goal of a House majority, and soon after the GOP took over the Senate as well. The firebrand Gingrich became Speaker of the House. "What is distinctive in the period after the Republican takeover in 1995," writes Aberbach, "is the level of oversight hostile not only to the intent and behavior of political appointees, but to the missions of many federal programs and agencies."[14]

Once largely immune to the tides of politics in the legislative chambers (the hot issue of Nicaragua during the 1980s excepted), the two Intelligence Committees soon proved vulnerable to this rising tide of partisanship. Lawmakers drifted into their separate party camps, casting votes and often verbal stones against the opposition. Stephen F. Knott attributes the polarization, in part, to a Republican wariness over President Bill Clinton's foreign policy initiatives and to "simple partisan payback for years of perceived Democratic hectoring of Republican presidents."[15] The nomination of Robert Gates for DCI in 1991 (his second bid for the office) was an important turning point, as Republicans rallied behind President George H. W. Bush's choice "as a matter of political loyalty and obligation."[16] Even though David Boren, the Democratic chair of SSCI, strongly backed Gates, too, the hearings and the final vote were significantly influenced by partisan considerations. Another confirmation hearing in 1997, during the Clinton administration, to review Anthony Lake's DCI candidacy also produced a partisan firestorm, with Lake finally withdrawing from the fray. The Lake hearings, characterized as "vitriolic" by a former SSCI staffer,[17] were no doubt the most bitter public exchanges among lawmakers in the Committee's history.

An additional dimension of oversight behavior emerged during this period. With an occasional exception, as in the case of SSCI Chair Richard C. Shelby (R-Alabama) in his final years on that Committee, Republican lawmakers on SSCI and HPSCI became less gimlet-eyed reviewers of intelligence programs than uncritical advocates of whatever the secret agencies wanted. The dominant Republican leader on HPSCI during this period, Porter Goss of Florida (a former CIA officer), found himself labeled an "unrelenting cheerleader" for the intelligence agencies.[18]

While Representative Goss was certainly more of an advocate than an adversary of intelligence, this description fails to capture the complexity of his tenure. Goss aggressively criticized the Clinton administration's neglect of intelligence. "'We don't care about national security,' said the Clinton people," Goss charged on a television talk show.[19] Further, he took a firm stance in favor of improving the management of the intelligence community, especially by strengthening the authority of the DCI. Under his tenure, HPSCI reports were often hard-hitting;[20] and he was the first and only

HPSCI leader to have an office in the Committee's suite near the Capitol Dome, spending more time on the premises than any previous chair. It is true, though, that Goss was considerably more supportive of intelligence programs than HPSCI Democrats, and he consistently sought to increase the annual intelligence budget. In 2004, President George W. Bush appointed Goss to the DCI position. By April 2005, he had been stripped of the DCI title, as that office was replaced by a new DNI; henceforth, Goss would hold only the title of director of the CIA. In this capacity, he served for just a little over a year longer, announcing his resignation (reportedly under pressure from the White House) in May 2006. He had the ignominious distinction of presiding over the decline of the CIA from its status as the nation's *central* intelligence agency to just one of 16 agencies in the intelligence community, leaving behind a corps of professional bureaucrats whose morale lie in tatters.[21]

In 2004, Goss's successor at HPSCI's helm was Representative Peter Hoekstra (R-Michigan). He came across as more of an intelligence cheerleader, lacking even the spurts of critical examination into intelligence programs occasionally displayed by Goss.

Era of Congressional Ambivalence (2002–Now)

In the midst of the partisan squabbling that plagued the Intelligence Committees, terrorists struck the United States on September 11, 2001. Now the Committees faced a much more serious matter than party differences: clearly, the intelligence agencies had failed to protect the nation and, by implication, so had lawmakers on the oversight panels. As in 1975, Congress again began to take its intelligence oversight responsibilities more seriously. The members of SSCI and HPSCI formed into a special Joint Committee to investigate the intelligence failure, holding extensive hearings in 2002. Much of the time during its inquiry the Joint Committee was on the defensive, experiencing first a brouhaha over decisions made by its first staff director (who was fired), followed by accusations of Committee leaks. Members even went so far as to allow an investigation of their Joint Committee by the FBI, one of the agencies it was supposed to be investigating. The Committee did manage, however, to highlight significant mistakes made by the intelligence agencies, especially the lack of communications between the CIA and the FBI; but it ran out of time after a slow start and called for the creation of a special national commission to carry on and widen its work.

In the aftermath of 9/11, a new attitude began to dominate SSCI and HPSCI and, indeed, the entire Congress: a sense of ambivalence toward intelligence accountability. On the one hand, the mistakes of 9/11 and the errors over predicting the presence of weapons of mass destruction

(WMD) in Iraq could hardly be ignored. On the other hand, lawmakers rushed to increase the espionage funding and authority and otherwise aid the secret agencies in the struggle against global terrorism. Some members of the Joint Committee, notably on the Democratic side, chided the secret agencies for their mistakes preceding 9/11; for the most part, though, the panel appeared reluctant to move aggressively toward major reforms. Increasingly, oversight on SSCI and HPSCI came to mean rallying behind the intelligence community in its war against terrorism and in support of intelligence operations in the second Gulf War—laudable enough goals, but only part of an overseer's responsibilities. Overseers are supposed to be both advocates and critics. According to an observer, the relationship between the oversight committees and the intelligence community had "degenerated into a mutual admiration society for secret agencies."[22]

The congressional ambivalence toward intelligence has continued, as revealed in the dispute over whether President George W. Bush violated the Foreign Intelligence Surveillance Act of 1978 by conducting warrantless wiretaps in the war against terrorism. The flap led to a decision by the Republican leadership on both Intelligence Committees to support the President and dismiss the allegations of FISA violations. In response, the SSCI Vice Chairman, John D. Rockefeller IV (D-West Virginia), charged that the Committee was "basically under the control of the White House, through its chairman" Pat Roberts (R-Kansas).[23] In turn, Roberts blamed the Democrats for bringing partisan politics and "gotch 'ya oversight" into the realm of sensitive intelligence operations. The experiment in accountability begun by the Church Committee in 1975 faced the prospect of failure, as the wrangling between Republicans and Democrats threatened to undermine all hope of a dispassionate, careful scrutiny of intelligence programs.

SHOCK AS A STIMULUS FOR OVERSIGHT

The research on intelligence oversight on Capitol Hill indicates that efforts of lawmakers to supervise the secret agencies have been "sporadic, spotty, and essentially uncritical."[24] The chief cause of this inattentiveness derives from the nature of Congress: lawmakers seek reelection and usually conclude that passing bills and raising campaign funds is a better use of their time than the often tedious review of executive programs. This is especially true of intelligence review, since the examination of America's secret operations must take place for the most part in closed committee sanctuaries, outside of public view. Absent public awareness, credit-claiming vital to reelection prospects becomes difficult.[25]

An analysis of intelligence accountability indicates a pattern in recent decades: a major intelligence scandal or failure, a shock, converts perfunctory "police patrolling" into a burst of intense "fire fighting." This fire fighting is then followed by a period of dedicated patrolling that yields remedial legislation or other reforms designed to curb inappropriate intelligence activities in the future.[26] Sometimes the high-intensity patrolling can last for months and, if the original shock creates a media tsunami, even years. Once the firestorm has subsided and reforms are in place, however, lawmakers return to a state of relative inattention to intelligence issues.[27] This pattern is depicted in Figure 5.1.

Intense media coverage of intelligence abuses or failures may not be enough in itself to sound a major fire alarm, stimulating lawmakers to don their fire-fighting jackets and seek reform in the heat of failure or scandal. Such considerations, as the personalities of congressional overseers, especially committee chairs, as well as the existence of a divided government, can play a role, too.[28] In 2006, the media coverage of possible presidential abuse of the Foreign Intelligence Surveillance Act was extensive. The Republicans controlled the White House and both houses of Congress,

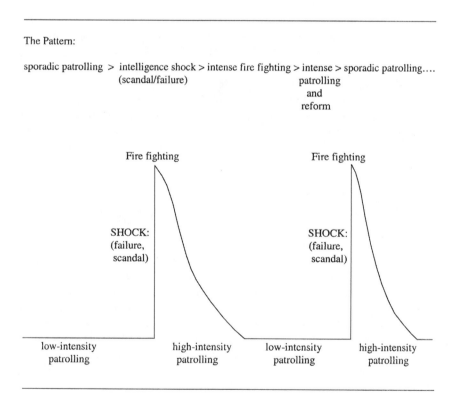

Figure 5.1 The Dominant Pattern of Intelligence Oversight by Lawmakers, 1975–2006

however, and they successfully resisted Democratic calls for an investigation into the allegation of wiretap abuse.

CHIEF OBSTACLES TO OVERSIGHT

Motivation

Nothing is more important to effective oversight than the will of individual lawmakers or executive overseers to engage in the meaningful examination of intelligence programs. "Determination is the key. Members [of Congress] have to be willing to break arms and legs," emphasizes a staffer with three decades of experience on the Hill. He concluded: "Not too many are willing."[29] In 2003, a former special assistant to DCI Casey urged former lawmakers and other officials on the Kean Commission, created to further investigate the 9/11 attacks after the Joint Committee inquiry, to pursue their responsibilities with utmost seriousness. The Casey aide advocated a "helicopter-raids-at-dawn, break-down-the-doors, kick-their-rear-ends sort of operation,"[30] although this was hardly the approach to legislative oversight endorsed by his Congress-bashing boss during the 1980s.

Such exhortations for better oversight to the contrary notwithstanding, the day-to-day reality has been starkly different. As this level, flaccidity has been the hallmark. "Congress is informed to the degree that Congress wants to be informed," former DCI William E. Colby once noted, pointing out that several overseers had expressed little interest in being briefed by the CIA.[31] Recalled another DCI, Admiral Turner: "I believe the committees of Congress could have been more rigorous with me [during the Carter administration]...it would be more helpful if you are probing and rigorous."[32] Were he alive, no doubt DCI Casey would disagree, probably with scatological emphasis. Several lawmakers also have quite a different view than Colby and Turner, preferring the role of advocate over critic. For them, the President and the DCI know best in this sensitive domain: better to follow their lead than to second-guess and perhaps harm America's national security. In their view, efficiency trumps accountability, especially in the war against global terrorism.

Executive Branch Cooperation

Vital for effective accountability, too, is the cooperation of the White House, the Justice Department, and the intelligence agencies in working with Congress. Lawmakers know about intelligence activities only to the extent that the President and the DCI permit them to know.[33] As James Currie puts it, oversight works "only if there is honesty and completeness in what the members of the intelligence community tell their congressional overseers."[34] Yet this *sine qua non* is often missing.

In 2002, the Joint Committee complained about stonewalling by the second Bush administration. During that probe, DCI George Tenet tried to put the Committee on the defensive in public hearings with edgy responses to questions about 9/11. Allotted 10 minutes to speak, he went on in a "somewhat defiant tone" for 50 minutes, despite a request from co-chair Bob Graham (D-Florida) that he abbreviate his remarks.[35] Tenet also refused to declassify information the Committee had asked to make public. He often also withdrew intelligence witnesses the Committee had called to testify just before a scheduled hearing. "Witnesses are requested, refused, requested again, granted, and then at the last minute refused again," groused a Committee member on the Senate floor.[36]

When word leaked that the staff had cautioned members about the likely elusive responses of a scheduled CIA witness, Tenet blasted the Committee for prejudging the veracity of CIA officers. The staff, though, could hardly be blamed for reminding members that in past inquiries CIA witnesses had not always been forthcoming. On the contrary, some had misled Congress, even under oath during the Iran-Contra investigation.[37] Moreover, officers from the CIA had "flat lied" to SSCI in 1995–1996, according to a senior staffer, when the Committee attempted to investigate the Agency's ties with a controversial military officer in Guatemala.[38]

With a growing dissatisfaction over Tenet's belligerent posture before the Joint Committee, co-chair Graham "toughened his stance toward the intelligence agencies when the administration began to stonewall," recalls a staff aide on the panel.[39] When the DCI refused to provide SSCI with CIA documents on Iraq and then failed to appear at a closed Joint Committee hearing, Graham accused the CIA of "obstructionism" and said that its behavior was "unacceptable."[40] A former Hill staffer who follows intelligence closely concluded that the CIA had "stuck its fingers in the eye of the oversight committee, which—under Graham—was waking up very late to the fact that it is being rolled."[41] Though Graham and Shelby were clearly agitated, most of their colleagues seemed to shrug off the intelligence community's behavior, choosing instead to concentrate on the terrorist threat.

CONCLUSION

Intelligence oversight since 1975 has been relatively robust compared to earlier years, yet it falls far short of goals espoused by the Church Committee and other panels that have championed serious intelligence supervision. Most lawmakers have been desultory in their oversight duties, responding to fire alarms, carrying out probes into domestic spying (1975), improper covert actions (1987), counterintelligence vulnerabilities (1995), and major intelligence failures (2002–2005), but giving insufficient attention to the day-to-day police work that might uncover weaknesses in the first place and eliminate the need for hurry-up *ex post facto* fire fighting.

For the most part, the experience in intelligence oversight since 1975 has been a story of discontinuous motivation, *ad hoc* responses to scandals, and reliance on the initiative of only a few members of Congress, mainly the occasional dedicated chair, to carry the burden. Absent is a comprehensive approach to intelligence review that mobilizes most members of SSCI and HPSCI behind an approach that includes a systematic plan of police-patrolling, without waiting for fire alarms. Responding after the fact to intelligence failures and scandals in today's dangerous world is not good enough. Overseers must try harder to prevent surprises like the 9/11 attacks from occurring in the first place, as well as abuse of power by the secret agencies.

What are the ingredients for better intelligence oversight? Of foremost importance is greater devotion to police-patrolling instead of waiting for fire alarms, which in the closed world of intelligence are unlikely to sound until a major scandal or disaster strikes. More specifically, lawmakers need to pay closer attention to the following:

- the accuracy of an administration's threat assessments, as the controversy over Iraq's alleged WMD threat in 2003 reminds us;
- the balance between human and technical collection;
- data-sifting capabilities;
- the perspicacity of its analytic reports;
- charges of intelligence politicization; and
- efforts designed to achieve institutional and computer integration for "all-source fusion" of intelligence in Washington (horizontal integration), as well as down to the state and local levels (vertical integration).

Truly meaningful oversight would also give closer scrutiny to covert action and efforts by the Department of Defense to develop its own capabilities in this area, which are currently poorly supervised by Congress. One would hope to see, too, a renewed focus on counterintelligence. This will involve appraising the merits of the British Security Service or an MI5-like unit in the United States, reviewing the current efforts to guard against another Aldrich Ames, and building protections against hostile electronic penetrations of America's intelligence computer systems. Among other issues lawmakers need to examine more closely are the merits of greater authority for the newly created office of DNI, to overcome the powerful centrifugal forces in the U.S. intelligence community. On the civil liberties side, overseers must revisit the procedures of the FISA Court, as well as the adequacy of protections for the rights of law-abiding Muslim Americans.

Specifically on the question of global human rights, the congressional oversight committees should insist on better and more frequent use of U.S. intelligence satellites and reconnaissance aircraft to monitor Darfur in the

Sudan and other suspect locations in the world for evidence of human rights abuses. During the Balkan Wars in 1999, for example, America's satellites detected evidence that mass graves had been freshly dug in the villages of Pusto Selo and Izbica in Kosovo. These photographs permitted UN investigators to search for further evidence of atrocities that could be used in trials against the murderers. Low-flying drones augmented the satellite data by crisscrossing Kosovo each day with cameras fastened to their bellies. So-called Jstars (Joint Surveillance Target Attack Radar Systems) and Apache helicopters can be a part of the reconnaissance sweeps.

Better incentives must be created as well to encourage the involvement of officials in oversight, such as public praise by congressional leaders, along with the granting of choice committee assignments and other perks to lawmakers who have demonstrated skill and devotion to the hard work of maintaining accountability over executive agencies. It would be useful, further, to establish regular meetings between rank-and-file overseers and the DNI, rather than having the DNI meet with just a few select members of the oversight committees.

Congressional jurisdictional lines for oversight need to be restructured, so that SSCI and HPSCI are given more authority over the full intelligence community, in place of the tangled strands that currently exist with the armed services, judiciary, and homeland security committees. Vital, too, are measures to make the government less secretive, including more SSCI and HPSCI open hearings, more online reports about the activities of the oversight Committees, and fewer classification actions by the executive branch.

Despite its flaws—especially excessive partisanship—along with too much advocacy and too little criticism by overseers, the U.S. system of intelligence oversight is strong compared to other nations. It represents a dramatic improvement over the relative absence of meaningful accountability in the United States before the intelligence investigations of 1975 and the establishment of Senate and House Intelligence Committees. These Committees are independent from the executive branch and have a capacity to probe intelligence programs, using subpoena and budget powers as leverage. A number of laws allow the Committees access to information about intelligence activities *before* they are implemented, not just after something goes wrong. The Committees also have sizable staffs with extensive intelligence expertise.

Clearly, though, further reforms are needed to improve intelligence supervision, and the time has never been more propitious for reform. Enormous incentives exist: the prevention of another 9/11 attack and better monitoring of WMD around the globe. If lawmakers will take the time to address these oversight deficiencies, the United States will be in a position to achieve a better balance between security and liberty.

6

Parliamentary Oversight of Intelligence: The German Approach

Christian Heyer

The greatest threat to democratic societies today is no longer that of a foreign military invasion but the risks to internal security resulting from international terrorism, proliferation of nuclear or other weapons of mass destruction, serious drug-related crime, international organized crime, and illegal migration.[1] The challenges unleashed by the terrorist attacks of September 11, 2001, underline the urgent need to balance our commitments to security on the one hand and democracy on the other hand. This can be achieved only if new powers to meet the new security challenges are accompanied by renewing the emphasis on the oversight of security and intelligence agencies.

Intelligence services perform a valuable service in democratic societies by protecting national security and good order. But the services operate clandestinely, and the nature of their work requires them to fulfill their obligations in secret. Even retrospective disclosure of individual operations could harm the long-term activities of the intelligence services, as this could provide insights into the working practices of the services, the identity of the employees and secret contacts, or their areas of operation. However, security services are also government agencies that exercise public authority. The notion of government agencies operating in secret run counter to the principles of an open society. Nevertheless, and ironically, the existence of an open society requires defense by secret services. To strike a balance between these conflicting demands means that the intelligence services must be subjected to comprehensive democratic accountability and civilian control.[2] There is a widespread belief that security policy is a matter best left to the executive branch as it has the necessary knowledge and can act quickly. The legislative branch tends to be regarded as less suitable for dealing with security issues.[3]

However, oversight of the intelligence services cannot be left to the executive branch alone without inviting abuses, at least potentially. As with all areas of government operation, parliament is the most appropriate institution to review, monitor, and scrutinize them. For a democracy to stay vibrant and healthy no area of state activity can be allowed to remain a "no-go" zone for parliamentary oversight, including the intelligence services. The existence of parliamentary oversight, in fact, can work to the benefits of the secret services and helps to build up and sustain public confidence in the agencies by reassuring the general public that individual rights are respected and public money is properly spent. Furthermore, since most people watched by the secret services do not usually know they were under surveillance, they would not be able to seek judicial protection of their rights unless and until they became aware that they might have been subjected to such surveillance, if this was done illegally. In light of this inherent limitation in the judicial branch's effectiveness to balance this particular area of government activity, the case for effective parliamentary supervision is even stronger. Indeed, parliamentary oversight of the intelligence services should apply both in general terms and in specific cases in order to ensure that the basic rights of individual citizens are properly protected. Having established the importance of parliamentary oversight, I examine in the rest of this chapter how parliamentary control operates in Germany. I start with a short survey of the German Intelligence Community, which is followed by an examination of how the most important individual control bodies of the German Bundestag, the Parliamentary Control Panel and the G10 Commission, work.

THE GERMAN INTELLIGENCE COMMUNITY

In Germany the term "intelligence service" refers to an organization that gathers and evaluates information on foreign, internal, and security policy situations through both open and clandestine channels. Intelligence services in Germany have no executive powers. They may not be attached to any police authority, and they may restrict basic rights only where the law specifically permits them to do so. In order to preempt them from undermining the fundamental pillars of democracy, the intelligence services are organized as three separate agencies at the federal level in Germany, each with clearly defined objectives and areas of operation:

- The Federal Intelligence Service, or Bundesnachrichtendienst (BND), is the foreign intelligence service.
- The Federal Office for the Protection of the Constitution, or Bundesamt für Verfassungsschutz (BfV), is the domestic intelligence service.
- The Military Counterintelligence Service, or Militärischer Abschirmdienst (MAD), is part of the armed forces.

The Federal Intelligence Service or BND is a federal agency that comes under the Head of the Federal Chancellery. Its primary task is to collect information about foreign countries that is relevant and valuable to the making of the foreign and security policies of Germany. The BND acts as the Federal Government's early warning system for troubles abroad, particularly where German interests are involved. This means it focuses its attention and resources on crisis-prone regions and regions where members of the Federal Armed Forces are deployed. It also accords high priority to monitoring dangers such as international terrorism, proliferation and illegal technology transfers, international organized crime, the international arms trade, international drug trafficking, money laundering, and illegal migration. The legal basis for the BND's work is the BND Act.[4] It currently employs approximately 6,000 members of staff.

The Federal Office for the Protection of the Constitution (BfV) is a federal agency answerable to the Federal Ministry of the Interior. Its main task is to gather and evaluate information on extremists and activities by German nationals and foreigners that endanger the security of Germany, as well as on the activities of hostile intelligence services inside Germany. In light of the new terrorist threats and their international nature, the BfV has also been tasked with monitoring activities directed against "international understanding or peaceful coexistence." The BfV Act governs the structure, procedures, and working of this agency.[5] It has a current strength of approximately 2,400 members of staff.

The Military Counterintelligence Service (MAD) is a part of the armed forces and comes under the jurisdiction of the Federal Ministry of Defense. Its organization and operations are governed by the Military Counterintelligence Act.[6] It is a domestic intelligence service and is responsible for performing the same functions that the BfV has, but on behalf of the Federal Armed Forces. Its current establishment provides for approximately 1,300 officers and support staff.

THE PARLIAMENTARY CONTROL PANEL

Over the years a system of control has developed in Germany that seeks to strike a balance between the diverging interests—the need to maintain secrecy on the one hand, and the need to exert effective control on the other. This system of parliamentary control has developed over time and has been steadily refined. It was in 1978 that the Parliamentary Control Panel—then known as the Parliamentary Control Commission—was put on solid legal footing for the first time. Its hands were strengthened by the introduction of extensive additional powers in 1999 with the revision of the Control Panel Act.[7] In accordance with public expectations the German system makes it a point to emphasize that the Bundestag owns its Control Panel. It means that the Bundestag alone is responsible for appointing and, where necessary, removing members of this body, as is the case with all parliamentary bodies exercising the oversight function in its name.[8] This is to ensure the Control Panel enjoys legitimacy and commands trust. For the same reasons it is also given a broad mandate and is required to represent a cross-section of the political groups within the Bundestag.[9] Indeed, the Bundestag elects members for the Panel from among its members at the beginning of each electoral term. As required by law this plenary meeting of the Bundestag must set out the number of members on the Panel, their composition, and working procedures in a resolution at the beginning of a new parliament, so that it will be adjusted to reflect the varied composition of a new parliament. Membership lasts until a new Control Panel is formed after a general election. The Chairmanship of the Panel, however, alternates annually between a member nominated by the parliamentary majority and a member nominated by the minority

An unusual requirement for members of the Bundestag to join the Control Panel is for them to secure the support of a majority of fellow members of the Bundestag. This is not a requirement imposed on membership of other parliamentary committees. It is intended to ensure that a majority in the Bundestag is convinced that those elected are qualified and will observe secrecy. The rationale is that with the Control Panel enjoying the express confidence of the parliament it should help to eliminate mistrust between the executive branch and the Control Panel.

This size of the Control Panel is deliberately kept small in order to retain confidence of the intelligence community, as information provided by it will need to be treated confidentially by members of the Panel. The current Panel consists of nine members, which can be compared to 41 members in the Budgetary Committee. They include three from the Christian Democratic Union/Christian Social Union parliamentary group, three from the Social Democratic Party parliamentary group, and one member each from the Free Democratic Party (Liberals), the Party of Democratic Socialism (Left), and the Alliance 90/The Greens parliamentary groups. It reflects the strengths of the political parties in the Bundestag.

Mandate of the Control Panel

There are two dimensions to parliamentary oversight of the intelligence community. The first concerns operational details and the other questions of policy and finance. If the scope of the Control Panel were to be restricted only to the latter, it would not have the power to monitor and ensure that government policy in this sphere is carried out efficiently and properly. It would also have meant the Control Panel would not be able to check if the secret service agencies have conducted themselves in accordance with the law and respected the fundamental rights of the individual.[10] In reality, the Parliamentary Control Panel is given the mandate to scrutinize both dimensions.

As provided for under the Control Panel Act, the Federal Government is obliged to report comprehensively to the Panel on the general activities of the German intelligence services as well as on operations of particular importance. The Panel can also call on the Federal Government to report on other operations. What this means in practice is that the Federal Government must provide as complete as possible the information required by the Control Panel to monitor its intelligence activities, the general procedures governing the operations of its intelligence agencies, as well as the results achieved by these agencies. The Control Panel also exercises budgetary scrutiny and control over the intelligence services. It not only examines the draft annual budgets prepared by the intelligence services, but also discusses issues concerning the structure, personnel, projects, and plans of the services. It is only after the Panel has completed its consultation with the services that their budgets, together with recommendations from the Panel, are submitted to the Bundestag's Confidential Forum of the Budgetary Committee, the formal parliamentary committee responsible for reviewing government budgets.

In addition the Control Panel is responsible for monitoring postal and telecommunications surveillance. While it does not look into individual cases, it examines the periodic reports provided by the responsible Federal Minister and checks that the operating procedures and the rights of individuals, including the privacy of posts and telecommunications, are duly respected. In this respect its most important task is to appoint the members of the G10 Commission, which is responsible for approving all the surveillance measures at the federal level.[11]

Meetings

Although the Control Panel is formally required to meet only once every three months, it does so much more frequently. Individual members of the Panel also have the right to request information about specific issues to be made available to the Panel at any time. A regular meeting of the Panel usually starts with a formal statement by the Minister, which is supplemented by information provided by the heads of the three intelligence services. The supervision that the Panel exercises is carried out by discussions among members of the Panel, the Minister, and the senior members of the intelligence services. Such discussions generally allow members of the Panel to influence and guide the work of the intelligence services. The discussions focus on getting the government to explain and justify what its agencies have done and often results in more guidelines being drawn up to govern current and future operations. The atmosphere is one of cooperation rather than adversarial questioning.

Confidentiality

The deliberations of the Parliamentary Control Panel are, by law, strictly confidential. The staffs of the Federal Government and of the Parliamentary Control Panel, who are allowed in its meetings, are all required to undergo strict security checks before their attendance is cleared. This does not apply to members of the Control Panel who are elected representatives of the people and are, as such, not obliged to undergo any special security checks or vetting.

Special Powers to Obtain Information and Documents

For a parliamentary oversight body to function effectively it must have sufficient power to obtain information and documents from the government and directly from the intelligence services, if necessary. The precise scope of the power of access for each parliamentary oversight body depends on the specific roles that it is asked to perform. For one whose functions include reviewing questions of the effectiveness and legality of government activities, as well as upholding human rights, it needs greater access to specific information than one whose remit is solely one of monitoring general policy.[12]

In the case of the Parliamentary Control Panel, it enjoys a wide range of statutory powers of control:

- At the request of the Panel or an authorized member of the Panel, the Government is obliged by law to provide all the documents and files of the services to be inspected.
- The Government has to make it possible for the Panel's members to visit the services at any time.
- Upon request, the Government must enable the Panel to question staff in the services at any time.
- In addition, with the agreement of a two-thirds majority of its members the Panel can appoint an external expert to conduct inquiries into specific cases for the purpose of exercising the Panel's duty of control; the results of such inquires should be reported directly and exclusively to the Panel.

The powers put at the disposal of the Control Panel are wider than for other parliamentary committees. They are intended to give the Panel leverage to secure the cooperation of the government and the intelligence agencies. Indeed, the provision of such powers underlines the seriousness that the Bundestag attaches to its responsibility of oversight in the matter of intelligence activities. In exercising such powers, the Control Panel tries to get actively involved and bring its influence to bear on the executive branch. The intention is not to detract from the government its responsibility, but to ensure the Bundestag can make its own input meaningfully rather than merely make its judgments on this important and sensitive area of government activities *expo facto* only.

The power of the Control Panel to access all government files is, needless to say, not absolute. The Federal Government can indeed refuse the Panel access to specific documents, but only if there are compelling reasons. They can be related to the need to protect the sources of the intelligence, to protect the privacy of third parties, or if the documents concerned touch upon the decision-making process within the Federal Government. In the event that the Federal Government refuses a request from the Panel to provide certain information, the Federal Minister concerned, which means the Head of the Federal Chancellery in the case of the BND, must provide a detailed justification to the Panel.

Beyond its power to call for government documents, the Panel is given additional authority to obtain information about any potential abuses by the intelligence services. They include the right for members of the intelligence services to bring service-related matters to the attention of the Parliamentary Control Panel concerning the work of the services. In so doing the intelligence service office concerned must not seek to advance personal gains and must aim only at improving the services' fulfillment of their duties. The officer should also resort to this option only if the management of the intelligence service has failed to follow up on proposals submitted to improve the agency in question.

In addition, ordinary citizens may also contact the Panel about activities of the intelligence services that affect them directly. They ensure that the Panel has access to information beyond those provided by the government and its intelligence agencies and can investigate serious accusations against the activities of the intelligence services.

Its Own Accountability

As a parliamentary committee, the Control Panel reports periodically to the Bundestag and informs the general public of its work. Given the need to maintain confidentiality, its reports to the Bundestag tend to be very general in nature. Nevertheless, the Control Panel does inform the Bundestag in general terms on matters concerning the clandestine surveillance activities of the intelligence services and on the exercise of new powers assigned to the intelligence services under the Counter-Terrorism Act of 2002, as well as new measures that were introduced.

The Control Panel is also not the only parliamentary body given the responsibility to exercise the power of control. Other bodies, such as the Bundestag itself, *ad hoc* committees of inquiry, the Interior Committee and the Defense Committee of the Bundestag, as well as the G10 Commission have parallel control responsibilities as well. But the primary parliamentary control of the intelligence services is exercised by the Control Panel maintaining a high standard of secrecy in its deliberations.

The need to maintain confidentiality notwithstanding, the Control Panel also publishes an appraisal of current operations, for which it will require approval by a two-thirds majority of its members.[13] It should be emphasized that such publications include only the assessments of the Panel and do not include specific information about operations or operational matters. They are intended, on the one hand, to reassure the general public that proper scrutiny has been performed and, on the other hand, to deter the intelligence services from improper conduct.

THE G10 COMMISSION

The G10 Commission is not a parliamentary body but a special commission appointed by the Parliamentary Control Panel to fulfill the requirements laid down in Article 10 of the German Constitution. It consists of four full and four alternate members, though all are entitled to speak and raise questions freely. Its members are not usually members of the Bundestag, though they can be. They are usually "elder statesmen" with a very good knowledge of the technical, political, and judicial aspects of intelligence work and are usually members of political parties. To be selected as chairman a member must qualify to hold a judicial office. Members of this Commission hold their offices as unpaid public service and discharge their responsibilities independently. The Commission deliberates in private and meets once a month.

Origins

The German Constitution upholds every citizen's right to the privacy of correspondence, posts, and telecommunications. It prohibits surveillance of telecommunications unless specifically allowed by law and ensures members of the public can exchange opinions and information over the telecommunication networks without fear of them being intercepted by the state surreptitiously and used against them. The specific legislation that permits and regulates government monitoring of communications between individuals is the Article 10 Act, better known by its abbreviation in German: G10—hence the name of the Commission, which is responsible for approving surveillance measures ordered and implemented under the G10 Act and conducted by the Federal intelligence services. The importance of the G10 Act and the G10 Commission has been enhanced in recent years, as the surveillance of telephone lines, Internet connections, mobile phones, and so on is now one of the most important means available for countering global terrorism.

In accordance with the G10 Act there is a division of labor among the intelligence agencies in monitoring electronic and other telecommunications. While cases involving individuals are as a rule handled by the BfV or by the MAD, "strategic restrictions" fall into the domain of the BND. It should be recognized that inherent in the monitoring of communications by the intelligence agencies is the fact that the subjects whose communications are put under surveillance usually have not, or at least not yet, committed any crime. Where criminal offenses have already been committed, they would normally be referred to the police or other law enforcement agencies.

How It Works

The G10 Act lays down in detail the procedures used to implement surveillance operations. It is up to the Federal Minister of the Interior to specify the areas of risk for which the strategic telecommunication surveillance may take place. At the moment the risk areas include, for example, the following:

- international terrorism,
- proliferation of weapons,
- serious drug-related crime, and
- internationally organized money laundering of particular importance.

Within the framework approved by the Parliamentary Control Panel, the G10 Commission decides whether requests for specific surveillance of the telecommunications traffic by the intelligence services are legal and necessary. The Commission also has to approve the search terms used by the BND in monitoring telecommunications.

Before a request is formally submitted to the Commission by the Federal Government, the staffs of the secretariat of the G10 Commission make a "preliminary assessment." Since such staffs must themselves qualify to hold judicial offices and have acquired the appropriate technical expertise, they would inform and advise members of the Commission of any special, legal, or material aspects of an individual case before it is put to the Commission for a decision or, indeed, during Commission meetings. The Commission then decides whether the surveillance measures are legal and necessary. Its decisions are binding on the intelligence agencies. This means the G10

Commission is the organ that actually controls surveillance and sanctions operations that interfere with the basic rights of individuals as provided for in the G10 Act.

What does this make the G10 Commission—an executive agency, a parliamentary organ, or a sort of administrative court? It is not an executive organ since it is not subject to instructions from a higher bureaucracy. It is also not really a parliamentary body because it lacks the dependence and reporting obligations typical of such bodies. While the G10 Commission resembles an administrative court in terms of its practice and self-perception, its decisions do not have the force of legal judgments. This is because they are likewise subject to judicial review, as the subjects of surveillance are entitled to seek redress in a court of law following notification. What complicates matters further is that while the G10 Commission exercises a judicial rather than a political control function, its authority exceeds that of a court of law, as it exercises not just legal control, but can also refuse to approve an operation that it considers to be either unnecessary or otherwise inappropriate. No court of law in Germany has such powers. In view of the Commission's special position, it is probably best to let it be defined legally as a governmental body *sui generis*.

The control that the G10 Commission exercises is real and is not limited to assessing the ministerial instructions on and requests for surveillance. It vets the entire process of how the Federal intelligence services collect, process, and utilize data monitored. It also checks that the statutory provisions on the protection and labeling of data and on deletion and transfer protocols are complied with by the agencies concerned. In exercising its extensive control authority, the Commission can delegate its power to its staff, so that they can demand information, inspect all relevant government documents, and visit all relevant offices to discharge the oversight responsibilities effectively. In addition, the Commission receives complaints from citizens and assesses whether the authorized breach of the basic rights of a person was conducted in accordance with Article 10 of the Federal Constitution. On average it receives and handles between 20 and 30 such complaints every year.

CONCLUSION

All in all the system of parliamentary oversight of the intelligence services in Germany works well. It has managed to establish a balance between the need to protect secrecy on the one hand and to ensure the proper conduct of the intelligence services on the other. But there are also a few problems that require fine-tuning. The confidentiality requirement means that the rest of the parliament is not sufficiently informed by members of the Control Panel. As a result a debate is going on in the Bundestag on whether members of the Panel should be given the scope to inform the heads of their respective parliamentary political parties of their work and, indeed, to provide more information to the general public about their work. Another inadequacy lies in the fact that members of the Control Panel, and, for that matter, members of the G10 Commission, have too many other obligations to allow them sufficient time to conduct any intensive investigations themselves. Furthermore, the Control Panel also suffers from a lack of strategic focus. Instead it is largely preoccupied with investigating into scandals and reacting to media reports. It has not devoted itself sufficiently to analyze systematically the working of the intelligence agencies. Such shortcomings notwithstanding, the German approach to parliamentary control of the intelligence sector has, in general terms, successfully established the necessary basis of trust in relations between intelligence services, government and Parliament, although minor adjustment to this system will certainly be conducted in the not so distant future.

7

An Appropriate Legal Framework for Dealing with Modern Terrorism and WMD

Richard G. Stearns

Can an effective campaign against terrorism be waged within the constraints of the rule of law? The rule of law has procedural and substantive components. By the shorthand expression "rule of law," we mean in the first instance that in fixing culpability certain fundamental procedural norms will be observed—that an accused will have the right to an attorney (or at least be afforded a fair opportunity to represent himself or herself), that he or she will be informed of the charges and the evidence against him or her, and that he or she will be permitted to gather and present exculpatory or mitigating evidence to an impartial tribunal. The rule of law also has a substantive component. Procedural protections enable, but do not guarantee, the protection of human rights.[1] There are types of evidence, like confessions extracted by torture, and institutional practices, like the merger of the accusatory and the adjudicatory functions, that a civilized system of justice best not tolerate.[2]

We care about the rule of law because its assurances of fundamental rights and processes confer legitimacy and predictability on public decision making, giving both government and citizens a means of conforming to reciprocal expectations of behavior. And the alternative, living in a Hobbesian state of nature, has little appeal to most of us. While the strict application of the rule of law may seem the intuitively moral choice, the resulting constraints can be maddeningly frustrating to government authorities attempting to address real or perceived threats. Judges, who are the custodians and administrators of the rule of law, are conservative by nature, rule bound, and generally unhappy when forced to make hurried decisions. These are admirable qualities, but as the recent trial of Zacarias Moussaoui (among others) illustrates, they are ill suited to coping with a true emergency or responding to an enemy that perceives the rule of law as a weakness to be exploited.

In the context of the struggle against terrorism, the rule of law must be distinguished from the rules of war that apply to conventional military conflicts. Captured terrorists are not ordinarily eligible for formal treatment as prisoners of war (POW) under the Geneva Conventions because, as Adam Roberts observes, they typically operate outside of the parameters of these international treaties. The Conventions require that captured combatants be members of the armed forces of a belligerent state or a legally recognized party to the conflict, that they operate according to the laws of war under a responsible chain of command, and that they wear a distinctive insignia and carry their arms openly. Nevertheless, there are good arguments for extending POW treatment to terrorist prisoners. These include the preservation of public and international support for antiterrorist campaigns and the depriving of terrorists and their sympathizers of any grounds for arguments based on a supposed moral equivalency.[3]

In this chapter, I try to explain why al Qaeda, because of its determination to obtain and use weapons of mass destruction, represents a threat to the West and the international legal order that exceeds that posed by any other terrorist organization past or present. I set out my assessment of the likelihood of a group like al Qaeda actually acquiring or developing chemical, biological, or nuclear weapons. I then describe some of the reasons why domestic and international laws have largely failed in their attempt to come to grips with this new terrorist threat. I end with my own views as to the application and adaptability of the rule of law to what has perhaps unwisely been declared a "war on terror."

THE THREAT FROM MODERN TERRORISM

Distinguishing terrorist groups by type is useful if one believes, as I do, that it is a mistake to treat terrorism as if it were a unitary system of belief rather than a methodology or political technique. Not all terrorists share similar attitudes or goals or even operate under the same lack of ethical and political constraints. For delusional cults like the Solar Temple or the Branch Davidians, terrorist acts—usually self-inflicted—are often intended to hasten a millenarian event or a passage to a better place. For anarchist groups like the Russian Narodniks and the Bader-Meinhof gang, targeted assassinations were a method of ridding society of "those who are really responsible for the evil deed."[4] For the Marxist ideologues of the Khmer Rouge and Shining Path, terror was a means of reshaping human nature to conform to a utopian vision of perfection, however grotesque. For irredentist groups like the IRA (Irish Republican Army), the Tamil Tigers, and the Basque ETA (Euskadi Ta Askatasuna), terror served (and in some instances, still does) as an instrument for accomplishing political ends. These are the groups with which societies best cope, if only because their objectives are for the most part comprehensible. One may disagree with the idea of a united Ireland, an autonomous Tamil homeland, or an independent Basque state, but it is difficult to dismiss these aspirations as irrational or even unachievable. A similar point can be made about the Sunni insurrection in Iraq. As gory as are the methods of the Zarqawi al Qaeda faction in Iraq, its goal of preventing the usurpation of the power historically exercised by the Sunni Arab minority over the Shi'a and Kurdish majority is a rational one. Separatist groups for the most part understand, if they do not always respect, the principle that indiscriminate killing of civilians alienates the audience upon whose sympathy and support they depend for success and even survival. In a somewhat different category are criminal syndicates that use terror as a means of economic coercion: these include traditional organized crime groups as well as guerilla movements like the Colombian FARC (Fuerzas Armadas Revolucionarias de Colombia) and the Provisional IRA that, whatever their ideological pretensions, have over time found criminal activity to be more profitable than politics. Finally, there are serial killers like the "Washington, D.C. sniper" John Allen Muhammad and the "Unabomber" Theodore Kaczynski, whose motives are better explained by psychopathology than by ideological belief, but whose terrorist deeds have as profound an impact on the public consciousness as any politically motivated act of terror.[5]

Within this taxonomy, Osama bin Laden is a decidedly rational actor for whom terrorism is an efficacious means to a larger end. Bin Laden's objectives, whether achievable or not, have a fundamental coherence, although they tend to shed pragmatic content as bin Laden shifts from shorter-term political goals to longer-term religious objectives. After mujahideen fighters successfully expelled the Soviet Army from Afghanistan (with substantial covert assistance from the United States and Saudi Arabia), bin Laden focused his insurrectionary zeal on the "near enemy,"[6] those Muslim rulers whom he considered corrupt pawns of the West, notably the Saudi royal family. The failure of the Arab masses to heed the call to revolution, and the crushing of jihadist rebellions in the mid-1990s by the security forces of Egypt, Saudi Arabia, and Algeria, led bin Laden to rechannel his efforts into combating the "distant" enemy—the "Zionist Crusader alliance" on which he declared war in an undernoticed 1996 manifesto.[7]

The calculations behind al Qaeda's attacks on U.S. forces in the Middle East, the American embassies in East Africa, and the Madrid railway station are self-evident and, in the latter case, accomplished their objective.[8] A motivating factor behind the 9/11 attacks was bin Laden's conviction, based on the withdrawal under fire of U.S. troops from Beirut and Mogadishu, that the United States could be intimidated into a similar retreat from the entire Muslim world. This was not a wholly irrational calculation, although it proved to be an error in judgment that might have permanently crippled al Qaeda and the jihadi movement had it not been for reciprocal miscalculations by the United States in expanding the "war on terrorism" to include the invasion of Iraq.[9]

Most of the world's billion or more Muslims (census estimates vary widely) neither sympathize with jihadist violence nor have any desire to live under a repressive theocratic dictatorship of the kind espoused by bin Laden. Nor is modern-day Islam the only religion ever to be seized upon by fanatics as a flag of convenience—the Roman-era Jewish Zealots, the medieval Ismaili Assassins, and the warring Christian factions of sixteenth and seventeenth century Europe, like the jihadists, drew on religious fervor to support essentially political ends. The Holy Book of Muslims, the Qur'an, while it does not set out a chronological history, is similar to the Old Testament in its illumination of God's message with historical examples drawn from the life of the Prophet Muhammad and his companions. The story told in the Qur'an follows the Old Testament cycle of persecution, exile, survival, war, and ultimate triumph. Like the Bible, the Qur'an can be read selectively to reinforce whatever predilections a believer chooses to bring to a reading of its text. There are Qu'ranic verses that read as a virtual declaration of war on nonbelievers,[10] as there are verses (although fewer in number) that counsel toleration and respect.[11]

To gain insight into bin Laden's thinking, it is useful to consider not only what he has said, but also the writings of others that have shaped his religious and political ideas. The intellectual foundations of al Qaeda rest primarily on the teachings of Sayyid Qutb, a Muslim Brotherhood militant and the most able of the theoreticians of modern jihad.[12] Bin Laden's absorption in Qutb's thinking is largely owed to the influence of his deputy commander, Ayman al-Zawahiri, an early Qutb disciple and the leader of Tanzim al-Jihad, the most lethal of the Egyptian jihadist groups. Bin Laden and Zawahiri forged an enduring friendship during their service on behalf of the Afghani resistance in the 1980s. In 1989, Zawahiri joined bin Laden and Sheikh Abdullah Azzam in the founding of al Qaeda.[13] Although Zawahiri, because of his obsession with the overthrow of Hosni Mubarak, was a late convert to the idea of global jihad, he nonetheless tutored bin Laden in Qutb's bloodthirsty view that proper jihad requires the infliction of "the maximum casualties against the opponent."[14]

Although Qutb was initially an admirer of the West, two years of study and travel in the United States persuaded him that the proper practice of Islam could not coexist with what he perceived as Western licentiousness and depravity. The mission of jihad[15] is, in Qutb's words, to destroy the "kingdom of man to establish the kingdom of heaven on earth" in the form of a pristine Islamic kingdom governed by a restored Caliphate. Qutb believed that Islam was not only the superior religion, but also the only religion acceptable to God. In Qutb's view, a correct Muslim life could be lived only by strict submission to Shari'a law as the Prophet and his companions practiced it. A legal order based on anything other than God's decree was, according to Qutb, apostatical or heretical and unworthy of obedience.[16] As Qutb defined it, the duty incumbent on all Muslims was "to destroy all forces that stand in [the] way of liberating mankind from any shackle that prevents the free choice of adopting Islam."[17] This recasting of jihad from a quest for inner redemption into a compulsory duty to fight to establish global Muslim suzerainty is the singular contribution of Qutb and other neofundamentalist theologians to modern Islamist terrorism.[18]

Al Qaeda represents an order of dangerousness the magnitude of which distances it from traditional terrorist groups with more parochial goals. This is so for four reasons. First, al Qaeda in its present orientation is not focused on any national or regional objective, but sees the world at large as its theater of operations.

Second, while its leadership has fragmented under Western military pressure, al Qaeda as an organization has metastasized into a franchise, lending (willingly or not) its famous mark to groups like Abu Sayyaf, al-Ittihad al-Islami, and Jemaah Islamiyah, who are waging their own versions of jihad. Despite crippling losses in its structure of command and control, al Qaeda continues to recruit and inspire the formation of jihadi cells within Muslim immigrant populations in Europe, Canada, and the United States.[19]

Third, al Qaeda, despite its reactionary religious orientation, has a thoroughly modern appreciation of the uses of technology. Al Qaeda has a sophisticated understanding of the Internet, telecommunications, and the world banking system. It has used these tools to link its operatives, disseminate propaganda, and raise and funnel financial support for its operations. While the overthrow of the Taliban regime in Afghanistan cost al Qaeda most of its territorial base, al Qaeda today is a virtual organization more dependent on cyberspace than physical space.[20] Hundreds (if not thousands) of sites on the Internet disseminate al Qaeda propaganda and offer instruction in everything from proper religious practice to the making of ricin and the launching of surface-to-air missiles.

Fourth, and of more immediate significance, is al Qaeda's determination to acquire and use weapons of mass destruction against its Western enemies,[21] this despite the Qu'ranic injunction against the wanton killing of children and other innocent noncombatants.[22] In May 2003, Saudi Sheikh Nasir al-Fahd, encouraged by bin Laden, published a fatwa entitled "A Treatise on the Legal Status of Using Weapons of Mass Destruction Against Infidels."[23] Al-Fahd invoked the Old Testament principle that one may treat others in the manner that one has been treated. Because in al-Fahd's esti-mate, American weapons had been used to kill 10 million Muslims, it was permissible to kill 10 million Americans in retaliation "with no need to men-tion any other argument." In a 2002 letter addressed to "the Americans," bin Laden further justified al Qaeda's attacks on civilians in the United States by arguing that Americans, by voting and paying taxes to their government, had forfeited any claim to noncombatant status.[24]

A weapon of mass destruction need not be a device of any great sophisti-cation. The bombs used in the 1993 attack on the World Trade Center and the 1995 attack on the Alfred P. Murrah Federal Building in Oklahoma City consisted of a mixture of commercial fertilizer (ammonium nitrate) and number 2 home heating oil, a simple but powerful explosive used to great effect by the IRA. Al Qaeda's inspiration to convert heavily fueled commer-cial airliners into piloted missiles was an idea of grisly genius, but one based on a very conventional weapons technology. It is worth remembering that the terrorists' weapon of choice remains today a century-old invention—dynamite.

In assessing the potential threat posed by the possibility that al Qaeda might acquire or develop weapons of mass destruction, it is useful to differ-entiate these weapons by type. They fall into four categories: conventional explosives, including sophisticated compounds like semtex; chemical weap-ons such as sarin and VX[25] gas; biological agents like anthrax; and radiation devices, including nuclear weapons and the so-called "dirty" bomb.[26]

Chemical agents are classified by their effect on the body: blood agents like hydrogen cyanide (prussic acid), blistering agents like mustard gas, choking agents like chlorine and phosgene, and nerve agents like sarin.[27] Chemical agents are difficult to detect and can cause death on a massive scale if effectively deployed, but are extremely dangerous to manufacture in uncontrolled conditions. While it appears from videotapes seized in Afghanistan that al Qaeda had conducted crude experiments with various chemical gasses,[28] the releases of sarin by the Japanese cult Aum Shinrikyo (Supreme Truth) in the resort city of Matsumoto in 1994 and (with a more devastating effect) in the Tokyo subway system in 1995[29] are the only doc-umented instances in which a terrorist group has successfully deployed a homemade chemical agent against civilians with any success.

Biological agents are generally cheaper to produce and are more lethal than chemical weapons.[30] Biological agents can be weaponized in three forms: bacteria, such as anthrax or plague; biotoxins (nonliving substances engineered from living organisms), such as ricin; and viruses, like Ebola and smallpox. Bubonic plague, the bacterial disease that precipitated the Black Death, killed an estimated third of the population of fourteenth-century Europe. While bacterial diseases are not difficult to culture, they require direct contact to spread and can usually be contained with antibiot-ics and quarantines. Biotoxins, like botulinum and ricin, are among the most toxic poisons known and are reasonably easy to produce. Ricin, to take an example, is extracted from castor beans, using a simple process explained in a patent issued to the U.S. Army in 1952 (which can still be found on the Internet). Because biotoxins are not infectious and do not replicate, they are more effective as an assassin's tool than as a means of causing mass death. Exotic viruses like Ebola and Marburg are incurable and have a lethality rate of nearly 100 percent. The culturing of exotic viruses, however, is difficult and almost certainly beyond the means and sophistication of al Qaeda and like-minded groups.[31] Smallpox, unlike Ebola and Marburg, does not require physical contact to spread and can be easily cultured. Smallpox has a fatality rate of roughly 30 percent or higher, depending on the amount of residual vaccine in an infected population. The weaponization of smallpox, however, presents two significant obstacles to a terrorist group. Smallpox in its wild state was eradicated in 1977 as a result of a worldwide campaign undertaken by the World Health Organization, although it is conceivable that a specimen could be cloned from the corpse of someone who died earlier of the disease or that rogue specimens were diverted from the bioweapons program secretly undertaken by the Soviet Union in the 1980s.[32] An even more formidable deterrent is the "blowback" effect of a smallpox epidemic; that is, a successful smallpox attack in Europe or North America would almost certainly become a worldwide pandemic before running its course.[33]

A nuclear weapon would, of course, offer al Qaeda the most spectacular result in terms of destruction and imagery. A commonly discussed expedient would be for al Qaeda to steal or purchase a weapon from the leaky Russian arsenal, which is believed to still contain as many as 8,000 nuclear warheads.[34] In 1997, the late General Aleksandr Lebed, then head of Russia's National Security Council, told the American TV news magazine 60 Minutes that over a hundred "suitcase" nuclear bombs were missing from the Soviet stockpile. (By suitcase bombs, Lebed presumably meant either atomic demolition devices or tactical battlefield weapons.) Lebed also revealed the unsettling fact that many of the Soviet weapons, unlike their American counterparts, had not been rigged with coding locks or environmental sensing devices.[35]

Another frequently discussed terrorist scenario involves the Improvised Nuclear Device or "garage" bomb. The building of a working nuclear weapon requires five things: an expertise in physics, a supply of uranium-238, an enrichment strategy, milling equipment, and a means of delivery.[36] The knowledge required to design a nuclear weapon is not beyond the grasp of a graduate-level student of physics, and a good deal of reliable information is available on the Internet, although the assembly of a nuclear weapon requires a high degree of technical skill and collective effort.[37]

The major obstacle al Qaeda would face in attempting to build a nuclear weapon from scratch is the acquisition of a sufficient amount of fissionable material to fuel it.[38] According to the International Atomic Energy Agency (IAEA), the minimal required amounts of fissile material are 25 kilograms of uranium-235 or 8 kilograms of plutonium-239. The actual amounts are classified, but are significantly smaller than the official IAEA figures.[39] Weapons-grade fissile material circulates on the black market. Over the past decade, there have been seizures of appreciable amounts of smuggled material in Germany, Eastern Europe, and Central Asia. Most of the seized material has been uranium-235, a total of some 16.4 kilograms, with enrichment rates ranging from 20 to 90 percent. Only 0.4 kilograms of the more hazardous plutonium-239 have been recovered.

The source of almost all black market weapons-grade material to date has been Russia. There is no evidence that countries like North Korea and Pakistan are involved in the black-market sale of fissile material (although the renegade Pakistani nuclear engineer A.Q. Kahn sold the nuclear know-how developed by Pakistan to Libya, North Korea, Iran, and possibly Syria and Saudi Arabia). The frequency of interceptions of smuggled fissile material has sharply declined over the past decade, largely because of the U.S.-led effort to assist Russia in securing its nuclear stockpile. Moreover, most of what is offered on the black market as weapons-grade fissile material are either scam substitutes like radiological medical waste, depleted uranium, osmium, or mythical substances like "red mercury." Of the some 550 incidents reported worldwide involving seizures of nuclear materials, all but a handful have proved to be hoaxes. There is no evidence that organized crime is involved in the theft or transshipment of fissile material, although organized crime has profited from a number of the scam sales. Al Qaeda is the only known nonstate actor currently in the market for nuclear materials. Finally, there is no analogy between the smuggling of drugs and the black-market sale of fissile material. While drugs, because of their reliable consumer base, are in constant demand, the market for nuclear materials is idiosyncratic, and, unlike drugs, smuggled nuclear materials (because of their radioactivity) are fairly easy to detect.

The more dangerous and plausible al Qaeda scenario involves a dirty bomb. A dirty bomb is a simple device constructed by wrapping a conventional explosive with low-grade nuclear material, such as strontium, cobalt-60, or cesium-137, substances that are regularly marketed for medical, food irradiation, and other commercial uses.[40] While the physical damage from a dirty-bomb explosion might not be great, the ensuing panic, fueled by exaggerated fears of the effects of radiological contamination, would wreak substantial financial and psychological damage.[41]

SEEKING AN APPROPRIATE LEGAL FRAMEWORK

The international legal regime regulating weapons of mass destruction is based largely on treaty obligations.[42] These treaties trace their origins to efforts undertaken in the mid-nineteenth century to codify the rules regulating the conduct of war. These efforts led to the 1925 Geneva Protocol banning the use of poisonous gas and bacteriological weapons and the 1949 Geneva Conventions dealing with the treatment of prisoners of war and civilian populations.[43] More recent treaties of interest include the 1968 Nuclear Nonproliferation Treaty, the 1972 Biological Weapons Convention,[44] and the 1993 Chemical Weapons Convention.[45]

The Conventions differ widely in their effectiveness. The nuclear and chemical treaties depend for enforcement on inspections by the IAEA and the Organization for the Prevention of Chemical Weapons, respectively, inspections to which a signatory state, at least in theory, must submit. The Nuclear Nonproliferation Treaty, while banning all but the five member states who had detonated nuclear bombs prior to January 1, 1967, from building nuclear weapons, also guarantees the right of signatories to acquire nuclear technology for peaceful purposes.[46] The components essential to the peaceful uses of atomic energy—reactors, centrifuges, milling equipment, switches, and fuses—are, however, many of the same components that are required to build a nuclear weapon.[47] Unlike the Chemical Weapons and Biological Weapons Conventions, the Nuclear Nonproliferation Treaty does not require member states to penalize the unauthorized acquisition of nuclear materials by private persons. The Conventions, despite well-founded criticisms, are nonetheless important because outside of a treaty context there is no prohibition under international law against a state developing or possessing weapons of mass destruction.

The effort to develop international rules of law addressing terrorism has been frustrated by the inability of diplomats and academicians to achieve a consensus definition of terrorism. As a result, international conventions addressing terrorism have focused on specific subjects like the protection of heads of state, diplomatic personnel and civil aviation, and on criminal acts associated with terrorism, like hostage taking and airplane hijacking. Attempts to craft an internationally accepted definition of terrorism in the 1960s and 1970s foundered on sympathy, real or calculated, for "wars of national liberation." The major stumbling block today, as David Bosco notes, "in one word, is Israel."[48] Muslim countries in particular are reluctant to endorse any definition of terrorism that might be used to undermine the legitimacy of the Palestinian resistance to Israeli occupation. United Nations Security Council Resolution 1373, enacted in the wake of the September 11 attacks, called upon member states to cooperate in the suppression of terrorist financing and to enact domestic laws imposing severe penalties for terrorist crimes. The Resolution, however, offered no insight into what was considered to be a "terrorist act."

It would seem reasonable that for an act to be deemed terrorist, it should at a minimum constitute a serious crime under the generally accepted law of nations. A draft resolution offered by Russia in the wake of the Beslan school massacre sought to define terrorism as "any act intended to cause death or serious injury to civilians or taking of hostages with the purpose to provoke a state of terror, intimidate a population or compel a government or an international organization to do or abstain from doing any act."[49] The Russian proposal, despite its focus on means, was criticized on familiar grounds: the failure of the resolution to more precisely define what was meant by "any act" and the potential of insult to the practitioners of wars of national liberation.[50]

As Adam Roberts has observed, "What is perhaps easier to define than the grand abstraction of terrorism is *terrorist* acts."[51] Following on this thought, it is perhaps even easier to define *who is a terrorist* by emphasizing act over motive, perhaps as follows: "Any person who, as a principal or an accessory, commits murder, robbery, kidnapping, arson, extortion, rape, or any other crime recognized as a violent offense under the law of nations, or who utilizes a weapon of mass destruction against a civilian population, or who attempts or threatens to do so, with the purpose of coercing or intimidating a government to act or refrain from acting, shall be deemed a terrorist under international law." While there may be much to criticize in this formulation, I have attempted to hew to the distinction drawn in international law between *jus ad bellum*—the right to use force—and *jus in bello*—the law governing how force is to be used. It might be perfectly possible to fight for a just cause as a "freedom fighter," while nonetheless using unjust (terrorist) means.[52]

The interest of a national State in erecting legal defenses to terrorism is in most instances provoked by a terrorist incident that is sufficiently horrendous to generate public pressure on authorities to act. The governmental response follows a predictable pattern. First, terrorist acts are made serious crimes under domestic law, and if the threat is external, the State asserts jurisdiction over extraterritorial acts that are intended to violate its sovereignty or to harm its citizens. The example of the United States is typical. Prior to the Palestinian hijacking of the cruise ship *Achille Lauro* and the murder of Leon Klinghoffer, the United States had only two antiterrorism laws in its federal criminal code. Both statutes were enacted during World War I and were intended to deter German saboteurs and any potential German-American collaborators.[53] The principal statute under which crimes that would today be labeled terrorist were then prosecuted was not a terrorism statute at all, but rather the Arms Export Control Act, a customs statute enacted to impede the flow of weapons technology to the Soviet Union and its allies.

If the threat persists, the typical response is to give police greater powers to detain suspects, to expand the authority of law enforcement officials to engage in electronic eavesdropping and surveillance,[54] to restrict speech that is perceived to incite or promote terrorism, and to place limitations on the power of courts to review actions taken by law enforcement agencies. This was the pattern followed by the French in response to the Algerian terrorist attacks on metropolitan France, by Spain in addressing ETA's secessionist campaign, the United Kingdom in dealing with the IRA,[55] and the United States in reacting to the September 11 attacks.[56] In some circumstances, as in Israel's battle with the Palestinian intifada, extreme measures, including kidnappings and targeted assassinations, or in the case of the United States, the rendition of suspects to countries with unacceptable human rights records, have been officially sanctioned. Despite the controversy aroused by restrictions on traditional civil liberties, from a politician's perspective the costs of overreaction are almost never outweighed by the risks of underreaction.

There is, of course, an inherent weakness in a response to terrorism that depends on the collective will of individual states. Often, the most timid member of the coalition will determine the steadfastness and effectiveness of the mutual resolve. The international legal system is hobbled by inconsistencies among sovereign legal systems in their definitions and penalties for terrorist offenses and by differences in the applicable evidentiary laws, as well as by structural inefficiencies created by judicial, as well as police and prosecutorial corruption and incompetence. There are corresponding weaknesses in a system of international regulation of weapons of mass destruction that depends on nation states applying national law, or on international inspection regimes that are either nonexistent or insufficiently rigorous. Organized crime and terrorist groups like al Qaeda skillfully exploit the gaps in enforcement created by these weaknesses.

A philosophical divide also exists between the European preference for a counterterrorism strategy based on a law enforcement model emphasizing detection, containment, disruption, and prosecution, and the Bush administration's advocacy of preemptive intervention, including the unilateral resort to military force whenever deemed necessary. The dichotomy between the European and American approaches is not, however, as absolute as it is often depicted. The law enforcement model was the official policy of the United States during the Clinton administration, and rhetoric aside, is the model still largely followed by the Federal Bureau of Investigation and the U.S. Department of Justice.

There are, of course, inherent difficulties in any approach that attempts to treat terrorism purely as a criminal matter to be dealt with by police and courts. The priority of law enforcement is to gather and analyze historical facts in order to assign culpability for past events. In a military-intelligence setting, the emphasis is on predictive facts that can be used to shape or deter future events. In an intelligence context, one might be quite willing to act on evidence the quality of which would not satisfy a court looking to determine guilt. This tension between historical and predictive facts explains the collapse of several significant terrorism prosecutions in Europe and the United

States in which prosecutors proved unable to satisfy courts with the quality of evidence gathered through confidential intelligence sources.

To return to the question posed at the outset, what role should the rule of law play in the struggle against terrorism? Walter Laqueur argues that while juridically based procedures might be adequate in containing terrorist groupings that are small and not very dangerous, when it comes to dealing with large-scale groups like al Qaeda, those governments that accede to the principle of asymmetrical warfare—the idea that they are bound by the rule of law while their terrorist opponents are not—will, according to Laqueur, "be severely, possibly fatally, handicapped."[57] In Laqueur's view, governments should undertake retaliatory campaigns against terrorist organizations like al Qaeda only if they are willing to apply massive military force.

Philip B. Heymann, a Harvard Law School professor and Deputy Attorney General in the Clinton administration, offers a more nuanced view.[58] Heymann argues that the metaphor of war neither accurately describes the challenge that terrorism presents nor the means that must be used to confront it. The war metaphor also confers an undeserved dignity on terrorists by according them a status akin to that reserved for sovereign states.[59] Heymann points out that terrorism runs the gamut from sporadic attention-getting violence fomented by dissident extremists, to sustained campaigns of intimidation undertaken by small groups, to the threatened deployment of weapons of mass destruction for the purpose of large-scale and indiscriminate killing. While military means may be the only appropriate response to the last, the criminal law supplemented by a more effective use of intelligence resources is, in Heymann's view, capable of coping with most terrorist threats.

While I agree with Laqueur's argument that a struggle of the dimension posed by al Qaeda cannot be won without at least some resort to preemptive means, I also agree with Heymann that the choice need not always favor preemption at the expense of the rule of law. There are four instances in which the rule of law has functioned, if not always efficiently, at least with reasonable effectiveness. It works when terrorists see themselves as stakeholders in the system, either because they view the courts as a pliable forum in which to advance their cause or because penal sanctions are simply seen as a necessary cost of doing business.[60] The rule of law has played a valuable role in developing successful strategies for coping with separatist groups whose aim is not to overthrow the entirety of the existing order, but to carve out their own geographical or political space. It is also an efficient means of redressing an apocalyptic terrorist event that is unlikely to be repeated because of the death or capture of the group leader.[61] And finally, the rule of law works well in dealing with criminal syndicates that use terrorist means to pursue conventional criminal activities. Al Qaeda, however, poses a more difficult problem as the recently concluded trial of Zacarias Moussaoui illustrates.

In August 2001, Moussaoui, a French citizen of Moroccan descent, was arrested by U.S. authorities on immigration charges. At the time, Moussaoui was enrolled in a Minnesota flight school to learn to fly passenger jets. His lack of interest in landing or takeoff techniques aroused sufficient suspicion to cause his instructors to alert authorities to his bizarre behavior. Moussaoui was eventually indicted as the missing 20th hijacker in the September 11 plot. On May 4, 2006, he was sentenced to life without parole in a maximum-security prison after having been spared from execution by a federal jury.

At its conclusion, the Moussaoui trial was widely heralded as proof (in the words of a member of the 9/11 Commission) that "we have a system that works." On more sober reflection, however, the praise heaped on the civil justice system may be undeserved. It took 4½ years, the production of over a million documents, endless disputes over defense requests for access to secret information, and tens of millions of dollars to bring the Moussaoui trial to closure. The trial would have taken much longer and involved even greater expense had not Moussaoui, against the advice of his attorneys, insisted on pleading guilty to six counts (three of which carried the death penalty) of an indictment charging him with conspiring with al Qaeda to fly airplanes into U.S. government buildings. According to Moussaoui's account, he had been designated by al Qaeda to pilot a fifth passenger plane into the White House.[62]

Moussaoui's conviction would be a triumph for the criminal justice system, albeit an expensive one, if there were any truth to the popular belief that Moussaoui is a high-level al Qaeda operative. Far from being a master terrorist, Moussaoui appears to be a mentally unstable al Qaeda aspirant suffering from *pseudologia fantastica*—the uncontrollable impulse to make heedless and grandiose statements. Moussaoui was never the 20th hijacker that he claimed to be (as the government eventually conceded). Rather, prosecutors argued to the jury that had Moussaoui come forward with what he knew prior to September 11, the attacks could have been foiled. This seems very doubtful, as there is no evidence, apart from Moussaoui's own ravings, that he had any advance knowledge of the details of the September 11 plot. While Moussaoui stands as the only person convicted of participation in the September 11 attacks, the true masterminds of the conspiracy, Khalid Shaikh Mohammad and Ramzi Binalshibh are somewhere in U.S. custody and, to date, have not been charged with any crimes. It must be asked whether even a society with the financial and legal resources of the United States can afford many more prosecutions like that of Moussaoui.[63]

The United States is not the first society under terrorist threat forced to rethink the capacity of its existing legal institutions to adapt. After fundamentalist republicans in Ulster regrouped under the banner of the Provisional IRA during the sectarian upheavals of 1969, Irish republicanism was transformed from a civil rights movement seeking to protect Catholic interests into an armed offensive against British governing institutions, including the judicial system. By 1972, the Ulster courts had become paralyzed as the result of physical intimidation (including murder) of jurors and witnesses by Catholic and Protestant paramilitaries.[64] In response, the British government introduced a number of measures suspending or limiting rights that had been previously extended to terror suspects. Among the innovations were the Diplock courts,[65] juryless tribunals presided over by single judges who were not strictly bound by common-law rules of evidence. The French engaged in similar institutional introspection after the upsurge of Algerian terrorism in the 1980s. The law of September 9, 1986, consolidated jurisdiction over terrorist offenses in the Paris regional court, giving birth to an elite cadre of magistrates with broad powers to oversee terrorist investigations. Spain also turned to the centralized investigating magistrate model, which has conferred near-celebrity status on Baltasar Garzón, the intensely energetic judge who, among his other sensational cases, indicted former Chilean dictator Augusto Pinochet for human rights abuses.

What is the appropriate legal framework for dealing with the next September 11 attack or worse? Bruce Ackerman has put forward a provocative idea—the adoption of an "emergency constitution" on the European model that would suspend (for the most part) the judicial power and (with limited Congressional oversight) authorize the President to take (for a defined period of time) whatever measures he or she deemed necessary to avert a follow-on strike.[66] It is difficult to do justice to Ackerman's proposal in a sentence, but his idea strikes me as not only unworkable, but dangerous, as powers ceded to the executive at the expense of other branches of government will prove very difficult to reclaim. My preference would be to simply admit that there are terrorist cases that in appropriate circumstances are best consigned to properly constituted military tribunals, preferably conducted under the auspices of the Uniform Code of Military Justice and the Geneva Conventions, with the right to seek review of material errors of law in the Article III courts.[67]

Five years have passed since September 11. The lack of political will that led Congress to reject the recommendations of three separate blue-ribbon Commissions convened to study the structural weaknesses of U.S. institutions charged with addressing the terrorist threat is as palpable today as it was then. When the next devastating attack on the U.S. mainland occurs, as it almost certainly will, without a well thought-out plan in place, the temptation to turn to authoritarian measures in the name of security may be irresistible. For those who are committed to the rule of law (and I count myself among them), it is important to acknowledge its fragilities as well as its strengths. Not every problem has a legal solution. There are challenges posed by terrorism that require flexibility and compromise. Rigid insistence on the rule of law as a value that transcends all others, even at the risk of collective suicide is, as Justice Jackson famously warned, simply too high a price to pay.[68]

8

Human Rights and Human Intelligence[1]

Alex Danchev

"What are you after? Do you think you'll bring this fine case of yours to a speedier end by wrangling with us, your warders, over papers and warrants? We are humble subordinates who can scarcely find our way through a legal document and have nothing to do with your case except to stand guard over you for ten hours a day and draw our pay for it. That's all we are, but we're quite capable of grasping the fact that the high authorities we serve, before they would order such an arrest as this must be quite well informed about the reasons for the arrest and the person of the prisoner. There can be no mistake about that. Our officials, so far as I know them, and I know only the lowest grades among them, never go hunting for crime in the populace, but, as the Law decrees, are drawn towards the guilty and must then send out us warders. That is the Law. How could there be a mistake in that?" "I don't know this Law," said K. "All the worse for you," replied the warder.

—Kafka, *The Trial*

The Global War on Terror (GWOT) is nothing if not kafkaesque. The very idea, a never-ending, all-encompassing, worldwide sweep, seems to pay a kind of tribute to Franz Kafka and his demons. "Someone must have been telling lies about Joseph K., for without having done anything wrong he was arrested one fine morning."[2] The arbitrary nature of the proceedings of *The Trial* corresponds eerily with the proceedings of the GWOT. "I forgot to ask you first what sort of acquittal you want. There are three possibilities, that is, definite acquittal, ostensible acquittal, and indefinite postponement."[3] Anonymous functionaries (warders, whippers, doorkeepers, and assessors) shield the prominent people from direct contamination. Hand-soiling in high office is inconceivable. Joseph K. never sees the Judge or locates the High Court. He is allowed an Advocate, but the Advocate is also part of the system. "So the Advocate's methods...amounted to this: that the client finally forgot the whole world and lived only in hope of toiling along this false path until the end of his case should come in sight. The client ceased to be a client and became the Advocate's dog." Rendition and subjection are spookishly prefigured.

The queasy combination of bureaucracy and depravity, a total envelopment at once sinister and grotesque, foreshadows policy and practice at Guantánamo Bay, Abu Ghraib, Bagram, and numberless other "facilities" in nameless other places, whose common denominator is the camp. "The camp is the space that is opened when the state of exception begins to become the rule," as Giorgio Agamben has observed. "In the camp, the state of exception, which was essentially a temporary suspension of the rule of law on the basis of a factual state of danger, is now given a permanent spatial arrangement, which as such nevertheless remains outside the social order."[4] Amnesty International's "gulag of our times" comes to resemble Kafka's penal colony, where the guiding principle is devastatingly simple: guilt is never to be doubted.[5] In the penal colony the prisoner is not told the sentence that has been passed on him, or even if he has been sentenced at all. He learns it corporally, on his person. The commandment he is supposed to have disobeyed is inscribed on his body, in needlepoint, by an ingenious apparatus called the Harrow.[6]

Corporal instruction and corporal indignity feature large in the catalog of torture and abuse perpetrated by the "alliance of values," in Tony Blair's parlance.[7] They are now copiously documented. Kafkaesque, however, embraces something more intimate still. Beyond menace, Kafka's great subject is humiliation. In its infinite and exquisite variety, humiliation is instinct in his life and work. The damage is explored with agonistic lucidity. Cruel, inhuman, or degrading treatment or punishment, the melancholy litany of the Convention against Torture, Kafka knew inside out.

In Kafka's world, humiliation takes canine form. The dog marks the degradation. Thus the bizarre fate of the Advocate's client. Becoming a dog is a process of voluntary or involuntary self-abasement. Kafka had an obsessive interest in small animals and in shrinking himself to be like them. He understood the terror of standing upright, as he put it to his muse Felice Bauer, a terror shared by the abused of Abu Ghraib. "The exact information you want about me, dearest F., I cannot give you," he wrote to her on another occasion. "I can give it to you, if at all, only when running along behind you in the Tiergarten, you always on the point of vanishing altogether, and

I on the point of prostrating myself; only when thus humiliated, more deeply than any dog, am I able to do it."[8] This image of humiliation haunts his fiction. "In the Penal Colony" opens with an unforgettable portrait of the condemned man in chains, held like a lead by his guard, as if to anticipate the grinning Lynndie England and the cringing detainee, leashed and naked, known to the night shift as Gus. "In any case, the condemned man looked so much like a submissive dog that one might have thought he could be left to run free on the surrounding hills and would only need to be whistled for when the execution was due to begin."[9]

GUANTANAMO AND ABU GHRAIB

The collateral descendants of Kafka's warders and whippers seem to mimic his obsessions. From the interrogation log of Detainee 063, aka Mohammed al-Qahtani, the so-called 20th hijacker, at Guantánamo, we read the following excerpt:

11 December 2002
Detainee was reminded that no one loved, cared or remembered him. He was reminded that he was less than human and that animals had more freedom and love than he does. He was taken outside to see a family of banana rats. The banana rats were moving around freely, playing, eating, showing concern for one another. Detainee was compared to the family of banana rats and reinforced that they had more love, freedom, and concern than he had. Detainee began to cry during this comparison.

20 December 2002
Detainee offered water—refused. Corpsman changed ankle bandages to prevent chafing. Interrogator began by reminding the detainee about the lessons in respect and how the detainee had disrespected the interrogators. Told detainee that a dog is held in higher esteem because dogs know right from wrong and know to protect innocent people from bad people. Began teaching the detainee lessons such as stay, come, and bark to elevate his social status up to that of a dog. Detainee became very agitated.[10]

The interrogation log is remarkably detailed—shamelessly detailed—but it does not make it quite clear that the detainee was chained throughout or that during the latter session he was forced to perform this series of "dog tricks" while being led round the interrogation room on a leash. These were by no means the most offensive or invasive techniques employed by the interrogators, as an official inquiry has revealed. Among other ploys, the detainee was forced to stand naked in front of a female interrogator, to wear women's underclothes, and to undergo repeated strip searches (allegedly cavity searches) as part of the interrogation.[11] The detail, moreover, obscures the regime. Detainee 063 was held in isolation for some six months. During that time he was regularly interrogated for 18–20 hours a day, starting at midnight, kept awake by dripping water on his head or loud playing of Christina Aguilera music—"sleep adjustment" combined with prolonged sleep deprivation.[12] After an episode of bradycardia (slow heartbeat) during the most intensive period of interrogation, his condition gave sufficient cause for concern that he was hospitalized for observation. Meanwhile other concerns were raised, sometimes from unlikely quarters. FBI agents serving at Guantánamo went so far as to complain about "highly aggressive interrogation techniques," noting that al-Qahtani exhibited behavior "consistent with extreme psychological trauma (talking to nonexistent people, reporting hearing voices, crouching in a cell covered with a sheet for hours on end)."[13]

All of the techniques employed in the interrogation of Mohammed al-Qahtani were found to be legally permissible and officially authorized under the current dispensation. Partly for this reason, multiple inquiries into interrogation practices and detainee abuse have been reluctant to return findings couched explicitly in the language of the Convention against Torture (CAT). The CAT may be the first casualty of the GWOT. For a force for good, "torture" is as difficult a word as "genocide." Following the bland evasions of the Bush administration—that as a matter of policy detainees are treated "humanely and, to the extent appropriate and consistent with military necessity, in a manner consistent with the principles of the Third Geneva Convention of 1949"—inquirers have also been reluctant straightforwardly to acknowledge "inhumane" treatment.[14] The most forthright to date is Major General Antonio Taguba, who was tasked to investigate the conduct of the Military Police at Abu Ghraib, and who found that "numerous incidents of sadistic, blatant, and wanton criminal abuses were inflicted on several detainees."[15] Seymour Hersh believes that Taguba was offended by what he saw. The "extremely graphic photographic evidence" to which he refers in his report, it is now known, far exceeds the sample disclosed in 2004—dogs, hoods, electrodes, and all—amounting to well over 1,000 images and nearly 100 video files of suspected detainee abuse.[16] Taguba went further. "This systemic and illegal abuse of detainees was intentionally perpetrated," he declared, confronting the weasel arguments offered by tame apologists: that the abuse was confined to rogue elements ("a few bad apples"), that it was not so heinous a crime ("Animal House on the night shift"), and that the purpose was not to cause harm but to extract information (the lawyerly exculpation of "specific intent").[17] The Taguba Report will have none of this.

Others have been more circumspect or less searching. Their struggle is played out in the parsing of their reports. Allegations of abuse at Guantánamo were investigated by Brigadier General John Furlow and Lieutenant General Randall Schmidt. In the matter of Detainee 063, they concluded that "the creative, aggressive, and persistent interrogation...resulted in the cumulative effect being degrading and abusive treatment," a formulation twice repeated. There follows an awkwardly worded concession—"this treatment did not rise to the level of prohibited inhumane treatment"— and then a recommendation that the Guantánamo Commander "should be held accountable for failing to supervise the interrogation...and should be admonished for that failure."[18]

Carefully circumscribed as it may be, the call for accountability is startling. No action has more severely compromised the United States in its prosecution of the war on terror than its inaction when faced with irrefutable evidence of American wrongdoing—evidence gathered by its own internal inquiries—the conspicuous failure to trace responsibility to its source and hold commanders and policy makers accountable. The lack of accountability confirms the culture of impunity. Minimization aggravates provocation, as surely as cover-up compounds scandal. Humiliation demands expiation. The strongholds of certainty, inviolability, and "inherent power"—the nexus of the Office of the Vice President, Secretary of Defense, and Legal Counsel—are above such considerations. The occupants of these offices brazenly add insult to injury, that is to say, heap humiliation on humiliation. "Issues of senior official accountability" are passed like an unwanted parcel from inquiry to inquiry and never addressed.[19] In most cases the very nature of the inquiry, administrative investigations commissioned by army commanders in the field, directs the focus down the chain of command rather than up and caps the seniority of scrutiny at the rank of the investigating officer—too low.[20] Salami-sliced remits and tightly drawn terms of reference serve to delimit and defang, a strategy familiar from the serial inquiries into intelligence and weapons of mass destruction (WMD).[21] Investigation after investigation pleads exhaustion (at Abu Ghraib, for example, one on Military Police, followed by another on Military Intelligence); chronic redundancy prevails. Some reports are parasitic on other reports. The Schmidt Report borrows from the Church Report. The Church Report is patterned on the Schlesinger Report. The Schlesinger Report synthesizes previous reports. Duplication and repetition contrive to blur the outline and blunt the impact. And of course, for the practiced hand, different tactics are available. Findings can be rejected, or disputed, or ignored. Both the conclusion and the recommendation of the Schmidt Report were summarily rejected by the officer who commissioned it. In a classic demonstration of the art, he argued that, because the Guantánamo Commander had little experience of detainees before he took charge, he should not be held accountable for every aspect of prison operations.

In the camp, everything is possible. Al-Qhatani and his cohorts found themselves in an ethical, political, and legal limbo. Agamben calls this "bare life." Bare life is a fathomless existence of domination, degradation, and dehumanization. "In the detainee at Guantánamo, bare life reaches its maximum indeterminacy," he writes, a process exemplified in the deliberately indeterminate designation of its subjects.[22] The nondescript "detainee" is wonderfully apt to the purpose. Even better is "Person Under Control" (PUC), an expression originating in Afghanistan to replace Prisoner of War (POW), after the President decided that the Geneva Conventions or at any rate POW status did not apply there; it was carried over conveniently to Iraq. The expression neatly dehumanizes: it signifies less a person than a nonperson.[23] PUC is pronounced puck, as in "fuck a PUC" (administer a beating). An inquiry conducted by Human Rights Watch, based on the first-hand testimony of serving soldiers, found that the PUCs held at Forward Operating Base Mercury, near Fallujah, were "fucked" routinely, by anyone who pleased. They were also "smoked," under the specific direction of Military Intelligence. "Smoking" referred to forced physical exertion, sometimes to the point of unconsciousness, accompanied by food, water, and sleep deprivation. Smoking was central to the interrogation system in operation at the base. As one soldier put it: "[The Military Intelligence officer] said he wanted the PUCs so fatigued, so smoked, so demoralized that they want to co-operate." In short, they were tortured, almost daily, over an eight-month period from September 2003 to April 2004.[24]

Once introduced, torture is more readily accepted than admitted. Normalization is easy and insidious. Detainee 063 was a special case, but the techniques employed against him soon passed into general use. The Special Interrogation Plan for Mohammed al-Qahtani was approved in advance by the Secretary of Defense, Donald Rumsfeld, for a "high-value" detainee who had resisted the standard techniques for months on end, and who was believed to possess "actionable intelligence"—the interrogator's Holy Grail—which might prevent further attacks on the United States. The strategy was to establish and maintain total control, an objective straight out of Army Field Manual (FM) 34-52, *Intelligence Interrogation* (1992), the fundamentals of military doctrine. At least one official inquiry has suggested that the precepts set down in the widely used (but significantly revised) 1987 version of the manual may have been open to abuse by the untrained:

> The interrogator should appear to be the one who controls all aspects of the interrogation to include the lighting, heating, and configuration of the interrogation room, as well as the food, shelter, and clothing given to the source. The interrogator must always be in control, he must act quickly and firmly. However, everything that he says and does must be within the limits of the Geneva and Hague Conventions, as well as the standards of conduct outlined in the UCMJ [Uniform Code of Military Justice].[25]

The techniques embodied in the Special Interrogation Plan were applied to that end. Each had its rationale, expressed in the elementary psychology of FM 34-52. They centered on "Pride and Ego Down" and "Futility."[26] But they contained an additional element: "Increasing Anxiety by Use of Aversions," specifically, bringing a military working dog (MWD) into the interrogation room and ordering it to growl, bark, and bare its teeth at the detainee. The dog, like the detainee, was on a lead. The teeth were for show—this time—but the threat was for real. The image of humiliation appeared before him, large as life, unmuzzled. It was illicit, but easily justified ("exploiting individual phobias"). Crude notions about Arab fear of dogs and Muslim sense of shame mark the limits of cultural understanding.

The war on terror is a war of mutual incomprehension, a war of tribes, with something of the primitive about it. As the captors strip the captives of their dignity, insult their mothers, and profane their religious books, so the captives mock the captors in terms the latter cannot begin to comprehend—women with men's haircuts, men without beards. "In the American army I could not see a real man," said an Afghan returned to his homeland, no longer an enemy combatant, after three years in Guantánamo. "And they talk rudely about homosexuals, which is very shameful to us."[27]

The dog-shaped descent from subject to abject was designed to intensify the shame, sapping the will to resist. That was the hope or expectation. In the nature of the case, it is almost impossible to determine the success of the Special Interrogation Plan, even in its own terms. According to the internal inquiries, Mohammed al-Qahtani's resistance was eventually broken, and he provided valuable intelligence. He is said to have confirmed more than 20 detainees as "UBL bodyguards" who received terrorist training at Al Farooq, "an Al Qaeda facility," and were active fighters against the Northern Alliance in Afghanistan. He is also said to have provided detailed information on meetings with the well-guarded Osama bin Laden himself, and on "the dirty bomber" José Padilla, "the shoe bomber" Richard Reid, and "the terror suspect" Adnan G. El Shukrijumah, alias Jaafaral the Pilot, one of the FBI's most wanted.[28] How valuable was this intelligence, given the time elapsing, the overinflating, the self-justifying, the scaremongering, and the marginal status of most of those identified, including disaffected ex-cons like Padilla and Reid?[29]

The vexed question of value is a difficult one to answer. The baseline is important. "At the time, we didn't even understand what Al Qaeda *was*," admitted a Military Intelligence officer familiar with the practices at Guantánamo. "We thought the detainees were all masterminds. It wasn't the case. Most of them were just dirt farmers in Afghanistan."[30] John Walker Lindh, "the American Taliban," was at Al Farooq; it was in fact a training camp for the Al Ansar group, of which he was a member. Lindh was a foot soldier, and a novice. Now that they had him, however, the Administration had high hopes of making an example of him. Al Qaeda and conspiracy to mass murder topped the charge sheet. When he was captured, in December 2001, he was stripped, gagged, strapped to a board, and exhibited on the evening news. After that he was kept from time to time in a pitch-dark steel shipping container. The commanding officer at Mazar-i-Sharif, where he was being held, told his interrogator that "the Secretary of Defense's counsel had authorized him to 'take the gloves off' and ask whatever he wanted."

The elaborately constructed case collapsed, for want of evidence and understanding. Quite apart from the public exhibition and the private coercion, it transpired that the interrogator, who was new to the job, had consistently replaced the word "Ansar" with "Qaeda" in his report.[31] One expert who interviewed Lindh at length came to believe that the root of the problem lay in the sheer depth of ignorance of U.S. officials, at all levels. "They were like babies. They didn't know enough about Islam or Afghanistan. It was totally alien to them."[32] For those who know nothing, anything is of value.

The al-Qahtani case has an alternative narrative. According to senior Pentagon officials, some of his most interesting confessions were not extracted under the interrogation plan, nor were they attributable to the use of any particular technique. They came more freely, or more unexpectedly, when he was presented with evidence that others were talking, especially Khalid Sheikh Mohammed ("KSM"), the alleged mastermind of 9/11.[33] Whatever the value of the intelligence, on this account "the take" was cumulative, unpredictable, almost adventitious. The correlation between human intelligence (HUMINT) and humiliation was moot.

The techniques approved for al-Qahtani embroidered on a long list of "aggressive interrogation techniques," otherwise known as "counterresistance strategies," requested for use at Guantánamo by its commander in October 2002. The request addressed a deceptively simple problem. "The current guidelines for interrogation procedures at GTMO limit the ability of interrogators to counter advanced resistance." In other words, the swelling population of the penal colony had produced a frustrating paucity of actionable intelligence. High-value or low-value, they yielded embarrassingly little—even supposing that the system was capable of distinguishing between them. More creativity was required. The new man at Guantánamo was Major General Geoffrey Miller. His mantra, "the rapid exploitation of detainees," entailed the functional integration of detention operations, interrogation operations, and collection management.[34] On this model, the "Gitmo" model, Military Police work hand-in-hand with Military Intelligence. The detention force "sets the conditions" for successful interrogations. Setting the conditions means softening up—a polite form of smoking. Rapid exploitation means coercive interrogation, *con brio*. The request from Guantánamo was a request for more latitude.

THE SEPTEMBER 11 SYNDROME

If the war on terror has a theme, it is the Lindh syndrome—or rather the September 11 syndrome—the itch to "take the gloves off" in order to achieve results against such a despicable and fanatical foe. In Cofer Black's pithy testimony, "there was 'before' 9/11 and 'after' 9/11. After 9/11 the gloves come off."[35]

Turning a traditional blind eye, the British, in their allotted role of bag carrier, are complicit also in this. "We have now to cope with a deliberate regression towards barbaric terrorism by our opponents," complains the Defence Secretary, echoing the casuists of the Justice Department.[36] Barbaric terrorism is not cricket.

On this analysis, the ground rules are as outmoded as the Geneva Conventions. "Good manners are timeless, spaceless, classless," writes Christine Brooke-Rose: "simply the ability to imagine the other. As an intelligence officer learns to do, if efficiently backed and not corrupted, experiencing a whole war from the enemy point of view."[37] Good manners were conspicuous by their absence at Abu Ghraib, as Gus, Taxi Driver, Gilligan, the Iranian, and Shitboy could testify.[38] The new normal is improvised, disorderly, and contingent. Bare life is precarious and often vicious. Exploitation, not imagination, is the watchword. The other remains incorrigibly other: not like us. One of the things Eliot Weinberger heard about Iraq was Captain Todd Brown saying, "You have to understand the Arab mind. The only thing they understand is force—force, pride, and saving face."[39] Breaking the barbarians is not a job for the squeamish.

The list of aggressive interrogation techniques was divided into three categories. Category I techniques were the most commonplace and the least aggressive (direct questioning; standard rewards and deceptions; yelling, but not directly in the ear). Category II techniques became the benchmark:

1. The use of stress positions (like standing), for a maximum of four hours.
2. The use of falsified documents or reports.
3. Use of the isolation facility for up to 30 days [with certain conditions attached].
4. Interrogating the detainee in an environment other than the standard interrogation booth.
5. Deprivation of light and auditory stimuli.
6. The detainee may also have a hood placed over his head during transportation and questioning. The hood should not restrict breathing in any way and the detainee should be under direct observation when hooded.
7. The use of 20 hour interrogations.
8. Removal of all comfort items (including religious items).
9. Switching the detainee from hot rations to MREs [Meals Ready to Eat].
10. Removal of clothing.
11. Forced grooming (shaving of facial hair etc).
12. Using detainees' individual phobias (such as fear of dogs) to induce stress.

Category III techniques went a little further:

1. The use of scenarios designed to convince the detainee that death or severely painful consequences are imminent for him and/or his family.

2. Exposure to cold weather or water (with appropriate medical monitoring).

3. Use of a wet towel and dripping water to induce the misperception of suffocation.

4. Use of mild, non-injurious physical contact such as grabbing, poking in the chest with the finger, and light pushing.[40]

Donald Rumsfeld was the man for latitude. He approved the request. On legal advice, the list was trimmed at the edges—Category III techniques were disallowed, except for the fourth—but Rumsfeld could not resist annotating the memorandum of approval with a scribbled addendum: "However, I stand for 8–10 hours a day. Why is standing limited to 4 hours?"[41]

In the bureaucratic politics of torture, this addendum is close to perfection. One of the very few vocal opponents of these measures in high office, Alberto Mora, General Counsel of the U.S. Navy, focused immediately on Rumsfeld's mischief-making intervention. Mora understood well enough that it could be construed as a jest, a throwaway line. But he also feared that it could become an argument for the defense in any prosecution of terror suspects; furthermore, it could be read as an encouragement to exceed the limits officially prescribed by the Secretary of Defense himself. Mora's was not an aberrant interpretation. Colonel Lawrence Wilkerson, Chief of Staff to the former Secretary of State Colin Powell, had a similar reaction when he saw the addendum. "It said, 'Carte blanche, guys,'" Wilkerson explained to the investigative reporter Jane Mayer. "That's what started them down the slope. You'll have My Lais then. Once you pull this thread, the whole fabric unravels."[42]

The techniques approved for Guantánamo migrated to other camps in other countries. Migration bred corruption. In Iraq, in August 2003, under intense pressure from Washington for actionable intelligence on the remarkably persistent insurgent deadbeats and former regime remnants, a familiar cry went up. From Coalition Headquarters a Military Intelligence officer sent an e-mail to his colleagues in the community. "The gloves are coming off gentlemen regarding these detainees, Col. Boltz has made it clear that we want these individuals broken. Casualties are mounting and we need to start gathering info to help protect our fellow soldiers from any further attacks." The e-mail betrayed some desperation. There was an appeal for "input" on effective interrogation techniques and an urgent request for a "wish list" of personal favorites.[43] Soon afterward, the go-getting Geoffrey Miller appeared with a team of specialists, on what was quaintly termed an assistance visit. Assistance was sorely needed. Even the terrorists knew about the parlous state of HUMINT in Iraq. Collection was haphazard, analysis disconnected. Documentation was practically nonexistent. Detention and interrogation operations were ramshackle and ineffectual. The ace of spades, Saddam Hussein himself, was still at large; a full-scale insurgency was building. Back in Guantánamo—by way of adding to the bizarrerie—interrogators would gather outside Mohammed al-Qahtani's cell, in a kind of barbershop chorus, and serenade him with the Rolling Stones' "Time Is on My Side." The joke (if it was a joke) was on them. The interrogator works against the clock. Time is the torturer's best defense: actionable intelligence is acutely time sensitive. Waiting for the barbarians to talk might take forever. For the embattled Coalition Provisional Authority, bunkered down in Baghdad, any solution could come not a moment too soon. Geoffrey Miller was sent to Iraq for a purpose. His report was a technocrat's blueprint. "The team used JTF-GTMO operational procedures and interrogation authorities as baselines."[44] Iraq was to be "Gitmo-ized."

Wherever Miller went, the dog was sure to follow. Dogs arrived at Abu Ghraib in November 2003. In the overcrowded Hard Site, where MI holds (detainees considered to be of Military Intelligence value) were penned higgledy-piggledy with miscellaneous criminals and various unknowns, dog tricks and "dog piles" of naked detainees were already part of the curriculum. "They forced us to walk like dogs on our hands and knees. And we had to bark like a dog and if we didn't do that, they start hitting us hard on our face and chest with no mercy."[45] The Military Police were setting conditions with a will. Real live military working dogs were immediately put to use, menacing and even biting detainees, sometimes for interrogation, sometimes for sport. Two Army dog handlers had a competition to see who could make a detainee urinate or defecate on himself, if sufficiently terrorized by Marco and Duco, dogs with better names than detainees. Other soldiers came to watch. Soon "doggy dances" were all the rage.[46] These antics appear to have been regarded as just that by almost everyone who participated in them, or witnessed them, or heard about them: a sizable constituency. So far from being concealed, they were a commonplace of prison conversation.[47] In fact, they were as disgraceful as they were unremarkable. Like the routine sexual humiliation, like the pervasive nakedness, the use or abuse of dogs was an accepted practice—all in a day's work—filmed by the perpetrators themselves, posing happy-snappy for the camera. The results became screen savers on their personal computers.

Abu Ghraib was the nadir of normalization. Many of the perpetrators were members of the 320th Military Police Battalion, reservists, undertrained and overwhelmed—ordinary men indeed.[48] They received every encouragement. Emboldened by the permissive atmosphere, egged on by Military Intelligence, they knew no bounds. There were interrogators who revelled in the use of dogs, not only to set the conditions, but also to "fear up" detainees during the interrogation itself. Some of them were civilian contractors, who appeared to enjoy a special license; some were regular soldiers, members of the 205th Military Intelligence Brigade, who should have known better. The Fay-Jones Report found that, over the period July 2003 to February 2004, no fewer than 27 Military Intelligence personnel "requested, encouraged, condoned or solicited Military Police personnel to abuse detainees and/or participated in detainee abuse and/or violated established interrogation procedures and applicable laws and regulations during intelligence operations at Abu Ghraib."[49] These were common-or-garden crimes. For some, they were overrated. They were certainly overmatched.

There was another caste at the prison, the untouchables of "OGA" ["Other Government Agency," a euphemism for the Central Intelligence Agency (CIA)], with their gangster tactics and their "ghost detainees." OGA were a pernicious influence at Abu Ghraib. Fay-Jones speaks with barely concealed distaste of their "unhealthy mystique." Their modus operandi is cloaked in mystery, but CIA sources attest to a shortlist of "enhanced interrogation techniques," introduced in March 2002, going far beyond the pussyfooting categorizing of the Department of Defense:

1. Attention Grab. The interrogator forcefully grabs the shirt front of the prisoner and shakes him.

2. Attention Slap. An open-handed slap aimed at causing pain and triggering fear.

3. Belly Slap. A hard open-handed slap to the stomach. The aim is to cause pain, but not internal injury. Doctors consulted advised against using a punch, which could cause lasting internal damage.

4. Long Time Standing. Prisoners are forced to stand, handcuffed and with their feet shackled to an eye bolt in the floor for more than 40 hours. Exhaustion and sleep deprivation are effective in yielding confessions.

5. Cold Cell. The prisoner is left to stand naked in a cell kept near 50 degrees. Throughout the time in the cell the prisoner is doused with cold water.

6. Water-Boarding. The prisoner is bound to an inclined board, feet raised and head slightly below the feet. Cellophane is wrapped over the prisoner's face and water is poured over him. Unavoidably, the gag reflex kicks in and a terrifying fear of drowning leads to almost instant pleas to bring the treatment to a halt.[50]

The application of these techniques at Abu Ghraib in November 2003 resulted in an OGA "death in custody," later ruled a homicide, caused by "blunt force injuries to the torso complicated by compromised respiration."[51] This was Detainee 28, Manadel al-Jamadi, identified by the CIA as a high-value target for his involvement in a number of bombing atrocities in Baghdad. He was alleged to have supplied the explosives. Detainee 28 had no time to talk. He died in a shower room within an hour of arrival. Disposal of the body is always a delicate business. In this instance it was placed in a body bag, packed in ice, and left in the showers overnight. The following morning it was removed, on a stretcher, as if to a hospital. During the night it was discovered by two of the Military Police, who took the opportunity to photograph each other, thumbs up, with the mutilated corpse.[52] So immortalized, Manadel al-Jamadi assumed a new alias: the Ice Man. In the prison his fate was well-known, as was the disposal of the body. There were few secrets at Abu Ghraib. Colonel Thomas Pappas, commander of the Military Intelligence Brigade, was reported as saying, "Well, if I go down, I'm not going down alone. The guys from Langley are going with me."[53]

In such a climate, it may be that torture and abuse were massively overdetermined, even if they were not directly ordered, solicited, encouraged, condoned, or simply ignored. And yet, even in these circumstances, degradation is not preordained.

The exercise of professional judgment, not to mention moral scruple, was possible at Abu Ghraib. It happened even at the height of the abuse. It was demonstrated in exemplary fashion by the response of three Navy dog teams, led by Master-at-Arms William Kimbro, who respectfully refused to indulge in any abuse and steadfastly resisted all entreaties to do so. The official account of this intriguing episode is a little circumspect, but the outline is clear. Recalled to the Hard Site one night after a fruitless search for explosives, Kimbro and his dog came upon three civilians, evidently interrogators, yelling and screaming at a detainee squatting in a corner of a cell. Agitated, the dog began to bark and lunge; the dog handler struggled to regain control. One of the civilians told the detainee that if he did not cooperate, then the interrogator would let Kimbro set the dog on him. That was not at all what William Kimbro had in mind. Dog and dog handler promptly departed. They were called back, but they did not return. The Fay-Jones Report takes up the story:

> Following this 24 November 2003 incident the three Navy dog teams concluded that some interrogators might attempt to misuse Navy dogs to support their interrogations. For all subsequent requests they inquired what the specific purpose of the dog was and when told "for interrogation" they explained that Navy dogs were not intended for interrogations and the request would not be fulfilled. Over the next few weeks, the Navy dog teams received about eight similar calls, none of which were fulfilled. In the later part of December 2003, Col. Pappas summoned MA1 Kimbro and wanted to know what the Navy dogs's [sic] capabilities were. MA1 Kimbro explained Navy dog capabilities and provided the Navy Dog Use SOP [Standard Operating Procedure]. Col. Pappas never asked if they could be used in interrogations and following that meeting the Navy dog teams received no additional requests to support interrogations.[54]

Offering his own commendation, Taguba reports succinctly that William Kimbro "knew his duties and refused to participate in improper interrogations despite significant pressure from the MI personnel at Abu Ghraib."[55]

Like the abuse, the pressure was systemic. It started at the top and trickled all the way down. Behind the dog is the dog handler. Behind the dog handler is the commander. Behind the commander is the policy maker. The Military Police set the conditions; the Secretary of Defense set the tone. The dauntless Donald Rumsfeld bears a heavy responsibility for the chamber of horrors that is Abu Ghraib, a metonym for the moral failings of this factitious war. Some part of that responsibility is the troubling issue of "pressure."[56]

Pressure from policy makers for actionable intelligence is uncomfortably reminiscent of pressure for usable intelligence in the campaign of persuasion that preceded the invasion of Iraq. With the passage of time the demand for proof has been superseded by the demand for results. It is almost as if the mythical WMD have mutated into the all too real MWD (Military Working Dogs) as the emblem of the war effort. The effect is corrosive, be it "sexing up" or "smoking" or worse. For the intelligence community the risks are clear. They go to the heart of the relationship between intelligence and policy. Politicization is a disease that can take many forms.[57]

The tensions caused by these frustrated desires do not end there. FBI complaints about interrogation practices at Guantánamo were not entirely altruistic. As the Schmidt Report explains, the different organizations involved had different priorities. "Law enforcement agencies were primarily interested in interviews that would produce voluntary confessions...admissible in U.S. Federal District Courts. Conversely, DoD [Department of Defense] interrogators were interested in actionable intelligence and thus had greater latitude on the techniques used during interrogations." The Administration recognized well enough that Increasing Anxiety by Use of Aversions, for example, that is to say the use of dogs, could have a significant impact on the admissibility of evidence in court. They did not care. The problem was finessed under the state of exception. Admissibility, they were advised, was a "lesser issue" for military commissions.[58]

The military approach prevailed. It is after all the GWOT and not the GLOT (Global Law on Terror). War-war is better than law-law. George W. Bush is the self-declared war president. The destination of choice is not the court but the camp. The arena is the interrogation room. This is the paradigm of the new normal. The interrogation is the fundamental engagement of the war on terror. The bare life of the detainee has come to define the Western way in warfare.

Interrogation is apt to be adversarial. Polite interrogation may not be a complete contradiction in terms, but it is evidently a rarity. Coercive interrogation is the thing. The singular history of the GWOT is the search for creative forms of coercion: methods permissible and effectual.[59] The emphasis on "creativity" is, on the face of it, surprising. Yet there is something theatrical, choreographed, about an interrogation—corded and recorded, as one might say—like a late work by Samuel Beckett, *Krapp's Last Tape*, perhaps, or *Eh, Joe*, with its night terror and mocking questions. "Anyone living love you now, Joe?…Anyone living sorry for you now?"[60] This is not so far from Mohammed al-Qahtani and the banana rats of Guantánamo Bay, the gruesome world of the Special Interrogation Plan, Pride and Ego Down, and Futility.

THE END JUSTIFIES THE MEANS?

In the end interrogation is a matter of question and answer. "The Socratic method intensified," noted Lichtenberg—"I mean *torture*."[61] Creative forms of coercion found expression in "smoking" and "fucking" and "water boarding." The Ice Man is not an isolated case. Nearly 100 detainees have died in the hands of U.S. officials in the global war on terror. According to the U.S. military's own classification, 34 of these cases are suspected or confirmed homicides; Human Rights First has identified a further 11 in which the facts suggest death as a result of physical abuse or harsh detention conditions. Eight people in U.S. custody have been tortured to death. The steepest sentence given to anyone involved in a torture-related death is five months in jail. Only 12 detainee deaths have resulted in punishment of any kind for any U.S. official.[62]

For an alliance of values, moral ruination is a particular hardship. The effort to reconcile the excusable and the inexcusable has failed, as it was bound to fail. Actionable intelligence remains elusive. Tactically, a lucky break may serve to capture a fugitive or secure a hostage.[63] Strategically, the picture is cloudy—blurred by known unknowns and unknown unknowns—but it is not evident that we are winning the war of HUMINT, in Baghdad or Basra, or for that matter in London or Leeds.[64] Barbaric terrorists seem to have an uncanny knack of strategic surprise. Arguments about "efficacy" are in any event too narrowly drawn. The larger truth is that the war of humiliation is already lost.

Humiliation breaks people. It makes them talk. This may or may not produce good intelligence. It surely widens the circle of shame. "The fact that such things could take place among us is a humiliation we must henceforth face. Meanwhile, we must at least refuse to justify such methods, even on the score of efficacy. The moment they are justified, even indirectly, there are no more rules or values; all causes are equally good, and war without aims or laws sanctions the triumph of nihilism." So wrote Albert Camus in a preface to his "Algerian Reports" in 1958. "And what is that efficacy whereby we manage to justify everything that is most unjustifiable in our adversary? Consequently, the chief argument of those who decide to accept the use of torture must be met head on. Torture has perhaps saved some, at the expense of honour, by uncovering thirty bombs, but at the same time it aroused fifty new terrorists who, operating in some other way and in another place, will cause the death of even more innocent people. Even when accepted in the interest of realism and efficacy, such a flouting of honour serves no purpose but to degrade our country in her own eyes and abroad."[65]

Observing the unfortunate client-turned-dog, Kafka remarks, "[I]t was humiliating even to the onlooker."[66] Antonio Taguba was not merely offended by what he saw of Abu Ghraib, he was humiliated. So is the United States. So are we all. As Walt Whitman knew, the damage is indivisible.

> Whoever degrades another degrades me,
> And whatever is done or said returns at last to me.[67]

Shame is enduring. In the Muslim world the story of the shame will be told, Scheherazade-like, for years to come. Awareness will seep into the United States and its satrapies like dripping water on the Western conscience.

Shame is Kafka's strongest gesture, Walter Benjamin said.[68] Joseph K. meets his end at the hands of two frock-coated warders, who lead him away, ceremoniously undress him, lay him out like a sacrifice, and produce a double-edged butcher's knife for the purpose, passing it between them suggestively, as if hoping that K. himself will take it up and do the decent thing.

> He could not completely rise to the occasion, he could not relieve the officials of all their tasks; the responsibility for this last failure of his lay with him who had not left him the remnant of strength necessary for the deed. His glance fell on the top storey of the house adjoining the quarry. With a flicker as of a light going up, the casements of a window there suddenly flew open; a human figure, faint and insubstantial at that distance and that height, leaned abruptly far forward and stretched both arms still farther. Who was it? A friend? A good man? Someone who sympathized? Someone who wanted to help? Was it one person only? Or were they all there? Was help at hand? Were there some arguments in his favour that had been overlooked? Of course there must be. Logic is doubtless unshakable, but it cannot withstand a man who wants to go on living. Where was the Judge whom he had never seen? Where was the High Court, to which he had never penetrated? He raised his hands and spread out all his fingers.
>
> But the hands of one of the partners were already at K.'s throat, while the other thrust the knife into his heart and turned it there twice. With failing eyes K. could still see the two of them, cheek leaning against cheek, immediately before his face, watching the final act. "Like a dog!" he said: it was as if he meant the shame of it to outlive him.[69]

Part III: Toward New Intelligence Systems

9

Preparing to Meet New Challenges

Peter Wilson

> The problem...is determined precisely by the fact that the knowledge
> of the circumstances of which we must make use never exists in con-
> centrated or integrated form, but solely as the dispersed bits of incom-
> plete and frequently contradictory knowledge which all the separate
> individuals possess....The problem is thus in no way solved if we
> can show that all of the facts, *if* they were known to a single mind,
> would uniquely determine the solution; instead, we must show how a
> solution is produced by the interactions of people, each of whom pos-
> sesses only partial knowledge.
>
> —Friedrich von Hayek, *The Use of Knowledge in Society*

There is nothing new about intelligence reform. Intelligence agencies have
always had to adjust to changing targets, changing operational environments, and changing demands for external oversight and control. Many of
the changes have been evolutionary—experimental "bottom-up" responses
by individual officers to a new intelligence requirement—rather than the
result of a deliberate top-down program of "reform." They have perhaps
been more successful as a result. This chapter therefore prefers to talk about
change rather than reform and tries to examine how intelligence organizations can continue to be flexible and can continue to change as rapidly as
the targets they are facing.

The current change that we demand of intelligence agencies is that they should become better at responding to a plethora of ill-defined threats from inchoate networks of individuals and small groups. Al Qaeda is of course the classic example of an informal network that currently exercises the intelligence agencies. But even several years before 9/11 at the end of the Cold War, Western intelligence officers were developing techniques and structures to deal with terrorist and transnational crime networks that unlike Communist intelligence agencies had no fixed structure, few identifiable personnel, and no formal headquarters that could be bugged or watched. Some intelligence officers referred to this as the "lack of brass plate" problem to capture the difficulties of targeting organizations that did not announce their presence with a brass plate at their front door.

The challenge of dealing with a large number of small threats contains two conflicting elements. Rather than rely on a small number of high-value secret sources, intelligence agencies have to become better at compiling and analyzing a much wider range of information from a greater variety of sources and partner agencies. This requires larger budgets, tighter management focus, and a greater emphasis on systems, efficiency, and coordination. However, intelligence agencies also have to remain flexible and allow their officers to be imaginative and to innovate. No intelligence agency wishes to be criticized for a "failure of imagination"—as the American agencies were criticized by Congress over 9/11[1]—but the need to foster imagination is often at odds with the aim of achieving efficiency and management control.

To borrow Donald Rumsfeld's language,[2] this chapter discusses the difficulties of dealing with the "known unknowns" of the plans of existing enemies and the "unknown unknowns" of surprise attack by new enemies using new techniques. The former requires discipline, analysis, and knowledge management; the latter requires imagination, insight, and innovation. Management mechanisms have to be sensitive to the difficulties of combining such diverse activities, and structures that have been developed to oversee more conventional fields of Government activity may not be appropriate for the management of intelligence.

DEALING WITH THE KNOWN UNKNOWNS

The classic way of understanding the intentions of a formalized, bureaucratic institution such as a Communist intelligence agency is to recruit as a secret source someone who sits in a key management position or someone who works in the registry. The bureaucratic structures and disciplined record keeping of a traditional institution mean that a few well-placed sources can provide widespread coverage of the most important activities of the organization as a whole.

While the actual act of conducting the intelligence relationship may be complex, *managing* the activity is relatively simple. The hard part of the job is in establishing the secret relationship and maintaining it securely. This requires a complex mixture of innovation and discipline by the officer who is running the case. But deciding who should be recruited is relatively straightforward, and the importance of their output tends to be self-evident. The activity is self-contained and carried out by a small number of highly professional intelligence officers. There is little need to coordinate with other departments or manage a database full of fragments of partial, conflicting, or unclear information. It is normally clear where scarce resources should be directed.

The challenge of dealing with an inchoate network of individuals and groupings is entirely different. There may well be no single person who has an overview of all the network's activities, and there are few bureaucratic structures such as a registry that can be targeted. A few well-placed sources cannot provide comprehensive coverage, and there is a need to analyze and manage a much wider range of sources of information and intelligence, including Web site postings; suspicions and tip-offs from a plethora of low-level, partially informed sources; and the travel bookings and financial transactions of people who may or may not be important in the network. The intelligence agency does not control all such information and has to establish and coordinate relationships with several other domestic departments including police, Customs, Immigration, and financial watchdogs, along with a wide range of partner agencies in other countries.

The need to develop the capabilities of foreign partner agencies provides a particular challenge. Intelligence agencies recognize that they will make little headway against terrorism and transnational crime unless they can work with effective and legitimate intelligence and security agencies in key partner countries. Western intelligence agencies are therefore beginning to be involved in a complex mix of management consultancy, reform, training, and institutional development for foreign agencies, making a new set of demands of intelligence officers who were recruited and trained to run one-to-one intelligence relationships, not to manage major institutional change.

The prime challenge of all this activity is management. The organization cannot cover all possible sources of information, so it has to make choices about where to direct its resources, even at the risk of being criticized in hindsight for ignoring the one piece of information that could have prevented an attack. Efficiency is at a premium to allow the widest possible coverage from a given level of funding. Increased budgets and rapid growth may be necessary, but they bring their own problems, as the organization has to recruit, train, and induct large numbers of new recruits into a lean organization that does not have many experienced middle managers to oversee the process and provide a steadying hand.

We might think of the traditional Cold War intelligence agency as being analogous to an Oxford college—orchestrating the activities of a small number of self-directed, highly professional, sometimes eccentric intelligence officers all doing their own thing in relative isolation from their colleagues and from the rest of Government. In this environment the stereotypically pragmatic intelligence officer was impatient with budget management, co-ordination meetings, bureaucratic structures, and strategic plans and was recruited for his ability to get on with the job alone or in small teams.

The modern intelligence agency is changing to be more analogous to a large modern company, emphasizing efficiency, coordination, structures, procedures, and good management practice. This process is well under way in many Western agencies and is a proper response to the changing threat, but it is certainly new territory for intelligence cultures that traditionally preferred initiative to doctrine.

DEALING WITH THE UNKNOWN UNKNOWNS

The challenges of efficiency and good management require that an intelligence agency structures itself to respond to the most pressing current threats. But such focus risks missing clues about new threats that cannot be dealt with by the existing structures. The classic example of this is the failure to predict 9/11 because of an artificial distinction between domestic and foreign threats—such distinctions had been useful in the Cold War, but could not respond to the new threat from al Qaeda.[3] There was perhaps a vicious cycle here—an initial failure of imagination to accept that a foreign network could launch a huge-scale domestic attack, a resultant failure to create new structures that could deal with such a threat, the inability of the existing structures to piece together the evidence and come up with a credible warning, and, therefore, no compelling reason to reform and no "raw material" that could challenge preconceptions and prompt the application of imagination.

Even before 9/11 there was a huge literature on the problems for a security sector in preventing surprise attacks—typically the challenge is not in finding the clues but is in piecing them together when they do not fit the structures, preconceptions, and concerns of the existing security institutions.[4] The fundamental problem is that it is difficult to take effective security action when the danger signals are still weak—reorganizing security structures, deploying military forces, implementing widespread preventive security, or carrying out large-scale monitoring of suspects simply cannot be justified until the danger becomes immediate in the minds of politicians and the public. As a result, action is often taken only when it is too late, and an intelligence sector that has to reorganize every time the threat changes will always be behind the action. A security sector needs the capability to overcome organizational constraints to pick up on weak danger signals, investigate them, and shape them into a coherent case that Government can take seriously and have a range of small actions—intelligence coverage and a general watching brief—that it can put in place until the signals are strong enough to justify major action.

So while intelligence agencies focus their efforts on restructuring to tackle the existing threats from al Qaeda and its international franchises, how can we also prepare for the next surprise, perhaps from homegrown terrorism that does not rely on the international links that intelligence agencies are working hard to detect and control? The answer is that intelligence agencies have to allow for imagination and innovation as well as focus and control. They have to listen to intelligence officers and others whose view of the emerging threat does not fit the Government's preconceptions. They have to allocate a portion of their resources to nascent threats even when there is not yet any clear evidence of danger or political pressure for action. Such activity by definition cannot be efficient—there will be false trails and wasted money, but intelligence agencies will have to spread their chips around the table and incur some losses rather than betting on one single understanding of the threats that they face.

The old model of the intelligence agency as Oxford College was well placed to manage such innovation. It trusted in individuals and it promoted imagination, even at the expense of a loss of efficiency and control. In general this was the result of a happy accident resulting from the nature of intelligence rather than from a deep understanding of innovation management. Intelligence activity is inherently rather *ad hoc*. The act of establishing a relationship with someone to the point where they will tell you secrets is very personal. It relies a great deal on luck and the characters of the individual intelligence officer and his target. Managers at headquarters do not try to manage the process too closely because they know they cannot second-guess the knowledge of the officer conducting the relationship. Senior officers understand the need for their subordinates to try several different approaches, only some of which would prove successful. The culture of successful intelligence agencies always therefore emphasized the need for individual initiative, risk taking, and a diversity of techniques, and individuals were recruited who could thrive in such a loose management system.

COMBINING EFFICIENCY AND INNOVATION

So even as intelligence agencies move to a greater emphasis on tighter management, some of the flavor of the old system has to be maintained. Senior managers in intelligence agencies have to manage a dual culture within their organization and consciously distinguish between the management styles that are suitable for highly efficient, evidence-based targeting of known unknowns and the more flexible and intuitive search for new threats and unknown unknowns.

There is no right answer on the structures required in order to achieve this balancing act. Major companies have battled with the problem for many years—how do you standardize behavior in order to be efficient while also responding flexibly to the challenge from the unknown entrepreneur working is his garage?[5] How do you allocate resources effectively while also allowing your R&D department to pursue radical research that may or may not lead to profitable new products? There are many management books suggesting different solutions, none of which is wholly convincing. The classic work on the subject[6] emphasizes that these are genuine dilemmas, and the more efficient you are in current markets the less agility you will have to dominate future markets.

The lesson is that there is no perfect intelligence structure that could achieve all that we ask of it. Reorganization is always tempting and politically expedient, particularly after a failure to counter a surprise attack, but it risks simply reinforcing the problem of designing a system around past experience rather than future threats. There is no substitute for a professional culture that responds pragmatically to the problems of the day, uses structures and rules when it is sensible to do so, but bypasses them when the need arises.[7]

DEALING WITH THE PRESSURE FOR ACCOUNTABILITY

In addition to the internal changes that have been taking place in intelligence agencies to respond to new threats, agencies have also had to respond to changing external demands for government control of public sector activity. Many of the resulting mechanisms such as judicial and parliamentary oversight have been beneficial—needless secrecy has been swept away and intelligence and security services have secured increased public and political support by being seen as legitimate, competent institutions acting within the rule of law in response to priorities set by the elected Government.

As we have identified, however, intelligence activity is an unusual process that requires a high level of trust in professional case officers to manage individual agent relationships and to have the courage to risk "wasting" resources by pursuing weak signals. The application of heavy-handed accountability mechanisms may make the intelligence agency's balancing act between efficiency and innovation more difficult if it reduces officers' abilities to take such calculated risks and to cut across structures and rules where necessary. The philosopher Onora O'Neill describes the general desire for accountability in the public sector as follows:

> The new accountability has quite sharp teeth. Performance is monitored and subjected to quality control and quality assurance. The idea of *audit* has been exported from its original financial context to cover ever more detailed scrutiny

of non-financial processes and systems. Performance indicators are used to measure adequate and inadequate performance with supposed precision. This *audit explosion,* as Michael Power has so aptly called it, has often displaced or marginalized older systems of accountability. In the universities, external examiners lost influence as centrally planned teaching quality assessment was imposed; in the health services, professional judgment is constrained in many ways; in schools, curriculum and assessment of pupils are controlled in pretty minute detail.[8]

The challenge for a modern intelligence agency is therefore threefold: to introduce rapidly, into organizations that traditionally had little appetite or need for conventional management, those management techniques that are useful for dealing with fragmented threats; to do so while maintaining the flexibility to identify new threats; and to deal with a general governmental push for comprehensive accountability that is already being seen as unsuitable for much professional work in the public sector and may be particularly inappropriate for intelligence agencies.

Governments and oversight bodies need to understand these subtleties, leave some slack in the system, and not place too much emphasis only on a cost-effective response to "clear and present" dangers. On the general problem of accountability and trust, Onora O'Neill rightly stresses:

> [A]ccountability requires more attention to good governance and fewer fantasies about total control. Good governance is possible only if institutions are allowed some margin for self-governance of a form appropriate to their particular tasks, within a framework of financial and other reporting. Such reporting, I believe, is not improved by being wholly standardized or relentlessly detailed, and since much that has to be accounted for is not easily measured it cannot be boiled down to a set of stock performance indicators. Those who are called to account should give an *account* of what they have done, and of their successes and failures, to others who have sufficient time and experience to assess the evidence and report on it. Real accountability provides substantive and knowledgeable independent judgment of an institution's or professional's work.[9]

MEETING NEW CHALLENGES

Intelligence services are currently well served by highly motivated, intelligent *generalists,* working within loose management structures, who have found it relatively easy to adjust to the new challenges presented by al Qaeda and other networks. The speed with which intelligence organizations have thrown off Cold War orthodoxies has been impressive and often driven by pragmatic responses by junior or middle-ranking officers to new threats and operational opportunities, rather than by some cumbersome process of reviews and reorganizations.

The legitimate need for secrecy has protected intelligence agencies from the wilder excesses of accountability as described by O'Neill. Unlike many government departments, they have not had to respond to transient head-lines with eye-catching initiatives. They have been able to focus on the most important issues, because they have not been paralyzed by an attempt to fol-low up every possible lead for fear of being criticized in hindsight for miss-ing a vital clue.

So once a threat has been fully identified by government, we can be rea-sonably certain that intelligence agencies have the professional skills, disci-pline, and flexibility to achieve results. Where the system as a whole needs to be improved is in the ability to identify and prioritize those threats in the first place. We need to widen the range of people who can contribute to the task, while also respecting the entirely legitimate need for intelligence agencies to keep their priorities and activities secret. The following propos-als may help to strengthen our overall ability to identify and prioritize new threats, without undermining the foundations of intelligence agencies' cur-rent success.

Prepare Shadow Intelligence Requirements

It is often argued that governments should listen to academics and other external foreign policy experts to better identify emerging threats. Examples are given of particular experts who, with hindsight, are seen to have gotten something "right" before the government did—perhaps by predicting the end of the Cold War or noting the emergence of Islamic extremism. It is sometimes asserted that external experts, free of the constraints of government and able to concentrate on a single issue for many years, are better at understanding complex foreign policy issues than diplomats or intelligence officers.

But academics and experts make hundreds of predictions every day, often in direct opposition to each other—and by probability alone some of them are going to get it right some of the time. What matters to a government that needs to allocate scarce resources is not to hear an ever wider range of voices predicting an ever wider range of threats. Instead we need to find a way to assess the many threats that are already being asserted, filter out the wilder claims, insert the serious concerns into government in a way that is credible to busy officials, and recommend action that is politically realistic while the signals remain weak. Such action requires a combination of academic, pri-vate sector, and government activity, and we need not claim that one form of enquiry is better or worse than another.

One possible way of contributing to this is for academics and other experts to propose their own intelligence requirements. At present in the U.K. system, the Joint Intelligence Committee (JIC) prepares intelligence requirements based on the priorities of Whitehall departments. This is an important method of identifying the highest-priority known unknowns and ensures that the intelligence and security agencies focus on the issues of most importance to government rather than pursuing their own agendas. It is an important tool for coordination and accountability. The requirements are rightly classified "top secret" because they are politically sensitive—the assertion of an intelligence requirement about an organization or government also implies a willingness to spy on it in order to meet the requirement.

However, what official intelligence requirements by definition cannot do is identify the unknown unknowns or ask intelligence agencies to answer the question, "What question is not in the requirements but should be?" There is no reason that some august body of external experts could not try to reach consensus on their own "shadow intelligence requirements," which free of government approval need not be politically sensitive and which could capture a wider range of expertise. The JIC and the intelligence establishments of other Governments would be free to incorporate the more sensible proposals into the official requirements and ignore the rest.

Be Better at Oversight

Current mechanisms of oversight tend to be rather backward looking and suffer from the failures pointed out by O'Neill—they try to identify mistakes, wasted money, and inefficiency. What is needed from oversight bodies is instead some positive advice about where the intelligence agencies should be focusing their efforts in the future and some guidance on how they will need to change the way they organize and operate. Members of Parliament or Congress have differing abilities to fulfill such a role, and it may be wise to widen the membership of oversight bodies to include other trusted individuals who can bring in their own experience from other fields and provide some positive, expert guidance. By analogy with the private sector, perhaps what is needed is a nonexecutive board rather than just an audit committee.

Develop Wider Professional Skills

We have seen that there is no perfect organizational or oversight structure to manage the conflicting demands of efficiency and innovation, and we have little choice but to rely on the professionalism of intelligence officers to work within and around whatever systems are put in place.

However, intelligence officers are rarely trained to understand the increasingly complex managerial issues they are being asked to handle. For many years training in operational effectiveness was enough—as we have identified there was little need for management systems or even for particularly sophisticated analysis during the Cold War. As a result there is no intelligence equivalent of a military staff college, where officers can step back from their day-to-day work and understand how organizational and political issues affect their activities. There is no intelligence equivalent of the military's bible *On the Psychology of Military Incompetence*,[10] which provides officers with a self-critical look at common military errors. There is no system to allow operational officers to digest the lessons of Congressional and Parliamentary intelligence investigations, to learn from academic work on surprise attack and analytical failings, or to borrow insights from the private sector on the challenge of combining discipline and innovation.

The lack of wider professional training means that intelligence officers often know less than their military counterparts about the worldwide successes and failures of their profession, about common professional pitfalls, and about views from the related worlds of academia, business, and politics. There are few fora where intelligence officers can interact with experts from other fields or even with people from other parts of government.

This is partly a natural result of secrecy. Many external "experts" actually know little about the realities of intelligence and confine themselves to childish attempts to find out secrets—as a result they carry little credibility with busy operational officers. The different approaches to training between the military and intelligence is also perhaps because intelligence officers are busier—the military has developed long training courses partly to give officers something to do when there is no war, but intelligence officers have no such downtime.

The major challenge therefore is not in creating more insights into intelligence, management, and reform but in finding mechanisms to transmit what already exists into the hands of the people who need to use it. Intelligence officers have never been busier and would find it hard to take the time to absorb external views, but this might be precisely the moment when they most need such exposure.

CONCLUSION

The 9/11 Commission called for greater imagination in dealing with new threats, but imagination entails mistakes, waste, disorganization, and lack of focus, all of which are against the grain of modern government. There is no perfect way of organizing for imagination, but the intelligence services, benefiting from a tradition of individual initiative, probably do it better than most arms of Government. A few tweaks to the political and oversight environment they operate in and a greater openness to external views could allow them to maintain and strengthen this tradition.

10

Efficient Resource Allocation

George Maior
Sebastian Huluban

After September 11, 2001, the issue of allocating resources for intelligence as a matter of establishing a proper relationship between intelligence professionals and government can be better understood if it is set in a wider context. This means searching for a new balance between providing more money and widening the qualitative aspects of the resource base, so that the end result can be understood in terms of achieving results across the entire spectrum of intelligence work.

Modern organization theory assumes that one of the basic rules of change management is to ensure a proper balance between efficiency and effectiveness, as well as between allocating material resources and creating incentives for creativity. The means to achieve this is to reinvent human resources policies and maintain an effective trade-off between the quantity and the quality of changes planned. If a trade-off becomes inevitable it is better to target effectiveness on the long-term rather than efficiency on the short-term.

It should also be recognized that the reform of intelligence policy processes does not necessarily affect the balance between liberty and security. Many public intellectuals believe that when faced with "extreme situations" governments tend to strengthen their intelligence capacity by curtailing freedoms and human rights. In this respect, it is often assumed that open societies and liberty are so sensitive and fragile that any improvement in security or heightened intelligence capacity would seriously impinge upon them. Any such concern should be balanced against the consideration of how much a community's sense of security will be adversely affected by having a state of fear regarding the sustainability of our liberty. As the events of September 11, 2001, show, we tend to underestimate the importance of our security for the sake of a taboo, the fragility of our rights—at our own peril. In the end, instead of focusing on how weak liberty is in relation to security, we may want to think about how strong the democratic institutions remain after all the issues have been considered and new challenges confronted.

FACING NEW CHALLENGES

In the context of the global war on terror, intelligence services are under permanent pressure to change. It seems to us there is a significant degree of similarity between the transformation required of intelligence services in the global war on terror and the amount of reform the defense establishments of the post-Communist countries had to undertake during the NATO accession process. In thinking about managing changes in the intelligence and security services in the post-9/11 world lessons can be learned from the experience of the transformation in Eastern Europe. The East European armed forces were required not just to transform themselves with a clearly defined goal, but into very dynamic forces that meet the standards of the Allied forces. The transformation of the East European armed forces, therefore, had to take into account two parallel dynamic processes, one completely driven by external forces. However, the comparison between these two requirements has its limits. The crux of the matter is a straightforward one: change management and transformation should not lead us to conceptual confusion. Transformation should not be pursued just for the sake of transformation.

What this means is that once intelligence organizations are reformed in line with new strategic directions, legal rules, and procedures, they should be encouraged to develop a new organizational culture and not be subjected to criticism based on their previous failings. Efficient resource allocation of the intelligence services in the context of the global war on terror is about transforming attitudes and minds rather than just changing and redrawing organizational charts. Consequently, monitoring and assessing this transformation could be very difficult for governments and politicians to understand and oversee.

The first and most important condition for reforming and improving the process of efficient resource allocation is to separate the general context, namely, the global war on terror, from the daily bureaucratic routines. It is very important to bear in mind that such changes should not be directed to serve only a specific and therefore limited political goal, namely, disman- tling and destroying al Qaeda and associated terrorist networks. By putting matters in a broad strategic context one can see that the future will bring unpredictable combinations of multiple threats and risks (and not just the classical surprise attacks[1]) that will be even more surprising than what we faced in 2001 or even dare to imagine.

Consequently, governments in the midst of reforming their intelligence and security services need to put things in a broad rather than a narrow, issue-focused framework; otherwise they will simply have to repeat the pro- cess when caught by new surprises lurking just around the corner. Hence, in order to avoid a state of perpetual reform, we should focus on planning. This cannot be done effectively if we try to make a conceptual and practical demarcation between the political strategic direction and the planning pro- cess. The argument we should like to put forward in this chapter is that we might want to revisit the classical principles of strategic theory and reinforce the link between the political strategic level and the planning process in the context of the global war on terror. We assume that the issue of allocating resources means properly matching strategic direction with the frameworks for planning and implementation. In other words, next to strategic vision there should be an appropriate strategic planning process that generates scope for both making the most of allocated resources and, at the same time, creates conditions for widening the resource base.

INSTRUMENT- VERSUS ISSUES-BASED PLANNING

The intelligence planning process is part of general government policy making. This means it is affected by domestic and international considera- tions as much as other key policy matters. It also implies that it varies in dif- ferent countries depending on the nature and the type of political system in which they exist. Thus, even within democratic political systems there are different types of intelligence processes and planning. For instance, parlia- mentary democracies have an intelligence process different from that of a presidential or semipresidential system. The issues of who initiates the policy-making process, who reports to whom, who is overseeing, and how the political veto players[2] are positioned are paramount in understanding the framework of intelligence planning.

It should also be recognized that intelligence is not just a classical domes- tic bureaucratic process.[3] It is also a key instrument supporting foreign pol- icy, next to the diplomatic service and the military forces. This is particularly true in the context of the global war on terror. Hence we should look at the intelligence policy-making process by putting this in the context of how intelligence planning should be adjusted according to the structure of the international system. It is therefore appropriate to start this examination by looking at how intelligence planning evolved, for instance, during the Cold War, before coming to grasp with the possible paths for changes required in the current war on terror.

During the Cold War, within the framework of a bipolar world, and because of the main strategic requirements of the day—geopolitical stability (status quo) and preservation of the nuclear strategic balance—the intelligence planning process was basically organized around two main instruments: collection and analysis. This type of planning process was well suited for the main purposes of the two blocs' intelligence services: to know and assess the other side's political and military leadership, national and foreign military bases, and conventional and nuclear capabilities. From a conceptual and practical point of view, this was basically an intelligence planning process hierarchically structured in order to address hierarchically organized targets.

Furthermore, in terms of organizational design, this process of planning intelligence had led to subsequent structural adaptations at the level of intelligence agencies. On the one hand, in terms of intelligence gathering or collection, the focus was mainly on the type of sources used: human intelligence (HUMINT), signals intelligence (SIGINT), imagery intelligence (IMINT), and so forth. In time this approach led to a discussion that ended up in confusing means and ends. Thus, with the advent of technology, SIGINT became more important in terms of input for intelligence assessment. In response to the start of the global war on terror, HUMINT has now been reemphasized. Whatever the merits between the two the real issue is not how to attempt a trade-off between human and technological sources of intelligence but to create and reinvent analytical frameworks, where the quantity of high-tech-based input can be more properly checked against the quality of information gathered and intentions assessed by human beings.

As far as analysis is concerned, the intelligence agencies created during the Cold War developed their own methods of collating and analyzing the peculiar intelligence they gathered. Horizontally, the main difference was among law enforcement services, independent or autonomous intelligence agencies, as well as military intelligence bodies. Vertically, almost every country also developed centralized structures responsible for the final evaluation of these different assessments without paying enough attention to the different organizational contexts upon which the agencies' estimates were produced in terms of gathering and analytical methods. Moreover, the fact that the organizational context was not taken into account led to a partial ignorance of the interorganizational and intraorganizational jealousies when bureaucracies compete. In this "silent" bureaucratic turf war over resource allocation, the intelligence process as a whole ended up being the loser.

It is now generally taken for granted that the events of 9/11 and the sub-sequent global war on terror brought about a change in the dynamics in the international system. It is obvious that the fall of the Soviet Union and the conclusion of the Cold War ended the bipolar world, but between 1991 and 2001 there were no significant attempts to reform the intelligence planning process accordingly. The realization that an overhaul was overdue came rather late—in the aftermath of the attacks on New York and Washington, D.C.

It was only then did a change of focus in the intelligence planning process happen, which came to lay new emphasis on collection and analysis toward an issues-oriented planning process, paying particular attention to terrorism and weapons of mass destruction. For instance, almost every Western country has created intelligence fusion bodies, usually called counterterrorism centers of some description as a result. In this new organizational context, the existing intelligence agencies are supposed to collate and assess the intelligence gathered on terrorism and other, more or less related, threats and risks, in a much more decentralized and network-like manner. Furthermore, these counterterrorism centers are developing interinstitutional connections with similar bodies in other countries. In this regard, the argument is quite clear-cut: transnational threats and risks require transnational intelligence exchange and cooperation.

However, there are at least two types of problems this change of focus on intelligence planning process brings. To begin with, we should not probably want to replace a hierarchical intelligence process with a rigid hierarchy of priorities in terms of intelligence missions or issues. It might be plausible to argue that an exclusive focus at both the national and international levels on a single, central mission or issue, namely, terrorism and/or weapons of mass destruction, may take us all away from seeing both the whole picture and the dynamics and nuances related to the permutation of threats and risks.

Furthermore, as long as there are no political bodies to oversee, at both national and transnational levels, the processes of how these new intelligence-fusion centers develop, there is a significant chance their final assessments will be treated with suspicion by political actors who are responsible for making decisions domestically. To sum up, one should probably develop the issue-based planning process rather than improve the classical planning process focused on collection and analysis. There are three main issues at stake here.

First, the issue-based planning process needs, first of all, incentives to put the global war on terrorism in a broader picture, and this can be achieved by reforming the national security and strategic policy councils. Another way is to generate a kind of "division of labor" at the multinational level. It seems that there is still inadequate recognition of the paramount importance of maintaining a "devil's advocate" in intelligence assessment in order to avoid such pitfalls as "groupthink." The tendency in transnational intelligence co-operation is too conducive to a "rally around the most powerful" (for instance, American assessments) instead of bringing alternative views to contest the dominant view and provoke further analysis. Unless countered, this tendency can unintentionally produce a dangerous vicious circle.

Second, the classical planning process focused on gathering and analysis may be made to complement the new focus on the issue-based planning process. In terms of collection and the classical debate between HUMINT and technical intelligence (TECH-INT—SIGINT, IMINT, and so on) it is important to bear in mind that before addressing the trade-off between them, one should first address their problems separately. Regarding collection and gathering, for instance, it is important to underline the fact that intelligence collection in terms of capabilities is just the simplest part in the general process of threat or risk assessment.

A classical formula states that threat equals capabilities multiplied by intentions. The reversed formula (threat equals intentions multiplied by capabilities) was also true during the Cold War. Unfortunately, both during the Cold War and especially in the context of the war on terror, it is much more important to devote more collection and gathering instruments on intentions rather than just on capabilities, as well as on perceptions and ideological emotions rather than on material resources.

On the one hand, despite a strategic requirement for more HUMINT, we must be aware that this takes a lot of time and money. In addition, the end results are much more dependent on intangible factors than on more money and resources. There is a high level of expectation in this area, especially after September 11 and, unfortunately, this is a long-term planning target rather than a short-term one.

On the other hand, in terms of SIGINT and IMINT, the main problem is, paradoxically or not, related to the speed and agility with which new technology is put in use. The classical satellite surveillance, for instance, has become a passive instrument for collection, since the practical opportunities to avoid tracking have become well-known—even in Hollywood movies. In order to create technological agility, more money is probably necessary to improve the cycle of innovation so that potential future targets cannot bypass it and consequently avoid surveillance.

Last but not least, we should notice that the debate regarding a trade-off between HUMINT and TECH-INT is worth being addressed more than just inside the intelligence community. In a wider strategic context, it is crucial to understand the nature of the conflict we are living in as a struggle between the existential and instrumental components of waging war. In this respect, as Christopher Coker rightly points out, "Terrorists play on our uncertainties and anxieties; our anxieties about the side effects of our technological advances, and in the case of September 11, our anxieties about the underside of globalization…We tell ourselves that the nature of war has changed…

As such, we are imperfectly placed to recognize that it is we, perhaps not others—who have lost touch with war's true nature."[4]

WIDENING THE RESOURCE BASE

We believe there is an interdependent relationship between the issue of planning and resource allocation and the achievement of a proper relationship between government and intelligence professionals. The main condition for understanding this interdependency is to look without any preconceived views at the consequences that our dynamic and rapidly changing times bring.

In a wonderfully written book—a veritable appeal to free up minds— Robert Cooper advances an interesting rule for the world of diplomacy: "When you have a problem, enlarge the context."[5] This recommendation applies to dealing with intelligence as well. This rather simple sentence may not fully respect all the rules of Aristotle's Organon logics of the classical world, but it may provide the basis for sound political and strategic judgments today. Following Cooper, we present three areas of the intelligence policy-making process where we might want to "widen the context" in order to enhance the chances of the social capital of knowledge for intelligence.[6] We take into account these three areas as a zone of qualitative, conceptual improvement rather than just quantitative and material resource allocation.

In an interesting study on reforming the U.S. intelligence community, Gregory F. Treverton asserts, when referring to the issue of improving analysis, "Analysts of the future will need to think more like homicide detectives, trying to see patterns amid complete information."[7] The idea of taking advantage of analytical methods from other disciplines is not a new requirement at all. During the Cold War, scholars were searching for more creativity in intelligence analysis by adjusting methodologies from other scientific disciplines. For instance, Walter Laqueur made an interesting attempt at comparing intelligence analysis with medical diagnosis.[8] Even in the context of the global war on terror, there are voices that ask for the application of Laqueur's approach. One such voice argues, "The comparison could even be extended to epidemiology and transnational movements by comparing rates of transfer of disease to rates of growth in terrorist recruiting activities."[9]

The problem with borrowing analytical tools and methods from other disciplines is that we probably want to be more scientific than it is necessary, and consequently we do not focus enough on research areas that are obviously closest to the intelligence policy sphere in terms of research design, such as predicting the future out of intangible factors and hard-to-quantify variables. For instance, the current debate in political science/comparative politics between predictive capacities of path dependency versus contingency analysis might be more useful in the issue-based intelligence planning process.[10]

Over the last few years, political science and international relations experts have taken advantage of the existing opportunities and already adopted methodologies from other disciplines such as rational choice, game theory, even complexity and chaos theories, to name but a few. As far as intelligence analysis is concerned, it would be more appropriate to take advantage first of methodologies used in political science and international relations rather than other, more distant disciplines. It is necessary to bear in mind that the paradigms of intelligence analysis and political science cannot be produced and tested in a laboratory. What is needed is a process of trial and error, through which one can test which methodology can best be applied to enhance the intelligence community's capacity to assess intentions.

Regarding the global war on terror the main analytical requirement for an intelligence planning process is to distinguish between short-term requirements and long-term trends. In other words, intelligence related to terrorism is assessed from a dual perspective:

- provision of updated (daily or even more frequent) assessments required for immediate operations or responses, and
- trend or pattern analysis, which is essential for both an operational response, and reports required by politicians and for strategic planning in general.

Unfortunately, some intelligence officers already complain, "We now do reporting. We used to do analysis. The dominance of question-answering is pervasive, even when it would not be expected."[11] What is at issue here is mainly a matter of perception. What this intelligence officer meant by "reporting" can probably be assessed by using the methods of contingency analysis. What he labels as "analysis" (the study of trends and the change in a variable on a longer time span) might be assessed by using other methodologies.

In the end, assessing terrorism is not necessarily a matter of making a distinction between reporting and analyzing, but an issue of choosing the best assessment methodologies. This is why intelligence analysts might be more interested in the methods used in the "neighboring" social sciences, where the topics to be evaluated (the change in human and social behavior) are much closer to intelligence analysis than those used in medical studies, for instance. In the end, the kind of methods we bring into intelligence analysis is a matter of strategic choice. In this respect, we should not forget that it would probably be better to select from similar disciplines, namely, those where you cannot isolate the cases/targets for analysis under a microscope. It is important to emphasize that creativity is a matter of choice from the proper context; when one has a problem, one should widen the appropriate context.

Probably one of the most important policy means in encouraging the development of a social capital of knowledge in intelligence is a new and fresh human resources strategy. As we have already stated, the process of change management cannot avoid the issue of human capital and, consequently, the personnel policies.

It is common knowledge that intelligence agencies need peculiar adjustments in terms of personnel in the context of the war against terrorism. However, it is worth paying attention to some of the policy mechanisms related to the new techniques in human resources management, especially if we accept that intelligence policy cannot be fully separated from the domestic and societal context.

First of all, the concept of a "job for life" has become increasingly obsolete, and many public sector employees have reacted by taking a far more active role in developing individual careers. This is particularly the case in many of the emerging Central and Eastern European democracies. Discussion on the so-called "portfolio careers"[12] is indicative in this regard. Thus, there is an increase in spiral and transitory careers and a subsequent decrease in the more classical linear and expert careers.[13]

As a consequence, intelligence agencies, and the whole security sector in general, should start to evaluate the structure of the social base of recruitment in terms of social values and patterns. Intelligence agencies might proceed at evaluating how large the current gap is between those who are currently aspiring to become intelligence officers (who are more "portfolio" oriented) and the insiders (intelligence professionals) who entered the system earlier and followed mainly linear or expert careers. This could be particularly important because, as we saw in the case of the Romanian military personnel policy reform, for instance, paying close attention to the possible gap between the newcomers and the linear career-like officers is one of the key ways to manage successfully the entire process of transformation.[14] Despite the fact that the comparison between defense and intelligence branches cannot be taken too far, there are at least two points here we would like to make.

First, in terms of both defense and of intelligence, the training of future professionals (military officers on one hand, and analysts, for instance, on the other) is mainly carried out in-house. Whereas this is somehow understandable for the military, it cannot be fully taken for granted in the case of intelligence analysts. As we argued before, choosing strategically—rather than randomly—in terms of what kind of methods for intelligence analysis we borrow might significantly influence the type of disciplines we should look for when recruiting new and fresh personnel. For instance, if one tries to use intelligence analysis methodologies borrowed from the medical community, one should be aware one cannot recruit more doctors for intelligence analysis. In contrast, the relationship between using more social sciences methodologies and recruiting more intelligence analysts specialized in the associated disciplines (political science, international relations, sociology, cultural studies, or even philosophy) seems more plausible.

To sum up, we suggest widening the resource base by creating the policy premises for a social capital of knowledge in intelligence analysis. We assume from the beginning there is a high degree of interdependency not only between resource allocation and intelligence-government relations, but also among the various sectors that need to undergo changes within the intelligence planning process.

CONCLUSIONS

After 9/11 the world of intelligence seems to be governed by the idea of reform and changes, but do all the people concerned adhere to it? Can we assert with certainty that politicians with the responsibility to oversee and supervise the intelligence agencies have transformed themselves in such a way that they can appropriately assess the degree of changes required from the intelligence services? We cannot offer a definitive answer to this question. What is, however, clear is that one cannot understand the scale and nature of changes required if one does not transform oneself accordingly. In other words, for politicians to oversee the reforms and changes in the intelligence agencies properly, they cannot retain the old mind-set and approach.

Robert Cooper's suggestion of "widening the context when you have a problem" can and should be appropriately applied at the strategic level, regarding the interface between politics and intelligence. It is important to underline the fact that in order to achieve intelligence policy planning through efficient resource allocation in the global war on terror one must do so with a wide strategic consensus. There are several key issues involved and the most important ones are highlighted below.

First, after September 11, mainly because of the huge amount of operational intelligence required for fighting the global war on terror, it might be understandable why some intelligence officers seem to feel they do not engage as much in analysis as they do in reporting or data collection. Their discontent affects the effectiveness of intelligence work. The issue here could become more serious than a matter of using the most appropriate methodological techniques, as we tried to explain above. This being the case we should ask whether the top political decision makers have paid enough attention to what needs to be done in order not to blur the classical distinctions between strategic, operational, and tactical levels of intelligence work and not to sacrifice the strategic level for the sake of operational, day-to-day intelligence. In light of the increasing high priority being put on operational matters in the war on terror, the top policy makers and those responsible for oversight should make sure a good balance is maintained between the conflicting demands on the limited resources put at the disposal of the intelligence community.

Second, it is essential that we reflect critically on the concept of war as we approach the threats from al Qaeda in terms of the war on terror. We should keep in mind that there is a significant distinction between the nature and the character of war.[15] On the one hand, the character of war might change, especially due to advances in new high-tech means of war. On the other hand, the nature of war tends to remain rather constant, and one of the main rules for understanding the true nature of war remains the capacity to distinguish between strategic[16] and operational requirements.

Finally, there are greater links between intelligence studies and international cooperation in intelligence than is generally recognized. Top policy makers may lament that the lack of intelligence studies programs and intelligence studies more generally at universities might have impeded the development of sound intelligence cooperation mechanisms, at least until the events of September 11. However, if we still see intelligence through the traditional and nationalistic prism, intelligence work will remain the last bastion of nationalism and prevent international co-operation though the challenges being faced are global in nature. We suggest that we must face up to this issue squarely, particularly among allies, such as NATO member states. Since we already have a NATO Defense College, which is open to both Allies' and partner countries' students, why should we not think about having a NATO Intelligence College? The problems intelligence agencies in the world face now are transnational in character, and an effective response must transcend national boundaries. Encouraging national intelligence agencies to work together should in the long-term strengthen the prospect of "making the world safer for democracies."

11

A New Approach to Intelligence Assessment

Isaac Ben-Israel

Although terrorism and weapons of mass destruction (WMD) are by no means new phenomena, in recent decades they have become a major security threat to many countries and require a corresponding shift in the focus of intelligence efforts.

This chapter analyzes the pitfalls of some of the most spectacular failures of intelligence in the recent past and draws on the Israeli experience to highlight the need for changes. The main purpose of this chapter is to provide an unconventional view on how intelligence should be assessed.

The basic lessons learned by the Israeli intelligence services during the failure of the October 1973 War are a good starting point. This intelligence failure stemmed from an incorrect interpretation of the data collected prior to the outbreak of hostilities. This is not the only way an intelligence service can fail. Hence I examine other types of failures in the next section. Although problems of assessment are not the sole cause for failure, they figure prominently in the most recent spectacular failings, such as the September 11 attacks and the WMD issue in Iraq. I suggest these problems occurred because an incorrect assessment methodology was adopted. The rest of this chapter therefore outlines an alternative methodology. In so doing I use the case of WMD in Iraq and the war on terror in Israel to provide concrete basis for my analysis. I then examine what really is required to reform the intelligence services.

THE YOM KIPPUR WAR (1973)

Normal human logic tends to be inductive: a baby will not put its hand twice in the fire. Once is enough for it to "generalize' and conclude that "fire hurts." Useful as it may be, inductive logic is false. Unfortunately, unless trained especially to avoid it, people tend to follow induction. This applies to intelligence analysts, too.

The failure of Israeli Military Intelligence to predict the surprise Arabic attacks on Israeli positions when the Yom Kippur War started in October 1973 illustrates this human tendency vividly. The Egyptian and Syrian armies successfully deceived Israel. Their preparations and deployment of their forces were conducted under the cover of a huge "exercise" that was named "Tahrir 41." Israeli intelligence knew the format of the Tahrir exercises very well: they had carefully studied the previous 40 such exercises.[1] Once the 41st exercise began, they immediately recognized the pattern and judged it to be just another exercise in the "Tahrir" series. Unfortunately for them, this time the Egyptians deviated from the regular pattern and crossed the Suez Canal.

Many believe that this assessment failure was a result of a certain fixed notion ("The Concept"), universally and rigidly held within the military establishment. It goes like this. Egypt would not go to war without a long-range air strike capability against Israeli airfields. Syria would not go to war alone. Hence, since Egypt had no such capability, the probability of war was very low.

Some consider the then-prevalent acceptance of this Concept as the root of all evil. The fact that the Israeli intelligence heads had an *a priori* concept about the necessary preconditions for the outbreak of hostilities is deemed to underlie their incorrect assessments. A good intelligence analyst, they say, must be free of all commitment to any single conceptual framework. Others counter that an intelligence estimate is not possible without some kind of a conceptual framework.

So, should all conceptual frameworks be eliminated? Can this be done? Is it possible to make an intelligence assessment without a conceptual framework? Does such a framework have any "positive" value? If so, how should a conceptual framework in intelligence be built? What risks lurk within it? How and when should it be dropped? These questions all connect with one central question: is it possible to find methods for intelligence estimates that are "better" and more "successful" than others? Or, to put it bluntly: how should one carry out an intelligence assessment?

In my view, Israeli intelligence did not fail in 1973 because it used a conceptual framework.[2] It is not possible to make an assessment without any such framework. In fact, the problem stemmed from an incorrect interpretation of the data. It was wrong because it was based on inductive logic. Induction is a poor method. It is a severe "illness" of human reasoning in general and of intelligence analysis in particular. The "cure" to this illness requires a major change in the logic of assessment. What is needed is to replace the invalid methodology of induction by a different and valid one, which should be deductive in its essence and based on conjectures and refutation.

TYPOLOGY OF INTELLIGENCE FAILURES

The intelligence failure in the Yom Kippur War was not unique. History is full of examples in which intelligence interpretations were wrong even though, with the benefit of hindsight, sufficient information had been available. The failure of Stalin to understand that Hitler was going to attack Russia in 1941 (Operation Barbarossa) and the Japanese surprise attack on Pearl Harbor[3] at the end of the same year are just two of the better known examples in this category.

It was usually the case that colossal failures like them were subsequently investigated, and several "remedies" offered. In many cases the problem was not one of "not knowing," but one of "not understanding." Reading the vast material written about these failures, one can certainly reach the conclusion that these intelligence failures were attributed either to subjective, that is, psychological, reasons or to objective, that is, organizational, causes.

The most common explanations belong to the psychological group: the interpretation was incorrect because analysts were overconfident and underestimated the other side, or because they were too vain to listen to other opinions, or because they suffered from groupthink, and so on.[4] The accepted remedy for psychological problems is to replace the persons (who probably had the "wrong personalities") with new and better people. How does one ensure that the new team will be free of psychological biases and prejudices? It is done by increasing the psychological awareness of the analysts, or by making them aware of the full spectrum of possible biases. Incorrect interpretations can be minimized also by pluralism, that is, by engaging large and independent groups in the process of intelligence production.[5]

Sometimes, the problem is not one of *wrong or incorrect interpretation* (which is always subjective), but a more "objective" one. It may happen that a vital report was not received by those who should have read it because of some technical or procedural problem—"it took a long time to process it," or "you were not cleared to read this kind of classified material," and so forth. In these cases the remedy usually involves some organizational change.

Although a relatively rare event, sometimes the problem does stem from a lack of vital information. This was the case, according to the U.S. Senate Intelligence Report (2004)[6] in determining the status of Iraqi WMD before the Iraq War in 2003. But, one may ask: given that this was the top priority

Table 11.1   Typology of Intelligence Failures (in the current literature)

	Enough Information in the System		Not Enough
	Wrong interpretation	Information had not reached the proper address	
Cause of failure	Psychological	Procedural	Organizational
Remedy	Psychological awareness pluralism	Organizational change	Centralization

question and the hottest topic addressed by the Western world for more than a decade, how could it still lack sufficient vital information? The answer is simple: there were too many intelligence agencies working on the same problem, with no coordination between them, and the "left hand" was unaware of what the "right hand" was doing. So, in this case, the remedy is the opposite: pluralism is bad, and centralization is what we need. Having central management will allow the coordination of all intelligence activities and be more effective in gathering the necessary information.[7]

Table 11.1 summarizes the different possibilities mentioned above. I hold a different thesis. I believe that Table 11.1 misses the most important cause for intelligence failure: namely, that intelligence agencies do not suffer only from psychological or organizational shortcomings. They suffer above all from dependence on inductive logic.

AN ALTERNATIVE METHODOLOGY

Similar questions about the role of conceptual frameworks may be asked, in fact, in almost every field where information is gathered under conditions of uncertainty, processed, and used for forecasting. Intelligence organization is nothing more than an institution for studying and clarifying reality, and hence there is a clear analogy between intelligence and science.

The intelligence field has its own peculiarities. It usually involves putting human life at risk, so the cost of error can be extremely high. Furthermore, security problems dominate and most conventional techniques for filtering errors cannot be used because of security restrictions. Not only is intelligence material itself considered classified, but the method of working as well. Classifying the methods used is itself a serious obstacle to the development of intelligence, since it prevents any open, systematic discussion of the methodological question of how the intelligence estimate should be made.

Nevertheless, the analogy mentioned above is strong enough to convince me to propose a method[8] based on the asymmetry between verification and refutation. Verification of a general statement is impossible. How many facts are needed to verify a general statement? How many falling apples have to be observed to verify Newton's law of gravity? No finite set of facts will ever be sufficient to verify a general statement. However, one counter-example is enough to invalidate a general statement. Hence, only refutation is logically possible, and we must abandon induction and adopt refutation as a method.

Some people accept the argument above and yet still claim that induction is useful. Perhaps we cannot verify a general statement, they say, but surely we can make it very probable. Well, how many supporting facts would be needed to make a general statement probable? Look at the following example, which is, of course, a hypothetical statement:

Every natural number is $\leq 10^{100}$.

This general statement is supported by 10^{100} numbers. Does this enormous set of supporting evidence make it *probably true?* Probability in intelligence estimates is usually not a measure of reality, but a measure of the belief of the analyst in his or her estimate.

The logic I propose consists of two stages:

1. **Creation:** making conjectures or hypotheses.
2. **Criticism:** eliminating wrong conjectures by refutation.

The importance of the second stage should be emphasized. Even without any systematic methodology, smart people often create alternative conjectures. However, once they create them, they tend to judge them by the weight of supporting evidence. This, again, relies on induction and is wrong: no amount of supporting evidence is enough to prove the validity of a general statement, and any prediction is always based on some general statements.

Instead of looking for corroborating evidence, one should look for evidence that can refute each of the competing hypotheses. If one is lucky one will end up with a conjecture that is not, at least as yet, refuted and thus can be relied upon unless and until refuted. The justification for adopting such a hypothesis is not because it is supported by evidence, but because it is not refuted by what can be found and known.[9]

One should treat intelligence evidence the same way that one treats hypotheses: intelligence evidence is never certain; its validity should be constantly questioned, and the best way to overcome this problematic nature of information is to utilize the same methodology[10] when confronted with intelligence reports, namely, trying to refute them with the help of contrary evidence.

To make the above method work it is necessary to accept some preconditions. The most basic one is that hypotheses must be made in a language that allows their validity to be tested. Tautologies and truism are useless and should not be used. Assessments like "Saddam Hussein will use chemical warfare if he has his back to the wall" or "he will use chemical warfare if and when he has no other alternative" are meaningless and useless as hypotheses. As they cannot be refuted they remain accurate whether Saddam will or will not use chemical weapons and are therefore valueless.

The other is to create an environment for refutation to happen. Real criticism is not always possible in all organizations and societies, especially not in closed and hierarchical societies such as intelligence agencies. In order to allow criticism and debate, one must create an environment of openness, in which relevant information is freely available and hypotheses can be freely refuted. Only then can barriers of compartmentalization and classification be broken.

In the methodology I have outlined above, *to estimate or to analyze* implies finding and testing evidence that counters the hypotheses.[11] The way to do this is to direct collecting agencies toward potentially contrary information. Hence, guiding the collecting agencies is an integral part of the intelligence process. The barrier between field operators and analysts, within intelligence organizations, becomes unclear. This raises the more general issue concerning the fading of traditional border lines between operators and intelligence officers, which is discussed later.

Allow me to return now to the first stage of my alternative proposed methodology. This involves the creation of hypotheses. "Creation" is a very elusive concept. It is hard to define, and I know of no methodology to teach creativity (though there are some methodologies that can expose hidden creativity, but it does seem as though one has to have this *a priori*). Nevertheless, it is clear that creativity has something to do with imagination: creative people tend to be more imaginative. Hence, in my view, imagination should play a decisive role in the assessment process, and one should look for imaginative and creative people to be included in any intelligence organization.

The second step, however, namely, criticism, is more technical and allows less room for imagination. It is one where strict disciplinary training in the analytical methodology should be emphasized.

BACK TO THE YOM KIPPUR WAR

For the sake of completeness, let me go back and discuss the virtues of my proposed method in the case of the intelligence failure of the Yom Kippur War. It is evident that the leaders of Israeli intelligence were misled by inductive logic. They knew every detail of the previous Tahrir exercises, and these were compatible with the movements of the Egyptian Army in October 1973. Thus it was only "natural" to conclude that another Tahrir exercise was being witnessed.

Could the estimate failure be avoided using the alternative methodology proposed above? The answer to this question is clearly in the affirmative.

If Israeli intelligence had used my proposed method, it would have had to search for contrary instead of for corroborating evidence. Assuming one had to choose between two hypotheses ("war" or "exercise"),[12] one has first to divide all intelligence reports into three groups:

- reports that refute the war hypothesis,
- reports that refute the exercise hypothesis, and
- reports that refute neither.

Doing this, one would immediately realize that the vast majority of evidence belonged to the third group and was therefore compatible with both hypotheses. For example, the movement of the 4th Egyptian Armored Division from its base near Cairo to the vicinity of the Suez Canal was compatible with previous movements carried out in Tahrir exercises, but was also compatible with the war option.

Sorting the reports in the way described above could have revealed that the exercise conjecture was not more strongly supported by the evidence, as was accepted by the leaders of Israeli intelligence. They had no reason to estimate that it was a much more probable option than the alternative view. It would reveal that on the face of it, the first two scenarios were both refuted:

- The war hypothesis was refuted by explicit Egyptian reference to this operation as the Tahrir 41 exercise. Of course, this was part of the Egyptian deception plan, but this was not known at that time to Israeli intelligence analysts.
- The exercise hypothesis was refuted by some dozens of reports that were not compatible with this being an exercise (for example, the hasty and unorganized evacuation of the families of the Soviet military troops from Egypt and Syria three days before the war started and explicit reports from reliable sources about the coming war).

It is clear that either the entire group of reports that refute the war hypothesis is wrong, or the entire group of reports that refute the exercise hypothesis is wrong, or neither hypothesis is correct. But here lies an important asymmetry: an army going to war is expected to try to surprise its rival and deceive it; an army engaged in an exercise is not expected to try to deceive its rival and convince it that it is preparing for war.[13]

INTELLIGENCE AND OPERATIONS

As a matter of fact, intelligence organizations are not identical with operational organizations. They keep their separate identities, separate channels for reporting and, in the military case, separate uniforms and chains of command. With some reflection, this situation raises a fundamental question. Since no operation can be planned and performed without an intelligence input, why are these two activities kept separate?

There are, of course, good reasons for this. Perhaps the most important is the need to ensure the secrecy of intelligence sources. Even within the intelligence organization there is a strong tendency for compartmentalization because of this need. So, it is better to keep them separate, if at all possible.

But, is this really possible? I suggest separation should be kept only in cases in which operations evolve slowly and are not too dynamic. For example, there is no problem using two separate departments, operations and intelligence, to plan an attack on enemy airfields. The operations personnel will be briefed by their intelligence colleagues and then go for their planning activity. The airfield and its runways will not go away and so, a short update, close to the time of attack, will suffice.

This is not the case in air-to-air combat or in a fast-moving mobile land campaign. In such cases, the battlefield is very dynamic and an early intelligence briefing is not enough. In order to prevail in such dynamic environments one requires a continuous flow of intelligence. Where is the enemy? What are the relevant targets? And so on. However, historically the amount of real-time information flow needed in these cases is so large that no one in reality can supply and manage it. The usual solution is to build up a force (for example, air interceptors or a ground division) that is able to act and react swiftly on the basis of its real-time judgment, independently of detailed prior intelligence. You shoot at targets that you see directly. So, here too, one can live with a separation between the departments of intelligence and operations.

Technology has changed this picture completely. Modern communications, command, control, and intelligence (C3I) systems allow one to transfer real-time intelligence to almost every operational unit. The use of standoff weapons creates a situation in which the shooter does not see the target and someone has to tell him where and when to shoot. Now, one can ask, is the separation between the two still justified? I do not think so. I believe that one should take advantage of what is offered by modern technology and merge intelligence and operations into one integral organization. I will come back to this point when examining the war on terror.

WHAT ARE RELEVANT DATA?

Let me rephrase the paradigm or, in my view, the wrong methodology, of induction: the more relevant data you have, the better is the quality of the intelligence product. But, then, what makes the data relevant?

The conventional inductive answer is that data are relevant when they can be connected to the research problem. My alternative approach implies that they are relevant only when they can (that is, have the potential to) *refute* one of the conjectures of the research problem. This approach has two immediate results:

1. "Confirming," "corroborating," or "supporting" data are not relevant. Psychologically, we tend to be very influenced by supporting evidence, and our confidence in our supported conjectures becomes very high. However, this is a logical mistake.
2. "No data" can also be "relevant." To illustrate this last point I use the example of WMD in Iraq.[14]

Was there sufficient relevant data to estimate whether the Iraqis had or did not have WMD prior to the recent war in Iraq? If one checks how many reports claimed that the Iraqis had ballistic missiles armed with chemical warheads, one will find dozens of reports. But they were not very conclusive. One came from a source that reported a vehicle he saw, crossing a certain junction near his village in the western desert, "which carried a ballistic missile." Another source reported that he heard from one of his relatives that some 50 Scud missiles were hidden in the desert, and so on. The overall estimate, emerging from these reports, and their accumulative weight, led American Intelligence authorities, as well as British and Israeli ones, to estimate that Iraq had hidden some 50–100 missiles in the desert after the war in 1991, some of them armed with chemical warheads. The same line of thinking led them to believe that the Iraqis were involved in developing nuclear and biological weapons and hiding these activities as well.

Now, one may ask, how many intelligence reports claimed that Iraq did not have such capabilities? None. There were no reports on vehicles, spotted in the desert, carrying no missiles. No one reported that their relatives heard that the Iraqis had not hidden something in the desert. And so on. There are many possible reasons for not having reports of this kind. One is that the Iraqis succeeded to conceal their actions. Another is that they did not have the WMD to begin with. Which case is true?

How should we solve this puzzle? Let us look again at the two conjectures we have here:

- the Iraqis have an operational capability to launch ballistic missiles, armed with chemical warheads; or
- they do not have such a capability.

According to my suggested method one should not be looking for supporting evidence but, instead, for contrary evidence. How can one refute the conjecture of having such capability? In order to do so one must ask oneself, what does it take to have such a ballistic missile launch capability? Well, one first needs missiles and warheads. However this is not enough. One also needs a unit to operate these missiles. This unit needs to be trained regularly.

Then, from time to time the equipment should be tested. In the meantime someone has to maintain the launchers, the missiles, the warheads, and the rest of the required equipment. Surely one does not expect to be able to dig the hidden missiles out of the sand, 12 years after they had been buried there, and launch them without doing all the activities mentioned above. Now, did the Iraqis have all these capabilities? As far as it could be ascertained, they did not. There was not even one intelligence report dealing with these subjects. Obviously, this does not prove that the Iraqis did not have such weapons. To answer these questions seriously one needed certain intelligence sources with good access to these activities. Some of these activities were not covered at all, some of them were covered partially, and some were covered very well. Ballistic tests, for example, were covered hermetically by American Defense Support Program satellites. The Americans could know for sure that no ballistic missile was tested in Iraq in the 12 years between the two wars. It was known to a high degree of certainty that the Iraqis had not acquired spare parts for the Scud missiles externally in these intervening years and that the Iraqis did not have any internal production capability for these items. Suddenly, these apparently "missing data" turned out to be "relevant data."

If the intelligence services in Israel and the Western World[15] had adopted the refutation method, they could not have avoided the final conclusion that the Iraqis did not have the operational capability to launch ballistic missiles with chemical warheads, though the Iraqis might have had some hidden missiles or warheads.[16] Using the same method to explore the other related questions (such as, did they have a nuclear project or a biological one?) would also have led to a negative conclusion. The Israeli and British Intelligence, and the CIA, were all wrong because they evaluated what they had in their files and looked for supportive evidence instead of the missing parts or contrary evidence.

TERRORISM AND INTELLIGENCE

Although Israel has suffered from terrorism since its foundation, in the four years starting from September 2000, the rate of terrorist activity climbed to an unprecedented level. Figure 11.1 summarizes the number of fatal casualties per quarter during those years.

While suicide terrorism has been used in the past, it was during these four years that it emerged as the main tool employed by the terrorists. Between September 2000 and September 2004, some 553 suicide attacks were attempted, and 135 of them were successful, killing 880 noncombatant innocent civilians, including women, children, and elderly people. After four years of combating terrorism in Israel, the rate of terrorism has dropped back to pre-Intifada figures, as can be seen in Figure 11.1.

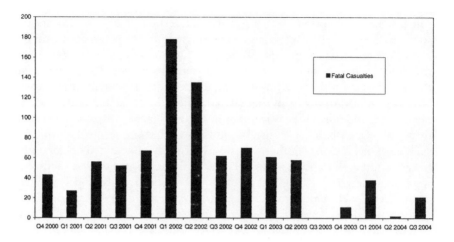

Figure 11.1   Distribution of Fatal Terrorism Casualties

Generally speaking, the turning point occurred after the war on terror was "separated" from the political issue of trying to come to an agreement with the Palestinian leadership. In April 2002, after Israel suffered 140 fatal casualties from suicide terrorism in the previous month, the wish to reach an agreement with the Palestinian Authority (PLA) was put aside (Arafat was declared to be "nonrelevant"), and Israel launched a full-scale campaign on the terrorist organizations, concentrating mostly on Hamas and Islamic Jihad. This campaign started by expanding intelligence coverage, mainly by entering those occupied areas[17] that had come under the control of the PLA after 1993. This, together with the erection of a security "fence," resulted, a year later, in an increase in the percentage of aborted terrorist acts from 40 percent (before April 2002) to over 80 percent.

How did Israel succeed in reducing the level of terrorism so substantially? There is no doubt that the key to this success is strongly connected to the capabilities of Israeli intelligence. Other key factors should also be taken into account. One of the immediate results of the reoccupation of Palestinian cities in the West Bank in April 2002 was a significant reinforcement of Israeli intelligence capabilities in these areas. Israel built up, during the previous 30 years, a good intelligence network in the occupied territories, but this started to deteriorate once Israel pulled out from the area and left it to PLA rule. The rebuilding of these capabilities was swift and, as a result, the drop in the number of successful suicide attacks was felt immediately (see Figure 11.1).

The rebuilding of Israeli intelligence capabilities involved a major organizational change in the Israeli intelligence community. The Shin-Bet—Israeli Security Agency—was given a bigger role within the intelligence community and took full responsibility for the occupied territories. New men and women were recruited, and the organization expanded quickly.

However, what is even more important was the adoption of a conceptual change. The classic border line between "operators" (including intelligence operators of sources as well as military units) and intelligence "analysts" was crossed and allowed to get fuzzy. At the same time, military units played an operational role tasked to arrest or eliminate a terrorist on his or her way to perform some terrorist act and an intelligence role tasked to collect some specific data on certain terrorist activities. The command chain was also altered, and the traditional distinction between "warriors and commanders" and "intelligence officers" was blurred. The reason for this change is the very dynamic character of the war on terror. Terrorists do not like to expose themselves and so act in an underground environment. Once a terrorist is detected and located, one has only a very short time to intercept him. Were the intelligence and operations to remain separate organizations, the chances of succeeding in this type of war would be very low.

In order to merge these two activities, proper tools need to be developed. One of the most important is the capability to form real-time intelligence assessments. As explained above, in order to do this, one should control intelligence sources in real-time, directing them to refute competing conjectures in accordance with real-time operational priorities in the field. The operational loop (controlling the "shooters" and generating "fire") and the intelligence loop (controlling the "sensors" and generating "intelligence") must merge into one real-time loop.[18]

It should be noted that in my proposed methodology, to make intelligence estimates is to create hypotheses and find evidence to contradict them, and hence, there should be no border line between the mission of tasking the sources and the analysis activity. The lessons learned in the context of Israeli success in the war against terror are compatible with this approach.

A NEW APPROACH TO INTELLIGENCE ASSESSMENT

What is the best way to reform intelligence organizations? There is no simple answer to this simple question. Some think there is no way to do this other than to demolish the existing ones and build new ones. This is the view of the late philosopher Paul Feyerabend who was, in principle, against any one dominant methodology in any field of science.[19] According to him,

> In second-world-war England, an improvement of intelligence work was achieved not by reforming the intelligence establishment via theory, but by introducing a second intelligence network, consisting of laypeople (in the field of intelligence) entirely: actors (like Noel Coward and Leslie Howard), scientists (like Turing) and others who had never done any intelligence work and were therefore unconfined by intelligence-prejudices (except the prejudice of

secrecy). I may be wrong, but such a replacement seems to me more effective than a new training for the old cadres.[20]

I am, perhaps, more optimistic. I believe once the incorrect methodology of induction is dispensed with and replaced by a critical approach, as described above, the rate of success of intelligence estimates will increase significantly. In my view, intelligence estimates should involve two stages. Feyerabend emphasizes the first: creation of hypotheses. I admit that this task can be helped much by including creative people, coming from either the scientific circles, such as Alan Turing or Francis Crick,[21] or from the arts, such as Noel Coward and Leslie Howard. The second stage, however, is more systematic and allows less scope for imagination. It involves the task of refuting the various hypotheses, with the help of solid information. In this task there is a huge advantage gained by utilizing knowledgeable and experienced people. So, in my view, an optimal intelligence organization should compose a mix of perhaps a small group of "creative outsiders" and a larger group of more experienced intelligence "professionals."

One of the immediate results of such a methodological reform will be a change in the concept of testing intelligence systems. If my proposal is adopted every hypothesis will be tested by checking to what extent it is refuted by the available evidence. I see such testing as the core of the estimate and analysis process. There is no need to wait for the verdict of history to find that one is wrong with one's analysis. Nor is it necessary for separate units to play the devil's advocate and offer alternatives to the official estimate. This testing of hypothesis against potential contrary evidence should simply become an organic and inseparable part of the analyst's work in producing intelligence estimates.

I am aware that my proposal runs counter to the traditional separation between operators and analysts. It is a difficult task and there are many obstacles to overcome. However, I believe this must be done because the war on terror and the proliferation of WMD are major security challenges against which the human race cannot afford to lose. I therefore conclude that successfully reforming operational strategies and the corresponding intelligence strategies is a matter of the utmost importance.

12

In Search of a New Intelligence System: The British Experience

Anthony Glees

There are today clear signals from Britain's intelligence and security community that it regards itself as "ready for reform." It has come to accept that there is an urgent need to reflect on the future nature of our intelligence system in order that government can deliver the best possible security in a rapidly changing and increasingly dangerous environment, at home and abroad.[1] Without thorough reform, public trust in the effectiveness of the community, already under great strain, will quickly dissipate altogether. It is not surprising that this is seen as a project of some urgency. The agencies have articulated their readiness to embark upon it not just in their evidence to the five inquiries into the intelligence failures dealing with Iraq but also in briefings under Chatham House rules at conferences and seminars. Theirs is not just an insular concern: all the great democracies of the West are coming to similar conclusions about the future of their intelligence and security services.

The impetus for reform stems from the intelligence failures connected with the Iraqi weapons of mass destruction (WMD) fiasco (very largely a matter affecting the Secret Intelligence Service, or SIS), the London bombings of July 2005 (a Security Service, or MI5 problem, currently being examined by the Intelligence and Security Committee), and the calibration of threat levels communicated to the public (a matter for MI5 and the Joint

Terrorism Analysis Centre, or JTAC, which is sited at MI5 headquarters in London). In 2002, for example, the Intelligence and Security Committee berated MI5 over its inability to provide the correct threat assessment for British visitors going to Indonesia, where, on October 12, 2002, over 190 people were murdered in a terrorist attack.[2] Then, at the beginning of July 2005, the Security Service once again got the threat level wrong, lowering it from level three to four rather than raising it.

It is significant to note that although the community is concerned with reform, and so is the British government, neither Her Majesty's Opposition nor the wider public is yet fully engaged with the issue. This is to be deeply regretted because the better the public debate, the greater the chance of success and the stronger the opportunity of successful reform.

BUILDING SECURITY AND PUBLIC TRUST

Lord Butler's case for a fundamental reform of Britain's security and intelligence community has been set out plainly in his compelling report.[3] He began his recommendations for change with a discussion of the need for better international cooperation (a point to which I shall return), going on to criticize the work of SIS and praising that undertaken by the Defence Intelligence Staff, the DIS, and suggested the latter should receive more funding. Butler also stressed the need for senior government ministers to have new "high-powered scientific advice" similar to that given by Lord Cherwell and Lord Zuckerman to previous governments. He asked that the Joint Intelligence Committee (JIC) be given more resources and its staff receive better training. Butler wrote, "We welcome the arrangements now being made to give the JIC more leverage...to ensure that the DIS serves wider national priorities as well as it does defence [ones] and has the resources which the rest of the intelligence community needs to support its activities."[4] This comment shows that the high quality of assessments provided by the DIS over Iraq was seen to deserve commendation, the misleading ones provided by SIS reprimand. Many of his recommendations are currently being enacted. In any event, reform is no longer just in the air. It is, in part, already under way. Analysis of its key features must inevitably be cautious. Most intelligence-led security work is conducted in secret. It therefore makes sense to ground any analysis of reform proposals with issues that the community has itself raised, through the individuals charged with doing so.

A security source has identified the reason why changes are deemed timely.[5] In the last five years, we learn, there have been nine attempted terrorist plots in the United Kingdom, of which seven were disrupted, and two were undiscovered, one of which—the July 7, 2005, bombings— was successful from the terrorists' point of view. Furthermore, it is assessed that the severity of the homegrown threat increased substantially after

2003—and that some 50 percent of plots are now "homegrown." MI5 judges that there are currently hundreds of potential terrorists in the United Kingdom, but it is not possible for the security services to take preemptive action.

What is our community doing to confront this threat? An excellent starting point for deeper probing is the remarkable speech given in The Hague, the Netherlands, in September 2005 by the Director General (DG) of Britain's Security Service, MI5.[6] After subjecting her ideas to critical examination, it will be clear how, and why, further development of many of them is of prime importance, while more broadly discussing the purpose and the place of a nonpractitioner academic's input into a future route map for the British secret agencies.[7] My comments are chiefly directed at the development of the Security Service, with some reference to SIS and the DIS.

In her speech to Dutch colleagues, Eliza Manningham-Buller set out her view of the future tasks of secret intelligence and security agencies in the aftermath of the London bombings of July 2005. Rather than put forward specific proposals for reform, the head of MI5 seemed to want to encourage debate, even "blue skies" thinking. She attempted to share with her audience the questions that are now at the back of her own and her service's mind as demonstrated by the title of her speech, "The International Terrorist Threat and *the Dilemmas* [my emphasis] in Countering It." A "dilemma" is something to be resolved, either alone or with friends. Significantly, although she does not spell this out, all her "dilemmas" rotate around real or perceived MI5 "failings," or "failures" (though not always ones on the part of MI5). The implication of her remarks is that if a solution to the dilemmas could be found, this would then represent the best way forward for British and, indeed, other intelligence services.

Her first dilemma was that, on the one hand, the secret agencies of the Western World all face a very similar threat requiring international cooperation ("one of the strengths we have in facing a global international threat is long-standing intelligence relationships of trust and cooperation in Europe and farther afield") *but* that cooperation could also be a major cause of weakness ("[while] we have a very strong interest in intelligence cooperation...if we splash intelligence around we shall soon have none of it ...I would never agree to a compulsory exchange of intelligence as that would compromise valuable sources of intelligence. There would soon be little to exchange").

What she says about this first dilemma, then, is that she would never consent to any directive that would establish, for example, a European Union intelligence and security agency to which the United Kingdom would be *obliged* to pass on intelligence. It is interesting, of course, that as the DG of MI5, she alone, of all agency heads, is permitted to make her own policy and is therefore well within her rights to state this so boldly.[8] Cooperation is fine, she says, but it appears to be simply on the basis of "as" and "when" she believes it is right. However, as is highlighted below, this is not quite as bold a statement as it would appear to be at first.

The DG's second dilemma was that "the attacks in London [of July 2005] were a shock and my service and the police were disappointed [sic] that we had not been able to prevent them" *but* that "we were not altogether surprised because of our understanding of the threat." On the one hand, the London attacks were, it might say, an "intelligence failure," but on the other we should not assume that they were unexpected. The intelligence failure was therefore limited while at the same time prompting further thought on how improved, predictive intelligence might be acquired as a matter of urgency to prevent attacks occurring in the first place.

Eliza Manningham-Buller fleshed out the difficulties of doing so where the justification of preemption is likely to take place in a court of law: "This is one of the central dilemmas of countering this sort of terrorism. We may be confident that an individual or a group is planning an attack but that confidence comes from intelligence [that is] patchy and fragmentary and uncertain...all too often it falls short of evidence to support criminal charges to bring an individual before the courts, the best solution if achievable. Moreover we need to protect fragile sources of intelligence including human sources."

Her emphasis on lawfulness is a key issue. She accepts that it is in the nature of her service that it has to rely, sometimes, on evidence that the courts will not accept. This is, in fact, a very real problem as shown by legal rulings on April 12, 2006, which condemned actions designed, *inter alia,* to prevent British citizens from going to Iraq allegedly to fight British troops there. As the Director General emphasized: "This is a central dilemma, how to protect our citizens within the rule of law...we value civil liberties and wish to do nothing to damage these hard fought rights. But the world has changed and there needs to be a debate on whether some erosion of what we all value may be necessary to improve the chances of our citizens not being blown apart as they go about their daily lives. Another dilemma."

In fact, these dilemmas consist of two quite different problems. One was the necessary and laudable desire of MI5 to work within the sphere of lawfulness. The other was the lack of clear predictive intelligence about the specific attacks in London of July 2005, in other words, tradecraft failings. The first is a serious issue. No one would suggest that MI5 or any part of the intelligence and security community should act unlawfully. But what follows from this is not that the matter be "kicked into the long grass," but that new laws should be passed that restore a pragmatic balance between human rights and protecting the security of each citizen from terrorist attacks. This would allow the security service to remain fully within the law while at the same time acting preemptively as an intelligence-led agency should clearly do. Police may be required to wait for a crime to be committed. A security service should intervene beforehand.

In order for a new "bodyguard" of legislation to be enacted, MI5 must convince the British political class that this is an urgent matter so that on occasion, and under continuous judicial scrutiny, MI5 may be given the benefit of the doubt. The hard truth is that, to date, MI5 has not been able to do so successfully. People have not taken their warnings seriously. Numerous figures, for example, the former antiterrorist chief at the Met (the Metropolitan Police), Sir David Veness, went out of their way in the 12 months before July 2005 to speak to groups of opinion formers, warning them that a terror attack on Britain proper was not a question of "if," but simply a question of "when."[9] They deserve much praise for doing so. But praise does not deal with the problem. Nor were they helped much by a former DG of MI5, Stella Rimington, who publicly questioned the need for identity cards, another measure many MI5 officers (and others) feel is necessary.[10]

The second problem, of course, can be addressed only by devoting more resources to the acquisition of secret intelligence about Islamist groupings who seek to attack us. MI5 and Special Branch need more agents. This, in highly compressed form, has to do with the three "R's" of intelligence work—requirements, resources, and recruitment. The last of these is plainly vital. Currently our agencies work a "selection effect" system (like a modeling agency) rather than a "treatment effect" one (like the Army). The former attempt to identify "stars" for whom training is less important than for the latter who realize they must make the person they want to see in their institution. If current recruitment systems are as good as they are claimed to be, why do our secret agencies have such obvious problems in recruiting ethnic minorities? The fundamental requirement for those wanting a career in intelligence is "insatiable curiosity." People either have this, or they do not. But once they do have it, it can be honed and trained and developed. Nor is it simply new recruits who need training: older staff who may have formed their own work pattern during a different historical era must be retrained.[11]

MI5 is expanding rapidly (there will be 800 more officers by 2007, bringing staff numbers from 2,000 in 2004 to 4,000, or to 3,000 officers by 2008 according to a different source).[12] Extra funding has, of course, been provided to the tune of a further £50 million per annum, especially to develop G Branch (which investigates international and Islamist terrorism). The size of MI5's budget is a state secret, but is thought by *The Sunday Times* to have been about £200 million in 2004.

Speaking at the Royal United Services Institute in February 2006, Chancellor Gordon Brown confirmed that as a result of the war on terror, there would be an overall increase in police numbers and funding—with the appointment of "nearly 16,000 more officers nationally and 6,000 more in the Met" so that "dedicated anti-terrorist resources will have doubled."[13] By 2008, he added, "a further £75 million will be added to the Met's counter-terrorism capability and a further £135 million for regional intelligence and investigation—in total investing £230 million more nation-wide. By 2008 the size of the security service will have nearly doubled. In total we will invest £2 billion a year on counter-terrorism and resilience—twice what we did before September 11th."

A difficulty with this is that public trust in both the necessity of enhanced security and in the products it provides appears to be diminishing. Prime Minister Tony Blair himself finds it hard to be believed on this matter by his fellow parliamentarians, and, as far as we can tell, by many in the legal profession. It is indeed of more than passing significance that he is *not* believed despite his habit of appealing to higher authority when national security is involved. It happened over the September 2002 Dossier on WMD, the release of which was to show that his fears were the outcome of the intelligence briefings he had received, or over his attempt to win support for his proposals in the Terrorism Bill 2005. In August 2005 Mr. Blair spoke of "a Security Service request that detention be extended" and the Home Office Minister said in October that "MI5 said three months detention was absolutely necessary."[14] But both Blair and the Minister, Hazel Blears, had got it wrong as MI5 did not stipulate the demand for a 90-day detention.[15] Members of Parliament, however, were plainly not convinced. One commentator has said, "If there is one blindingly obvious conclusion to be drawn from the Iraqi WMD fiasco, it is that to directly link a sensitive government decision with the privileged information provided by the intelligence services is wrong."[16]

Those who do not accept the need for new security measures use a simple rhetorical case: Blair claimed intelligence showed there was a threat from Iraqi WMD when there was in fact none. If he now says intelligence shows there is a threat from international terrorism he is likely to be wrong once again. A prominent Labour parliamentarian, Clare Short, has, for example, argued in this vein.[17] It is, of course, a logical fallacy to imagine that someone who may have got something wrong on one occasion will get everything wrong in the future, but the political fallout from the nonexistent WMD has been severe. Crispin Black, for example, wrote in July 2004 that Bush and Blair had "cooked the intelligence books on both sides of the Atlantic" and that "Blair has done considerable damage to the reputation of British intelligence and the intelligence process in general."[18] Even if today we can be sure that the problem with WMD intelligence was not that Blair invented it to suit his policy but that SIS passed faulty intelligence about WMD to the Prime Minister, the public's scepticism is not unwarranted.[19]

The government is still in denial about this. Sir David Omand, the government's security and intelligence coordinator from 2002 to 2005, has insisted, "We did not go to war because of specific pieces of faulty WMD intelligence although we all accept that there were some of these...." The causes he said "[m]ust be looked for in the change of attitudes in Government in the US and the UK after 9/11 when the vulnerability of modern urban life (including, in the future, to WMD) was revealed and highlighted."[20] Omand adds, "The intelligence on WMD in Iraq was not representative of agency performance" nor was there "any connection between it and the way that the analysis of intelligence is conducted in the war on terror." At the same time, Sir David accepts that "[p]olicy on protective security has to be made on the basis of rationality, in the light of the professional assessments made by JTAC and the Security Service and police." It is not hard to agree fully with this line.

Omand emphasized, "The key institution in this war, and an innovative one for the UK, was the construction of JTAC, the Joint Terrorism Analysis Centre based at Thames House, MI5's London headquarters but consisting of what is called 'all source intelligence analysis' since it brings together all the security and intelligence agencies." As we shall discuss, Sir David, at any rate, sees the evolution of a central intelligence and security organization in the United Kingdom as "an important concept." This would not make all intelligence officers members of the same organization but would, in Sir David's words, constitute "an acceptance of the value for recruiting and operations of the various specialised secret Agencies but to have a central capacity to plan, share support services—and train together." However convincing the detailed changes to the overall system may appear, political anxieties about recognizing the heavy blow to the credibility of political leaders and secret agencies because of the WMD issue and JTAC's own threat assessment difficulty are real obstacles to public support for reform.

Given this new thinking and the new resources apparently being put into this field, it seems likely that some of the biggest changes are likely to be made at the interface between intelligence-led policing and the intelligence agencies with the establishment of a national antiterrorist force to replace the old Special Branch.[21] We are certain to see the already considerable agent network run by the police in London expanded nationwide under the overall direction of the new regional MI5 offices.[22] More work will be done on terrorist "profiling" using skills acquired from an understanding of psychology and Islam. We can also expect an important boost not just for the DIS but also for other parts of the community, in particular JARIC (Joint Air Reconnaissance Intelligence Centre) whose national and international expertise in image intelligence are still insufficiently known about and insufficiently exploited.[23] JARIC's important work ought to feed into many other areas of intelligence activity. It has not always done so.

AN EFFECTIVE EUROPEAN SECURITY SHIELD

The Director General of MI5 is not the only leading secret agency chief to turn his or her mind to the future of the intelligence services.[24] Markus Ederer, the Deputy Director of Analysis at the German Secret Intelligence Service, the BND, has publicly pointed out that in December 2003 the

Member States of the European Union collectively defined the main threats in their EU Security Strategy as consisting of international terrorism, WMD, failing states, regional conflicts, and organized crime.[25]

He adds, "This threat analysis which is primarily characterized by transnational challenges and asymmetric threats, requires intelligence services, too, to update and change their modus operandi fundamentally." Ederer stressed, in particular, the need for preemptive action against terrorists and to second-guess their intentions by thinking "the unreasonable, the unexpected, the unthinkable (fly planes into buildings)."[26] Ederer must be right to argue that special attention needed to be focused on three matters in particular: developing what he calls a "culture of prevention: warning and response," "fighting the elephantiasis of reason," and, possibly most important of all, "fighting networks with networks."[27]

In respect of the first matter, he stresses the importance of preemption and better training: "Most of our current analysts as well as the newcomers lack the historical and cultural knowledge as well as the religious and sociological backgrounds of Islamic societies which are required to penetrate the minds of jihadi terrorists. Our intelligence-gathering systems rely heavily on traditional data collection and on measuring quantifiable facts. Correctly assessing perceptions as well as cultural and religious aspirations is a still underdeveloped and yet to be conceptualised discipline." Finally, his strategic reform involving the construction of "fighting networks with networks" is defined by him as a need to establish "a system of network-centric intelligence." This is essentially concerned with "enhancing lines of intra-service communication, questioning those firewalls which hedge bureaucratic competencies rather than secrets, as well as task force building are the needs of the moment."

He homes in on the very need that Manningham-Buller finds it hard to accept, at any rate accept lock, stock, and barrel. "We have," he insists, "to take the network idea further. Decisions on countering transnational or external threats to our societies are usually taken at a multilateral level —be it the United Nations, NATO or the EU. However, the intelligence assessments which serve as the basis for governments to take their decisions are produced autonomously at national level. Whilst there is some justification for that due to the very nature of the product, we are liable to generate more fissures in the International Community such as over Iraq, unless we advance to selective joint assessments internationally. As long as national threat perceptions are potentially divergent, how can policies at the international level be convergent?"[28]

Ederer provides an answer: "With the Joint Situation Center (SitCen) in its Secretariat General, the EU has made the hitherto widest-ranging attempt at international level to lay the groundwork for its Common Foreign and Security Policy (CFSP) by generating integrated situation and threat analyses. Made up of analysts from a total of seven EU member states at the moment, the SitCen essentially operates on the basis of the so-called watch list of about 25–30 crisis regions. Their joint assessments are to facilitate decision-making in the EU Council. The merits of this unique networking approach are clear: the knowledge base is broadened, pooling of different information from different services with different strengths, harmonisation of warning cultures, joint conclusions which necessarily help for unified decisions." He lauds, too, the appointment of Gijs de Vries whom he, perhaps surprisingly, calls the "EU counterterrorism Czar."

There can be few doubts, then, where the BND sees the future of intelligence and security work in the years that lie ahead. We must contrast Ederer's faith in Europe and its institutions with Manningham-Buller's scepticism. It will be recalled that Manningham-Buller's very first dilemma was that, on the one hand, the secret agencies of the Western World were all now facing a similar threat that required international cooperation, but that cooperation could also be a major cause of weakness particularly in compromising valuable sources of intelligence.

No serious intelligence analyst would suggest, of course, that what should be shared are the sources of a national secret agency. There are serious objections to this on many levels. What can, however, be safely shared are intelligence assessments that may be based on secret sources.

Even so, the DG of MI5 has—so far—delivered a clear and public "no," not just to Europe but to the Prime Minister himself (as she is entitled to do). There are good grounds for believing that, privately, MI5 may not be quite as sceptical. It has recently been suggested—with considerable emphasis—that the Security Service and SIS are already far more deeply involved in European institutional intelligence and security cooperation than one might assume.[29] Indeed, the focus is none other than SitCen (EU Joint Situation Centre). The British security community describes it in these terms: "The EU Joint Situation Centre or SitCen has duties which include early warning and monitoring of potential crises, support to crisis management operations run by the EU, and an intelligence analysis function. Such analysis is carried out by a Civilian Intelligence Cell within SitCen (SitCen/CIC), established in February 2002.

The SitCen/CIC's function is to prepare all-source assessments, drawing on assessed intelligence provided by Member States, in order to inform European policy and decision making. The SitCen Director is currently a British national on extended secondment to the Council Secretariat (it is believed that a British official set up the SitCen). In June 2004, the European Council endorsed a proposal by Javier Solana, the High Representative for the CFSP and Secretary-General of the Council, to expand the SitCen/CIC to enable it to cover all aspects of counterterrorism (i.e., internal as well as external). This was part of the package of measures agreed upon by the European Council in the wake of the Madrid bombings. A security source comments, "The UK is a strong supporter of the SitCen and in particular

the CIC, as a means of ensuring EU policy makers are better informed."
This statement would not have been made were it not true.

If, behind the curtain, so to speak, MI5 is rather more committed to European cooperation than its DG might allow in public, this chimes well with a view from the SIS. A former very senior figure in the secret intelligence community, speaking under the Chatham House rule, made a specific point of saying that cooperation within the European Union was an important way forward. When this person started his career, for a nation to have its own intelligence service was "the ultimate expression of national sovereignty." Today, however, "intelligence cooperation and liaison" are "at the front line." While it had to be accepted, he argued, that the United Kingdom "would always need a high level of coordination with the USA," it was an "ongoing issue as to whether the EU could coordinate in this area." The U.K. community had lost much of its "regional skills and knowledge," yet one needed such expertise "more than previously." It seemed plain that this person believed that the future was about international cooperation and coordination.

While it is plain that bilateral intelligence and security relations are strong and doubtless useful, they do not address all needs. Political realities may demand MI5 adopts a publicly stated Euro-sceptic line that insists that formalized and compulsory intelligence cooperation with the United States is good, but that it would be dangerous to extend this practice to our European Union partners, in particular, to the Big Five—Germany, the United Kingdom, France, Italy, and Spain.

Privately, however, things may be rather different. MI5 may dislike "enforced" cooperation, but be happy with voluntary collaboration. The trouble is, as the history of European integration tends to demonstrate, that without "enforcement," little of lasting value can be established. The political will to cooperate needs, it may be depressing to affirm, an expression in regulation. Newer EU partners (many of whom MI5 is doing much to train) may have to wait before joining SitCen, but they would expect to do so. A smaller state, like Austria, would have much to offer in specific areas. It is well-known to have outstanding human intelligence sources in the Balkans and to pay particular attention to the Islamist problem, since the Muslim faith has been a state religion in Austria since the end of the nineteenth century.[30]

However, British intelligence, if it goes down this route, will have to square up to the fact that there is still a blanket American refusal to share intelligence products with anyone outside the "quadrant" represented by the United States, the United Kingdom, Canada, and Australia. As everyone knows, these goods are so vital, and so enormous in quantity, that for the tap to be turned off would immediately push the three very junior partners into a different intelligence league altogether and certainly hinder Britain from her traditional ability to "punch above its weight" in world affairs.

No one should therefore minimize the enormous difficulties in establishing effective EU intelligence and security coordination. This is, indeed, a highly complex area that cannot be properly described here.[31]

Concrete successes in Europe of any kind are hard to achieve. One key plan—to require telecom companies to keep records of all calls and e-mails—which was part of the EU's strategy for combating terrorism produced in response to the Madrid attacks of March 11, 2004, had to be ditched.[32] Phone records had been used by the Spanish police to track down some of the Madrid bombers and by British police searching for the Omagh bombers. The proposal was simply to keep a list of date, time, caller, and recipient, but not content for one year and of e-mails for six months. However, the European Commission believed it should have been involved in the development of the policy and the European Parliament has said it would take national governments to court if they attempted to bypass the Commission. For those very reasons the DG of MI5 adduces that "international cooperation in the face of an international threat is essential," and further work should be given to constructing a European security and intelligence agency. The idea should most certainly not be dismissed out of hand.

OUTREACH AND ACADEME

One important and hitherto neglected means of addressing, if not solving, the dilemmas facing the British intelligence and security, and ensuring reform is successful, can lie through the development of outreach into academe and beyond and the involvement of academe in the full panoply of the teaching and training of intelligence officers. A proviso, of course, is that academics involved in this must be "persons of trust."

One of the frequent comments made by some, perhaps older and more jaded, intelligence practitioners to academic researchers, or at any rate to me, is that outsiders may have "opinions" on the agencies but simply do not have "the facts" to ensure their opinions should be taken into account. They are therefore rather useless unless they have very specific skills to offer. In fact, academics may have much to offer. There are, of course, areas of secret work about which they can know nothing.

What they can bring to this subject may be summarized as both narrow and broader professional skills. To the former belongs subject expertise. In the arts and social sciences, historians may bring an important element of collective memory to bear, necessary in a fast-moving world when all attention may be focused on one problem and then, at a moment's notice, be switched to another, quite different one. Those interested in literature bring an ability for close textual analysis and precision in wordsmithing. Political scientists who study institutions and processes may quickly detect the point at which what on paper seems like a perfect institution or a perfect regulation becomes an absurdity in the real world of political action. They may see where an alleged "reform," particularly in the interests of cutting expenditure, can in fact lead to great public danger. As Lord Butler showed clearly, the cuts in expenditure following the ending of the Cold War led to major cash problems, the early retirements of more experienced and more expensive staff, and a confusion of duties that allowed officers in the Requirements section to fail to exercise sufficient quality control.[33] Academics can warn both the community of the dangers of putting too much emphasis on "systems" and "processes" and ignoring the personal dimension to political power whether possessed by a politician or a civil servant. Ultimately, people will always be more important than institutions, but those working within them are usually the last to realize this.

To the broader skills every good academic should possess belong our training in, and our careers constructed on, the collection and analysis of information and on teaching and communicating it to others. We have skills that are certainly equivalent to some of the skills that intelligence professionals require. If Lord Butler is to be believed, as he should be, this more negative aspect of our duties is also shared by some in the intelligence community leading to some of the problems encountered in the WMD fiasco. Butler noted "the tendency [on the part of JIC members] for [their] assessments to be coloured by overreaction to previous errors." Later he said more famously that "the language in the Dossier may have left with readers the impression that there was fuller and firmer intelligence behind the judgements than was the case."[34] Academics will recognize the fault. However, we should not forget his conclusion that "the judgements in the dossier went to (although not beyond) the outer limits of the intelligence available."[35] This, too, is a point that academics will understand: they should go as far as they can, but not beyond what their evidence will bear. There are two good reasons why this should be so. First, academics like intelligence professionals must, in the end, make a judgment on what they are examining if it is at all possible to do so; if it is impossible, they should say so, as Lord Butler stresses this very clearly in parallel.[36] A judgment, of course, is just that. It is not a statement of fact and will never be so. Second, however, if they get things wrong their future credibility will suffer. That is, after all, why Lord Butler specifically discussed the idea that a "distinguished scientist" (not a political one) should be appointed as adviser to the Cabinet Office.[37]

Academics can also alert the community to the continuous need to question the constraints under which they operate, which are too often taken as "givens." I am struck by the extent to which the agencies have moved from being impervious to pressures from outside 30 years ago to being perhaps too anxious about making a strong case forcibly. It is not unknown that the security and intelligence community has been too often wrong footed in public and by Parliament (not always without justification, it must be added) and thereby placed on the defensive. This is not a good place for it to be, given its tasks. What is needed is more mature and careful criticism, set in the context of wanting the security and intelligence community to succeed at all times. A final step might be the establishment of an "intelligence college" or a "national institute of intelligence excellence" by the community and academe working jointly. This would provide an opportunity for world-class intelligence training, for the construction of relationships among intelligence officers who might otherwise be compartmentalized in their various agencies. It would permit serving officers to take some time out both for professional development but also research. Finally, if European and other partnership communities were drawn in to such an academy, it would necessarily provide our next generation of officers with the European and global awareness that will ultimately determine the success or failure of their mission in facing up to and defeating the global threat of terror.

13

Setting Priorities in a World of Changing Threats[1]

Richard J. Aldrich

In a world of changing threats, intelligence communities need to understand the spirit of the age. Identifying this correctly is all-important. This chapter argues that the defining feature of our epoch is globalization rather than the "new terror." The new terror is an important symptom of the pressures that global change has placed on states and societies, but it is not an underlying cause. Although the 1990s were an unhappy decade for intelligence agencies in which reform proved difficult, the emerging prescriptions that focused on globalization and an "information age" were not far off target.[2] However, since September 11, 2001, we have been distracted from these strategic issues. Important as terrorism is, the impending problems of organized crime, climate change, pandemics, and energy shortages demand more attention. Accordingly, the United Kingdom—and other countries—needs a new Global Threat Analysis Center, focused on broader issues of global security that can be examined through open sources. An exclusively open-source research unit would be able to connect freely with world university networks that are growing exponentially and would offer some assurance against the "groupthink" that has affected much of the Western intelligence community.[3]

TERROR OR GLOBALIZATION?

Since the devastating attacks on New York and Washington, D.C., conducted in September 2001, the world of intelligence has been focused on the "new terrorism." The last four years have seen a whirlwind of intelligence activity. Support for proactive counterterrorism has placed enormous strains on the key agencies and has required the acceleration of diverse activities. It has involved not only the difficult operations focused on preemption, but also support for retrospective prosecution. Security intelligence has had to connect with new programs designed to improve domestic resilience. Government departments and utility companies that rarely gave terrorism much thought are now avid consumers of advice and assessments from intelligence and security agencies. The intelligence demands for large-scale military operations overseas have also been growing.

The endless work of counterterrorism has been reflected in the dramatic growth of intelligence agencies on every continent. The assets of existing intelligence services have been "surged" toward the new targets and retired intelligence officers recalled to duty. In the United Kingdom the size of the Security Service (MI5) will soon be twice its Cold War establishment.[4] In the United States, intelligence spending for 2005–2006 stood at a record $44 billion and is still climbing.[5] Historically, growth is one objective that intelligence organizations have fulfilled without difficulty. Flexibility has proved more difficult to achieve. While the degree of effort exerted on current problems has been admirable, the focus on targeting the new terror has been disturbingly narrow, and perhaps misplaced. Many important issues, even issues connected to terrorism, are being neglected. We risk sliding back into an intelligence monoculture that is not unlike the experience of the Cold War. Arabic is the new Russian, and regular visits to Berlin or Vienna have been supplanted by sojourns in Cairo or Islamabad.

The challenge—now as ever—is to identify the objective nature of our epoch as a fundamental precursor to setting priorities. While in exile in Switzerland, Vladimir Lenin sat in the public library in Berne and read Carl von Clausewitz. It was not the first time that Lenin had immersed himself in Clausewitz, and he was something of an admirer. Both were influenced by Georg Wilhelm Friedrich Hegel and so shared the view that all conflicts are shaped by their underlying social and economic context. "To each epoch—its own wars," Lenin noted sagaciously in the margin.[6] The problem is that a new epoch now seems to come along about twice a decade. The Cold War seems rather distant, while the much-vaunted "end of history" proffered in the early 1990s was itself quickly consigned to the dustbin of history and overtaken by what seemed to be an era of new civil wars. By late 2001 we had entered the era of the "Global War on Terrorism," but this was abruptly canceled in 2005 when Washington announced the "Struggle Against Violent Extremism."[7]

We are not all that far from the second decade of the twenty-first century. What will be the nature of the "new threats" in 2010? A wide variety of experts, ranging from economists to biologists, suggest that the major security problems of the next decade will be of a different kind. A clash of cultures may still be with us, but we may also see countries fighting over increasingly scarce natural resources such as water and oil. Meanwhile, the largest killers of our populations are likely to be epidemics, famine, and climate change—natural events but exacerbated by injudicious human behavior. Although these are separate phenomena they are likely to hunt as a pack—and they will certainly hunt globally. Globalization will ensure that any shock to one part of the system will quickly be felt by the rest.[8]

Since the end of the Cold War, intelligence has been confronted with a bewildering range of threats and options. This makes it all the more important to identify the underlying themes and to decide "what has changed and what has not."[9] The so-called new terrorism is probably a symptom of more fundamental changes in the international system rather than a fundamental cause. Indeed some observers are increasingly persuaded that the new terrorism is not all that new. Advocates of the new terrorism have tended to argue that fundamentalists are not interested in political bargaining or political messages and simply wish to kill for the sake of killing. In reality, the timing of the bombing of Madrid in 2004 and the attacks on London in 2005 were highly political. We have been told to expect catastrophic events, perhaps with chemical and biological weapons, but instead the terrorists have mostly used conventional methods. It now seems that we will see more events like Bali and Madrid, but few 9/11s. Nevertheless, American-led intelligence doctrine has focused on preempting the so-called new terror. Its hallmark has been a pencil beam focus on "states" of concern, on particular groups, and on "getting" individuals.[10]

This chapter argues that, in fact, the important developments have been at a deeper level, involving global networks, connections, and processes. Arguably, the defining feature of our age and certainly the defining feature of the international system since the end of the Cold War is globalization. If there is a new terrorism, then much of its novelty actually derives from its "new" context—embedded within accelerating globalization. Globalization is fundamentally shifting the balance of advantage away from states in favor of terrorists and other miscreants. Although the attacks on London in July 2005 coincided with a major G-8 summit held in the United Kingdom that was focused on global issues, the transatlantic official mind has still failed to make the right connections. Globalization is making both crime and terrorism easier; it is rendering developed states and their economies more fragile and is making the work of intelligence services harder.[11]

Many economists have asserted that "globalization works," and there can be no doubt that increased trade volumes have lifted large regions of the world out of poverty.[12] Observers in the field of security studies are more inclined to assert that there are also costs. Around the world global trade has expanded unevenly, rewarding some, but punishing others. Globalized communications have offered profound cultural provocations to some groups. Simultaneously, it has provided the antagonized with new weapons and new ways of spreading their messages. Al Qaeda has used the Internet—the network of networks—for propaganda, for communications, and even to spread terrorist expertise. Globalization has created a "networked world" in which shadowy groups move elegantly, while states move clumsily.

Although the 1990s were messy, by the end of that decade the intelligence agencies had begun to recognize the connections between the various slippery problems of globalization.[13] While these problems did not present an immediate strategic threat, they were symptomatic of long-term trends. We need to refocus to these issues since they point the way to the next decade. Climate change, energy shortages, water issues, and pandemics are causing many more deaths than the recent bombings. Around the world, crime—particularly organized crime—currently kills and injures as many people as warfare. We only need to reflect on Africa to realize how these things interact—but do our intelligence priorities and structures reflect this world of changing threats? All of these issues require a more holistic approach to intelligence collection and a more sophisticated approach to analysis.[14]

THINKING NARROWLY OR BROADLY: BIORISK

What are the consequences of focusing our intelligence resources narrowly on the new terrorism and neglecting the wider aspects of global change, whether we define this in terms of economy or environment? Few issues illustrate the way in which intelligence needs to help policy makers achieve joined-up government than the problem of biorisk. Biological threats require states to produce sophisticated policies that cross the boundary from defense and foreign policy over into the realms of development, transport, science, and health. Biorisk also underlines how an excessive focus on the new terrorism potentially narrows our vision. If biorisk only means worrying about people who want to lay their hands on anthrax, then we can limit ourselves to fairly specific kinds of preparations.[15]

Should intelligence agencies confine themselves to worrying about bioterrorism, or should they focus more broadly on biorisk? At the strategic level of national assessments there is already growing consensus that intelligence should think about biorisk rather than mere bioterrorism simply because the two are increasingly connected. In the first decade of the twenty-first century we confront a range of biological challenges that are as diverse as they are alarming. Some of these are connected with the spread of expertise relating to a remarkable commercially driven biotechnological revolution that combines great promise with substantial possibilities for misuse.

At an operational level the responses that would be required to epidemic threats would not be dissimilar to those posed by a bioterrorism incident. Indeed, one of the most difficult tasks for intelligence in the face of major outbreak might be deciding whether this was an instigated attack or a natural occurrence. Both problems are multiplied by the accelerating scale of global travel and the capacity of disease to undermine governance across entire continents. Biorisk more broadly defined, whether it is the SARS virus, BSE (commonly known as mad cow disease), or the specter of AIDS in Africa, has confronted governments with new scales of problems that they have struggled to deal with. The United Kingdom's difficulties with BSE and later with Foot-and-Mouth Disease (requiring assistance from the military) underlined just how intractable these problems are. They also require sophisticated information exchange between elements of the state and private networks that are not accustomed to working with each other. In short, biorisk is a classically globalized problem respecting no borders or boundaries and for this reason is potentially the toughest test that governments may have to face.[16] Intelligence on biological risks remains remarkably underdeveloped precisely because it presents difficult architectural problems that are nonlinear. Yet early warning that might permit timely action is now essential to any chance of preventing the initiation of a global pandemic. Once it has escaped the locality where it has originated, there is little hope of containing it.[17]

Intelligence on biorisk is not only about early warning but also about support for policy making. Since 2002, biological threats have hit the headlines, and governments are now more prepared to make resources available. However, officials lack the kind of information support to allow sophisticated application of these new resources or to connect with wider issues outside their own countries. Donald A. Henderson, the former director of U.S. Office of Public Health Preparedness, recently noted that Congress had recently increased funds for public health preparedness from U.S.$500 million in FY2001 to $3 billion in FY2002. His department then had to set priorities for how to spend this windfall. However, efforts to deploy these new resources lack both intelligence support and a global dimension.[18]

A great deal can be done to address the conditions in which pandemics find their origins through the careful application of overseas aid and targeted assistance to improve the development of national health structures in developing countries. Overseas aid in the area of health connects directly with security because both terrorism and epidemics thrive wherever there are failed states. We might even see public health assistance—properly targeted through the imaginative use of intelligence—as a form of public health diplomacy. In the last two years vast sums have been spent on contracting public relations companies in the hope of somehow selling the image of the West more effectively, especially in the Middle East and Africa. What these programs lack is substantive evidence that the West recognizes that it shares security concerns with "the rest." Effective health assistance can provide material evidence of Western concern for that most basic of human rights—the right to life. Here the fight against disease and the battle for hearts of minds might find a material connection.[19]

In short, biorisk intelligence, broadly conceived, indeed globally conceived, allows us to look at the whole spectrum of health in a connected way. Yet our intelligence cover on biorisk is weak and fragmented precisely because these issues cross the security/health divide and because no single government agency owns this brief. The United States has only just begun to draw together an emergency infrastructure that crosses the security/health divide, placing those responsible for both pandemics and bioterrorist attack into one body: the Biomedical Advanced Research and Development Agency. This joined-up effort is commendable, but imaginative intelligence support for this agency is the missing component.[20] As early as 2000 the U.S. National Intelligence Council was looking at the threats posed by global infectious disease, but these things are typical of globalization threats that have languished since 9/11.[21]

What would a biorisk intelligence structure look like if it was required to look beyond the narrow subject of bioterrorism? Perhaps it might offer the opportunity for the creation of the first substantive UN intelligence agency. Self-evidently, globalization means that an outbreak of infectious disease is now a threat to public health everywhere.[22] The acceleration of disease needs to be matched by an acceleration of information. It is hard to resist the notion that some sort of "Biorisk Assessment Agency" working under the World Health Organization would be a good idea.[23] This is not a matter of simply tasking several people within a few national intelligence agencies to spend more time looking at existing disease-reporting sources. The whole realm requires a radical rethink to ensure that we can create a surveillance system for global public health that moves beyond the traditional conception of a national intelligence community.[24]

REMOVING BARRIERS: INTELLIGENCE VERSUS INFORMATION

Why have intelligence services struggled to address globalization since the end of the Cold War? States may have opened their borders since 1989, but intelligence remains a closed-off world. Secret services find it hard to share intelligence across national boundaries at a pace that is commensurate with the activities of their enemies. This is because secret intelligence agencies do not, as a rule, like sharing their information on anything other than a bilateral basis.[25] There are many good reasons why this should be the case, including the protection of sources. Where multilateral intelligence sharing has been achieved on any scale—for example, with signals intelligence—it has required a cumbersome system of special clearances and secure facilities. This problem has been visible wherever the international community has tried to build broad coalitions. The sight of National Intelligence Cells lined up inside compounds in the former Yugoslavia, supporting the same peace-keeping effort, but unable to intercommunicate, is a perfect symbol of how the old Cold War architecture has struggled to cope with a new international system. Experiments with European Union intelligence present another lackluster story.[26]

Some of these problems of cooperation and exchange are bound to persist, especially in the realm of counterterrorism intelligence. However, intelligence relating to many of the problems of globalization is not especially secret. Indeed one of the reasons that the British intelligence community began to develop a broader customer base in Whitehall in the late 1990s was precisely because much of the material on subjects such as organized crime was not especially sensitive and could be shared more widely. Crime, health, environment, and economy are amenable to attack with open sources or with sources of low classification. Fortunately, these are the very problems that require rapid and sophisticated multilateral cooperation among government, nongovernmental organizations (NGOs), and private organizations. Much of what we need to know in these areas is open-source intelligence—perhaps even mere information. The challenge is not collection, but instead reshaping our analytical structures to deal with a bewildering range of events. No linear Cold War–style intelligence agency, with its desk officers, will track these events imaginatively. Something new is required to look at global threats that employs information in imaginative ways.[27]

Most government bureaucracies, whether they work in the field of intelligence or not, are modern rather than postmodern. Put another way, they are Fordist entities, hierarchical, slow-moving, and unadaptive. Viable alternative models have emerged in the private sector and include RAND Corporation, Oxford Analytica, and Reuters. Writing in the late 1990s, Bruce D. Berkowitz and Allan E. Goodman were much taken with the model of Microsoft, with its flexible working groups and flat hierarchies. Structures need to be sufficiently permissive and open-ended to allow expert analysis from teams of people recruited for each task. They argued that an open structure, in which experts were seconded flexibly for a few months at a time, would soon outpace the old model of a pool of professional analysts. Where would the experts come from to populate this entity? They would mostly be seconded from universities, from private companies, from NGOs, and from journalism. One suspects that journalists would make superb open-source intelligence officers because they have that most important of all skills—selling the product to their masters.[28]

What should U.K. intelligence look like by 2010? What should its priorities be? Many things will change only incrementally and much of the secret architecture must remain. Indeed, if anything, the appetite for objective reporting from secret sources has increased because we have embarked on any number of large-scale military campaigns with operational intelligence requirements of a traditional kind. Even without those overseas excursions, the challenges of counterterrorism have prompted many to call for more secret work of a ruthless kind. Indeed many blamed the intelligence failures that preceded 9/11 upon a soft post–Cold War culture that was risk adverse and neglected long-term seeding operations in the realm of human intelligence. In the United States the managers of the 1990s have been publicly castigated for encouraging open-source reporting, pen pushing, and analysis while neglecting "real operations."[29]

In fact, the real issue is not what type of intelligence to go for, but how to achieve better quality. The international system is exceedingly complex. The new terrorism will be with us for a long time, but the old "new threats" of the 1990s have not gone away. If we are to deal effectively with the former, we need to understand and respond to the latter in a more sophisticated way. Resources have been found to double the size of MI5, and enhancements are under way at the Secret Intelligence Service and the Government Communications Headquarters. We have seen the creation of JTAC—the Joint Terrorism Analysis Centre. However, resources should also be found for a new and innovative open-source agency. The United Kingdom needs not only a JTAC, but also something that I might call a "GTAC"—a Global Threat Analysis Centre. This would be an agencified organization consisting of a few permanent staff who would buy open-source expertise on the issues of the moment. It would deal *only* with open sources, allowing it to engage with the wider world of information without the cumbersome air gaps dictated by secret intelligence.

What would GTAC look like? First of all, unlike some of our more recent enhancements it would be relatively cheap. It would have a small permanent staff of managers and a support element numbering less than 20, although its temporary staff would be larger. To encourage it to think differently from existing agencies, it would be based outside London—perhaps in Oxford. Some analysts would be brought in for short periods of a few months along the lines of research fellows at think tanks in London and Washington. Academics might choose to spend a semester with GTAC in Oxford as "Globalization Research Fellows." However, with an abundant bandwidth and no major security issues, many would be virtual contributors and need not be based in Oxford at all. Most importantly, working entirely with unclassified sources, reports would not just be drawn from U.K. universities or experts. They would be drawn from all around the world. An agency dealing only with open information and advice would also reassure the suppliers. Academics, journalists, and NGO specialists are sensitive about their liberal and humane credentials and would be more responsive to requests from an entity that looked like Oxford Analytica. Indeed, free market analytical entities are already busy commissioning precisely this sort of work.[30]

Universities are well prepared for this new role. Many of the world's major research universities have concluded that as single entities they are unable to address the global complexities of the twenty-first century effectively, and consequently they have formed their own alliances. In effect they are busily engaged in their own version of liaison. Universitas 21 and Worldwide Universities Network are just two examples of such emerging global knowledge alliances, and these are perhaps the academic equivalent of UKUSA. Strangely, governments have as yet shown remarkably little interest in the potential of these international knowledge leviathans.[31]

These proposals, which focus on finding the right experts, should not be confused with the "googlization" of intelligence advocated by some open-source enthusiasts. Merely using open sources or recruiting a group of eager graduates to surf the Internet is not enough. Regrettably, this seems to be the direction in which Washington has moved. In 2004, the presidential commission on intelligence regarding weapons of mass destruction (WMD) strongly recommended a major expansion of the open-source collection.[32] A new initiative was duly announced in early November 2005 by John D. Negroponte, Director of National Intelligence. Responding directly to the WMD Commission he announced a decision to create a new "Open Source Center." Located at the Central Intelligence Agency (CIA), this Center will develop the exploitation of openly available information to include the Internet, databases, press, radio, television, video, geospatial data, photos, and commercial imagery. This approach will capitalize on the established expertise of the CIA-directed Foreign Broadcast Information Service, which has long monitored international radio and television news.[33] However, it will also be an old-fashioned pool of analysts, not a flexible team of experts. Located within the leafy precincts of Langley, it is unlikely to be able to engage properly with the wider intellectual community or to offer much opportunity to escape "groupthink."[34]

"THE NAME'S BOND—PROFESSOR BOND"

The concept sounds a little improbable—a new model army of open-source intelligence analysts formed from the ranks of academics, hacks, and scribblers? Remarkably, it has been done before. In 1941, faced with a major convulsion in the international system and urged on by President Franklin D. Roosevelt, General William Donovan turned to the East Coast universities as an intelligence recruiting ground. Academics turned analysts formed the Research and Analysis Branch, the first unit of the wartime Office of Strategic Services (OSS) and forerunner of the CIA. Oxford itself was the site of another wartime experiment—the brief joining of Chatham House and the Foreign Office Research Department—much expanded to deal with wartime business and co-located at Balliol College, Oxford. Their tasks were similar to those of the American OSS Research and Analysis Branch.[35]

Recent history suggests that academics are more than up to the job. We might recall that some of the most important trends of the last few decades have been spotted by academics first. Of course, the issue here is which academic or freelance researcher one listens to. For every commentator who gets it right, two or three must surely get it wrong? Moreover, many academics prize originality and individuality over accuracy, generating a culture in which no expert would wish to be seen agreeing with another. This is, of course, a substantial problem. However, in many of the more specific cases the experts would be self-selecting. After all, how many experts are there who specialize on the social anthropology of the tribes of Afghanistan's Helmand province?[36]

Let us consider two cases—first, the end of the Cold War. The intelligence agencies got this wrong both in terms of predicting the event itself and the course it would take.[37] "Truth be told," remarks former Director of Central Intelligence Robert Gates, the American government, including the CIA, "had no idea in January 1989 that a tidal wave of history was about to break upon us."[38] Sir Percy Cradock, former Joint Intelligence Committee (JIC) stalwart, also freely concedes that the United Kingdom missed by a mile and has offered some cogent comments on why this was the case. Journalists like Timothy Garton Ash were more prescient. In 1983, he produced an account of the Polish Uprising of 1980–1981 and the fortunes of Solidarity. As early as 1983 he had made several important observations. First, he was already alert to globalization, noting that Solidarity was to a degree riding on the wave of a communications revolution, what he called a "tele-revolution," making innovative use of telexes, faxes, phones, and radio stations. Moreover, despite the imposition of martial law, he noted that this was a tide that would not turn back and predicted a hopeful future for Poland. About a third of the Communist Party members had joined Solidarity, so he was confident that there would soon be another upheaval.[39] Come the collapse of Communism in 1989, his columns in the newspapers were a better guide to what was happening than anything produced by the intelligence agencies.[40]

We might say the same of recent intellectual battles relating to Iraqi WMD. Although journalists were determined to call a "foul" regarding political interference in the realm of intelligence during the prologue to the Iraq War, in retrospect it looks as though at least 50 percent of the explanation was down to intelligence failure. This failure was characterized by colossal groupthink exacerbated by convergence among leading intelligence agencies around the world. The United States, the United Kingdom, Australia, Denmark, Israel, and Germany all got it spectacularly wrong and most have instituted searching enquiries to try and find out why.[41] Who, if anyone, got Iraqi WMD right? Many academics voiced their doubts. The reality is that the public writings of Glen Rangwala at the University of Cambridge would have proved to be a more reliable guide to what was going on inside Iraq than the output of the secret agencies.[42] It later transpired that the U.K. government's dossier on Iraq's security agencies proved to be largely lifted from a postgraduate student's doctoral thesis—perhaps the ultimate backhanded complement to the world of the academic intelligence expert.[43]

Outsiders were often rather good, even at the more secret stuff. Any handicap that they operated under by not being able to peruse a secure multilevel database was more than offset by the virtue of avoiding groupthink. In theory, friendly cooperation between the leading Western intelligence agencies should offer fresh insights and alternative perspectives. However, in practice what we have seen over the years is an unhealthy process of convergence. This has been identified by internal and external commentators alike as a worrying aspect of the baleful WMD intelligence experience.[44] Accordingly, an alternative analytical center would be valuable not only because it would be better at examining globalization-related issues, but also because it would put some grit in the oyster. Living outside the loop, it would have a much better chance of avoiding the unspoken assumptions that quickly become the orthodoxy in any large institution. Who will do better at predicting these trends and getting us ahead of the globalization curve—government intelligence services or a free-booting team of researchers with all the resources of a global network of universities? It is the latter facet that the United Kingdom, and other mature democracies, is currently missing and would not cost much to put right.

BEYOND BUTLER

We cannot pretend that the twenty-first century has opened well for Western intelligence agencies. Changes to intelligence are afoot in the United Kingdom, prompted by the recent Butler Report, but there is every sign that they are not radical enough. Moreover, while some problems have been identified, the way in which they were found, using an *ad hoc* enquiry, was rather alarming. After all, the United Kingdom has an Intelligence and Security Committee that is supposed to identify problems. It has been in operation for almost a decade, yet it failed to spot the obvious weaknesses that Butler picked up in his report, such as the historic underresourcing of the United Kingdom's central analytical process. Moreover, while Butler was keen to assert the importance of escaping groupthink, he offered few ideas as to how this might be done. Radical solutions suggested to him by those he talked to have been left by the wayside. Specifically, he shied away from the idea that outsiders might be invited onto the JIC. There is little in his report about open sources or opening windows into the wider world of the information age. In short, Butler's recommendations were hardly twenty-first century stuff.

At the management level the Butler Report also begs more questions than it answers. In an era of rapid global change, who will chart the path ahead for U.K. intelligence, and from where will it derive fresh ideas? Certainly not from the Ministerial Committee on Intelligence, which has never met during the last eight years. The Intelligence and Security Committee has shown itself to be fundamentally incapable of thinking about big issues. Meanwhile, Butler and his team of one-time consultants have delivered their report, collected their checks, and caught the train home. The United Kingdom certainly needs a new center focused on open sources—but it also needs to open its mind. One possibility might be a Prime Ministerial Intelligence Advisory Board staffed with some retired senior intelligence officers, but mostly composed of innovative outsiders. One thing is certain, current reforms both in the realm of analysis and management fall far short of what is required, and more innovative measures are needed to prepare us for a world of changing threats.[45]

Notes

CHAPTER 2

1. Mark Urban, *UK Eyes Alpha, The Inside Story of British Intelligence* (London: Faber and Faber, 1996), 48.

2. Peter Wright, with Paul Greengrass, *Spycatcher: The Candid Autobiography of a Senior Intelligence Officer* (New York: Viking, 1987).

3. "20/20 Vision," program featuring Cathy Massiter, broadcast by Channel 4, March 8, 1985.

4. "Panorama," program featuring David Shayler, transmitted by BBC 1, August 7, 1998.

5. Samuel P. Huntingdon, "The Clash of Civilizations," *Foreign Affairs* 72, no. 3 (1993): 22–49.

6. "Responsibility for the Terrorist Atrocities in the United States, 11 September 2001," British Cabinet Office document, undated, 2001.

CHAPTER 4

1. Philip H.J. Davies, "Intelligence Culture and Intelligence Failure in Britain and the United States," *Cambridge Review of International Affairs,* 17m, no. 3 (October 2004).

2. "Analysis" and "assessment" are conflated in this paper, though assessment arguably contains an extra dimension of judgment and prediction.

3. In Anthony Glees, Philip H.J. Davies, and John N.L. Morrison, *The Open Side of Secrecy: Britain's Intelligence and Security Committee* (London: Social Affairs Unit, forthcoming 2006).

4. The Foreign Secretary for SIS and GCHQ, the Home Secretary for the Security Service, and the Defence Secretary for the DIS.

5. See http://www.ignet.gov/randp/igbrochure04.pdf.

6. The Senate Select Committee on Intelligence and the House Permanent Select Committee on Intelligence.

7. HC 898, *Review of Intelligence on Weapons of Mass Destruction: Report of a Committee of Privy Counsellors,* July 14, 2004.

8. It is, however, addressed in Glees et al., *The Open Side of Secrecy*.

9. These are set out in the Intelligence Services Act 1994 (HMSO ISBN 0105413941).

10. In this chapter "Agencies" (capitalized) means SIS, the Security Service, and GCHQ; "agencies" (uncapitalized) covers worldwide intelligence and security organizations in general.

11. The ISC has also released sanitized versions of its *ad hoc* reports to Parliament, with the exception of two 1996 reports, one on an unnamed subject and the other on the Agencies' work in the area of economic well-being.

12. Now HM Customs and Revenue.

13. The ISC is dissolved at each election and reformed afterward; so far there have been four committees: 1994–1997, 1997–2001 (both chaired by Tom King), 2001–2005 (chaired by Ann Taylor), and 2005– (chaired by Paul Murphy).

14. This was no doubt helped by Tom King's early decision that only he or a nominee would speak to the media.

15. Frank Gardner, BBC News, March 30, 2006.

16. Intelligence and Security Committee, *Report into the London Terrorist Attacks on 7 July 2005*, Cm 6785, London, May 2006.

17. Sir David Omand is quoted in Glees et al., *The Open Side of Secrecy*.

18. Glees et al., *The Open Side of Secrecy*.

19. Ibid.

20. The United Kingdom does have Judicial Commissioners (the Interception of Communications Commissioner and the Intelligence Services Commissioner), but their functions are more limited than those of IGs.

21. It is an interesting question (which this chapter does not attempt to answer) why some democracies, such as France, do not have such a consensus.

22. *Report of the Joint Inquiry into the Terrorist Attacks of September 11 2001*, December 2002, xv.

23. Even if Saddam had possessed WMD, he would not have posed a threat unless he also had the intent to use them and the means to deliver them against U.K. targets.

24. *Sunday Times*, May 1, 2005.

25. It is, however, intriguing to speculate how key players will be variously categorized as "sincere," "deluded," and "cynical liars."

26. United States Senate Select Committee on Intelligence, July 7, 2004.

CHAPTER 5

1. This chapter is a revision of the author's earlier explorations into the relationship between the shock of failure and scandal, on the one hand, and intelligence oversight in the United States, on the other hand, beginning with a presentation at the "Geheimhaltung and Transparenz" Conference in Berlin (2004) and continuing with "Presidents, Lawmakers, and Spies: Intelligence Accountability in the United States," *Presidential Studies Quarterly* E34 (December 2004): 828–37; Hans Born, Loch K. Johnson, and Ian Leigh, eds., *Who's Watching the Spies? Establishing Intelligence Service Accountability* (Washington, DC: Potomac Books, 2005); Loch K. Johnson, "Accountability and America's Secret Foreign Policy: Keeping a Legislative Eye on the CIA," *Foreign Policy Analysis* 1 (Spring 2005): 99–120; and "Supervising

America's Secret Foreign Policy: A Shock Theory of Congressional Oversight for Intelligence," in *American Foreign Policy in a Globalized World,* ed. David P. Forsythe, Patrice C. McMahon, and Andrew Wedeman (New York: Routledge, 2006), 173–92.

2. Stephen F. Knott, *Secret and Sanctioned: Covert Operations and the American Presidency* (New York: Oxford University Press, 1996).

3. Select Committee to Study Governmental Operations with Respect to Intelligence Activities (the Church Committee), *Final Report,* Rept. 94-755, U.S. Senate, 94th Congress, 2nd Session (May 1976); David M. Barrett, "Glimpses of a Hidden History: Sen. Richard Russell, Congress, and Early Oversight of the CIA," *International Journal of Intelligence and Counter-intelligence* 11 (Fall 1998): 271–99; Loch K. Johnson, "Spymaster Richard Helms," *Intelligence and National Security* 18 (Autumn 2003): 24–44.

4. Public Law No. 93-559; 32, 88 Stat. 1804.

5. The Church Committee, *Final Report*; Loch K. Johnson, *A Season of Inquiry: The Senate Intelligence Investigation* (Lexington: University Press of Kentucky, 1986); Frank Smist, Jr., *Congress Oversees the United States Intelligence Community,* 2nd ed. (Knoxville: University of Tennessee Press, 1994).

6. Loch K. Johnson, "Congressional Supervision of America's Secret Agencies: The Experience and Legacy of the Church Committee," *Public Administration Review* 64 (January–February 2004): 3–26.

7. Public Law No. 95-511, 92 Stat. 1783.

8. Public Law No. 96-450; 407(b), 94 Stat. 1981.

9. Loch K. Johnson, *Secret Agencies: U.S. Intelligence in a Hostile World* (New Haven: Yale University Press, 1996), 89–94.

10. Author's interview with DCI William J. Casey, CIA Headquarters, Langley, Virginia (June 16, 1986).

11. Gregory F. Treverton, "Intelligence: Welcome to the American Government," in *A Question of Balance: The President, Congress and Foreign Policy,* ed. Thomas E. Mann (Washington, DC: Brookings Institution, 1990), 99–133.

12. Loch K. Johnson, "Legislative Reform of Intelligence Policy," *Polity* 17 (Spring 1985): 549–73.

13. Marvin C. Ott, "Partisanship and the Decline of Intelligence Oversight," *International Journal of Intelligence and Counterintelligence* 16 (Spring 2003): 69–94 (quote on p. 81).

14. Joel D. Aberbach, "What's Happened to the Watchful Eye?" *Congress & the Presidency* 29 (Spring 2002): 3–23 (quote on p. 20).

15. Stephen F. Knott, "The Great Republican Transformation on Oversight," *International Journal of Intelligence and Counterintelligence* 13 (Spring 2000): 49–63 (quote on p. 57).

16. Ott, "Partisanship," 82–83.

17. Ibid., 87.

18. Russ Baker, "Chill on the Hill," *Nation* (October 14, 2002): 11–14 (quote on p. 13).

19. Porter Goss, remarks, *Crossfire,* CNN Television (May 16, 2001).

20. See, for example, the Goss Committee Report, *Intelligence Authorization Act for Fiscal Year 2005*, House Permanent Select Committee on Intelligence, H. Rept. 108th Congress, 2nd Session (2004), which presented a harsh indictment against the intelligence agencies for their poor human intelligence (HUMINT) in the Middle East and Southwest Asia.

21. Dafna Linzer and Walter Pincus, "Goss Forced Out as CIA Director," *Washington Post* (May 6, 2006), A1; Mark Mazzetti and Scott Shane, "Director of C.I.A. Is Stepping Down Under Pressure," *New York Times* (May 6, 2006), A1.

22. Bill Gertz, *Breakdown: How America's Intelligence Failures Led to September 11* (Washington, DC: Regnery Publishing, 2002).

23. Charles Babington, 'Senate Intelligence Panel Frayed by Partisan Infighting,' *Washington Post* (April 29, 2006), A9.

24. Harry H. Ransom, "Secret Intelligence Agencies and Congress," *Society* 123 (1975): 33–38. This description of intelligence oversight seems to fit congressional approaches to accountability across the policy board, based on the author's observations as a Hill staffer for six years and, more importantly, the broad scholarly literature [see, for example, Joel D. Aberbach, *Keeping a Watchful Eye: The Politics of Congressional Oversight* (Washington, DC: The Brookings Institution, 1990); and Christopher J. Deering, "Alarms and Patrols: Legislative Oversight in Foreign and Defense Policy," in *Congress and the Politics of Foreign Policy*, ed. C.C. Campbell, N.C. Rae, and J.F. Stack, Jr. (Upper Saddle River, NJ: Prentice Hall, 2003), 112–138].

25. David Mayhew, *The Electoral Connection* (New Haven: Yale University Press, 1974).

26. The police-patrolling and fire-fighting metaphor is drawn from M.D. McCubbins and T. Schwartz, "Congressional Oversight Overlooked: Police Patrols and Fire Alarms," *American Journal of Political Science* 28 (1984): 165–79.

27. Johnson, "Accountability and America's Secret Foreign Policy."

28. See Loch K. Johnson, John C. Kuzenski, and Erna Gellner, "The Study of Congressional Investigations: Research Strategies," *Congress & the Presidency* 19 (Autumn 1992): 138–56.

29. Loch K. Johnson, author's interview with senior staffer, Washington, D.C. (February 4, 2003).

30. Herbert E. Meyer, "A Memo to the 9/11 Commission," *National Review Online* (January 6, 2003), http://www.nationalreview.com/comment/comment-meyer010603.asp.

31. *Hearings on Congressional Oversight of Covert Activities*, Permanent Select Committee on Intelligence, U.S. House of Representatives, 98th Congress, 2nd session (September 20, 1983).

32. Testimony, "H.R. 1013, H.R. 1317, and Other Proposals Which Address the Issue of Affording Prior Notice of Covert Actions in the Congress," *Hearings*, Permanent Select Committee on Intelligence, U.S. House, Washington, D.C. (April–June 1987), 66.

33. William H. Jackson, Jr., "Congressional Oversight of Intelligence: Search for a Framework," *Intelligence and National Security* 5 (July 1980): 113–47; and L. Britt Snider, *Sharing Secrets with Lawmakers: Congress as a User of Intelligence*

(Washington, DC: Center for the Study of Intelligence, Central Intelligence Agency, 1997).

34. James T. Currie, "Iran-Contra and Congressional Oversight of the CIA," *International Journal of Intelligence and Counterintelligence* 11 (Summer 1998): 185–210 (quote on p. 203).

35. Ken Guggenheim, "Tenet Defends CIA's Pre-9/11 Efforts," *Washington Post* (October 17, 2002), A1.

36. Senator Richard C. Shelby, remarks, *Congressional Record* (September 24, 2002), p. S9085.

37. Senate Select Committee on Secret Military Assistance to Iran and the Nicaraguan Opposition and House Select Committee to Investigate Covert Arms Transactions with Iran (the Inouye-Hamilton Committees), *Report on the Iran-Contra Affair*, S. Rept. 100-216 and H. Rept. 100-433 (November 1987).

38. Loch K. Johnson, author's interview with senior staffer, Washington, D.C. (February 6, 2003).

39. Loch K. Johnson, author's interview with senior staffer, Washington, D.C. (December 18, 2002).

40. Neil A. Lewis, "Senator Insists C.I.A. Is Harboring Iraq Reports," *New York Times* (October 4, 2002), A12.

41. E-mail communication to the author (October 4, 2002).

CHAPTER 6

1. Also cf. Hans Born and Ian Leigh, Legal Standards and Best Practice for Oversight of Intelligence Agencies, Oslo, 2005, p. 16.

2. Ibid.

3. Compare IPU and DCAF Handbook for Parliamentarians No. 5: Parliamentary Oversight of the Security Sector: Principles, Mechanisms and Practices, Geneva, 2003, p. 18.

4. Act of 20 December 1990 (Federal Law Gazette I. p. 2954), last amended by a law of 16 August 2002 (Federal Law Gazette I. pp. 3202, 3217).

5. Act of 20 December 1990 (Federal Law Gazette I. pp. 2954, 2970), last amended by a law of 16 August 2002 (Federal Law Gazette I. pp. 3202, 3217).

6. Act of 20 December 1990 (Federal Law Gazette I. pp. 2954, 2977), last amended by a law of 15 December 2004 (Federal Law Gazette I. pp. 3396, 3403).

7. Act of 11 April 1978 (Federal Law Gazette I. p. 453), last amended by a law of 26 June 2001 (Federal Law Gazette I. pp. 1254, 1260).

8. In contrast, other countries follow different practices. In the United Kingdom, for example, the head of government appoints (after consultation with the Leader of the Opposition) members of the parliamentary committee on intelligence and security, whereas in Australia the executive branch makes nominations but the parliament itself appoints them.

9. Also cf. Born and Leigh, Legal Standards and Best Practice, 85.

10. Ibid., 81.

11. See below for the G10 Commission.

12. Also cf. Born and Leigh, Legal Standards and Best Practice, 91.

13. Examples are as follows: April 2000: "Visit of BND Chairman Dr. Hanning to Chechnya served German Interests"; November 2005: "Observation of Journalists in the 1990s by BND Was Illegitimate—External Expert Appointed for Comprehensive Investigation."

CHAPTER 7

1. The Spanish Inquisition was meticulous in its observance of procedural norms. The Inquisitors recognized the right to the services of an advocate, the right (after formal accusation) of access to incriminating evidence, the right to call favorable witnesses and to impeach hostile witnesses, the right to a quasi-independent panel of judges, the right to demand the recusal of judges on grounds of bias, and the right to plead extenuating circumstances (for example, insanity, youthful indiscretion, or drunkenness). Despite these seemingly enlightened procedural practices, "[t]he number of acquittals were few." Henry Kamen, *The Spanish Inquisition* (London: Weidenfeld & Nicholson 1997), 199.

2. The temptation to countenance torture in extremity is not always easy to resist. See Bruce Ackerman, *Before the Next Attack: Preserving Civil Liberties in an Age of Terrorism* (New Haven: Yale University Press, 2006), 108–12, citing Alan Dershowitz, *Why Terrorism Works: Understanding the Threat, Responding to the Challenge* (New Haven: Yale University Press 2002), 142–63, and the U.S. Department of Justice "torture" memos attempting to justify harsh interrogation techniques.

3. Adam Roberts, "Counter-Terrorism, Armed Force and the Laws of War," in *Survival* 44, no. 1 (Spring 2002): 7–32. As Roberts further notes, POW status does not immunize a terrorist from prosecution for war crimes or other violations of international law committed before his capture.

4. The Russian anarchist Nicholas Morozov, quoted in David Bosco, "An Indefinable Problem," *Bulletin of Atomic Scientists* (January/February 2006): 46.

5. State-sponsored terror is beyond the scope of this chapter. One authoritative tabulation attributes some half-million deaths over the centuries to terrorists and guerilla practitioners of violence as contrasted with the 130 million people killed by their own governments in the twentieth century alone. See Clark R. McCauley, "Terrorism and the State: The Logic of Killing Civilians," in *The Making of a Terrorist: Recruitment, Training, and Root Causes,* ed. James J.F. Forest (Westport, CT: Praeger, 2006), 238, 246–47.

6. Attacking the near enemy before confronting the far enemy is enjoined by Q. 9:123. Citations to the Qur'an are to the M.H. Shakir, 1983 translation published by the Online Book Initiative, http://www.hti.umich.edu/k/koran.

7. Bruce Lawrence, ed., "Declaration of Jihad," August 23, 1996, in *Messages to the World: The Statements of Osama bin Laden* (London: Verso, 2005), 23–30. The reasons for bin Laden's (and ultimately Zawahiri's) shift in strategy in the mid-1990s are set out cogently in Fawaz A. Gerges, *Journey of the Jihadist: Inside Muslim Militancy* (Orlando, FL: Harcourt, Inc., 2006). Gerges attributes the decision to three factors: the availability of a large pool of hardened veterans of the Afghan war accustomed to warfare against a Great Power; the rejection by the Saudi royal family of bin Laden's offer to raise a force of mujahedeen to expel Saddam Hussein from Kuwait in favor of an American presence; and the conviction on the part of bin Laden and Zawahiri that the Western powers were ultimately responsible

for the defeat of the Islamist uprisings in Egypt, Saudi Arabia, and Algeria. Ibid., 177–80.

8. The initial July attack on the London transport system (if attributable to al Qaeda) appears to have been intended to have similar political repercussions. A parliamentary inquiry into the failure of the intelligence services to detect and thwart the July 7 attack, while attributing the bombings to an Islamist motivation, was equivocal on the issue of whether al Qaeda was directly involved or even had prior knowledge of the plot. The submission to Parliament specifically rejected as unsupported a statement by Ayman al-Zawahiri claiming credit for the bombings. *Report into the London Terrorist Attacks on 7 July 2005*, Intelligence and Security Committee, The Rt. Hon. Paul Murphy, MP, Chairman (Crown Copyright 2006), pp. 8–13, 27–28.

9. In a 1998 interview, bin Laden stated, "We have seen in the last decade the decline of the American government and the weakness of the American soldier who is ready to wage Cold Wars and unprepared to fight long wars. This was proven in Beirut when the Marines fled after two explosions. It also proves that they can run in less than 24 hours, and this was also repeated in Somalia." John Miller, "To Terror's Source: John Miller's 1998 Interview with Osama Bin Laden," quoted in Mary Habeck, *Knowing the Enemy: Jihadist Ideology and the War on Terror* (New Haven: Yale University Press, 2006), 168.

10. "And kill them wherever you find them, and drive them out from whence they drove you out, and persecution is severer than slaughter, and do not fight with them at the Sacred Mosque until they fight with you in it, but if they do fight you, then slay them; such is the recompense of the unbelievers." Q. 2:191. "Fight those who do not believe in Allah, nor in the latter day, nor do they prohibit what Allah and His Apostle have prohibited, nor follow the religion of truth, out of those who have been given the Book, until they pay the tax in acknowledgment of superiority and they are in a state of subjection." Q. 9:29. "O you who believe! do not take for intimate friends from among others than your own people; they do not fall short of inflicting loss upon you; they love what distresses you; vehement hatred has already appeared from out of their mouths, and what their breasts conceal is greater still...." Q: 3:118. "We will cast terror into the hearts of those who disbelieve, because they set up with Allah that for which He has sent down no authority, and their abode is the fire, and evil is the abode of the unjust." Q: 3:151. Cf. Deuteronomy 13:12–16 ("If you hear that in one of the towns...certain men...have led their fellow-citizens astray, saying 'let us go and serve other gods,'...it is your duty to look into the matter....If it's proved and confirmed that such a hateful thing has taken place among you, you must put the inhabitants of that town to the sword destroying it utterly and everything it contains....[A]ll its spoil you shall gather in the middle of its square, and then you shall burn in flames the city and its spoil, and it shall be come a ruin, never to be rebuilt.").

11. "There is no compulsion in religion." Q. 2:256. "You shall have your religion and I shall have my religion." Q. 109:6.

12. Sayyid Qutb, while the most incisive of the jihadi theorists, owed a large intellectual debt to others, particularly Ibn Taymiyya, the thirteenth century Muslim jurist who sought to purify Islam in the face of Mongol subjugation, Hassan al-Banna, the founder of the Muslim Brotherhood, and Sayyid Abul A'la Mawdudi,

the founder of Jamaat i-Islami, the largest Islamic party in Pakistan. Together with their shared conception of jihad, all four men were virulently anti-Semitic. A hadith (saying) attributed to the Prophet Muhammad is frequently recited by bin Laden: "The Hour will not come until the Muslims fight the Jews and kill them. When a Jew hides behind a rock or a tree, it will say: 'O Muslim, O Servant of God! There is a Jew behind me, come and kill him.'" See, e.g., "Terror for Terror," October 21, 2001, al-Jazeera interview with bin Laden, in *Messages to the World,* supra 125.

13. Sheikh Azzam, a Palestinian member of the Jordanian Muslim Brotherhood, collaborated with bin Laden in establishing the Afghan Service Bureau in 1984, a major conduit of fighters and materiel to the Afghan resistance. Azzam, a thoroughly educated scholar of Islamic law, was bin Laden's earliest mentor and spiritual adviser. Azzam, however, did not share bin Laden's enthusiasm for jihad against other Muslims, nor did he approve of the use of terrorism. In 1989, Azzam was killed by a car bomb while driving to a mosque in Peshawar, perhaps at the instigation of Zawahiri, or even bin Laden himself, although the truth is not known. Bin Laden blames the assassination on "Israel, in collusion with some of its Arab agents." See "A Muslim Bomb," December 1998 al-Jazeera interview with bin Laden, in *Messages to the World,* supra 77.

14. Steve Coll, *Ghost Wars* (New York: Penguin Press, 2004), 383.

15. Jihad is susceptible of two meanings. The Prophet Muhammad is said to have distinguished the "greater jihad"—"the struggle within one's soul," from the "lesser jihad"—the striving or fighting with unbelievers. Jihadists regard this hadith as a spurious invention, although it is consistently cited by mainstream Muslims who oppose jihadist methods.

16. "Any system in which the final decisions are referred to human beings, and in which the sources of all authority are human, deifies human beings by designating others than God as lords over men.... [T]o proclaim the authority and sovereignty of God means to eliminate all human kingship and to announce the rule of the Sustainer of the universe over the entire earth." Sayyid Qutb, *Milestones,* quoted in Mary Habeck, *Knowing the Enemy,* supra 62.

17. Sayyid Qutb, *In the Shade of the Qur'an,* quoted in Richard Bonney, *Jihad: From Qur'an to bin Laden* (Basingstoke: Palgrave, 2004), 219.

18. Qutb rejected the idea of jihad as limited to the defense of the Muslim community against external attack. He defined jihad instead as a call to unremitting warfare against the forces of unbelief in order to "open the nations for Islam." In traditional Islamic teaching, offensive jihad is understood as a collective duty exercised only at the direction of a legitimate political authority acting to defend Muslim territory from aggression.

19. While the population of the developed world has remained essentially stable at slightly more than a billion persons since 1950 and will rise at most to approximately 1.2 billion persons by 2050, population in the less-developed countries has soared from 1.4 billion persons in 1950 to 5.3 billion today and will reach nearly 8 billion persons by the middle of this century. Put in a different perspective, during the century ending in 2050, nearly 99 percent of the growth in the world's population will have taken place in the developing world. One consequence of this explosive growth in population has been the outward migration of economically marginalized young people toward Europe and North America. (According to one

estimate, the number of young Arab men with no prospect of real employment in their countries of birth is expected to exceed 50 million during the next two decades.) Muslims now constitute the majority of newly arrived immigrants in most Western European countries, including Belgium, France, Germany, and the Netherlands and are the largest immigrant group in the United Kingdom. Contrary to expectations, many children of Muslim immigrants reject the values of their adopted countries. For these young people, Islamist teachings offer a traditionalist alternative to the alien and threatening secularized society of the West—with its social and legal constructs promoting or tolerating the separation of church and state, the equality of women, capitalism, sexual permissiveness, and a consumer culture.

20. "Al-Qaeda today is no longer best conceived of as an organization, a network, or even a network-of-networks. Rather, by leveraging new information and communication technologies, al-Qaeda has transformed itself into an organic social movement, making its virulent ideology accessible to anyone with a computer." Jarret M. Brachman, "High-Tech Terror: Al-Qaeda's Use of New Technology," *The Fletcher Forum of World Affairs* 30, no. 2 (Summer 2006): 149.

21. "What al Qaeda wants, simply, is a tool to kill as many non-Muslims— Americans, Britons, Catholics, Jews, Christians generally, Israelis, and others—as possible in one stroke. It does not require symmetrical mushroom clouds or sophisticated intercontinental delivery systems, although it would take either. What al Qaeda wants is a high body count as soon as possible, and it will use whatever [mass destruction] materials it gets in ways that will ensure the most corpses." Michael Scheuer, *Through Our Enemies' Eyes: Osama bin Laden, Radical Islam, and the Future of America* (Washington, DC: Potomac Books, 2006), 198.

22. Bin Laden acknowledged the sensitivity of the issue among Muslims in taking credit for the September 11 attacks. "They say that the killing of innocents is wrong and invalid, and for proof, they say that the Prophet forbade the killing of children and women, and that is true.... [B]ut this forbidding of killing children and innocents is not set in stone, and there are other writings that uphold it." "Terror for Terror," October 21, 2001, al-Jazeera interview with bin Laden, in *Messages to the World*, supra 118. This argument is not complete sophistry on bin Laden's part. "Islamic law, unlike Western laws of war, does not recognize noncombatants per se as inviolable. While all those whom it is forbidden to harm are noncombatants, not all noncombatants are immune from harm by virtue of that status. The reasoning behind refraining from unnecessarily killing a noncombatant is more in line with the general principle of not causing unnecessary damage and not destroying what may be the spoils of war and hence the property of the Muslims...." Shmuel Bar, *Warrant for Terror: The Fatwas of Radical Islam and the Duty to Jihad* (Lanham, MD: Rowman & Littlefield, 2006), 47.

23. See Michael Scheuer, *Imperial Hubris: Why the West Is Losing the War on Terror* (Washington, DC: Potomac Books, 2005), 154–56.

24. "To the Americans," October 14, 2002, bin Laden Internet posting, in *Messages to the World*, supra 164–65. Bin Laden's epistle to the Americans also references, among other American flaws, debauchery, homosexuality, fornication, alcohol, gambling, usury, Jewish domination of the economy and the media, incest, the emancipation of women, AIDS (said to be an American invention),

environmental pollution, and lack of manners. "It is saddening to tell you that you are the worst civilization witnessed in the history of mankind." Ibid., 166–68.

25. VX is the most lethal of the V-series (skin penetrating) nerve agents developed at the U.S. Army's Edgewood Arsenal in the 1950s. VX has three times the toxicity of sarin when inhaled and a thousand times that of sarin when absorbed through the skin. One liter of VX contains a sufficient number of doses to kill 1 million persons. VX is essentially a compound distilled from phosphorous and sulfur. The production of VX is complex, requiring four separate reactions each of which yields progressively more volatile and corrosive compounds. See Jonathan B. Tucker, *War of Nerves: Chemical Warfare from World War I to al-Qaeda* (New York: Pantheon Books, 2006), 158–59.

26. An entire volume of al Qaeda's *Encyclopedia of Jihad* is devoted to methods of producing chemical and biological weapons.

27. Sarin is one of the G-series (respiratory) nerve agents discovered by German scientists at IG Farben in the search for more powerful pesticides. The G-series consists of a cyanide or fluorine base mixed with organophosphorous compounds. The German inventors gave the original GA-series agent the name Tabun. In the manufacture of sarin, methylphosphenic dichloride, a chemical intermediately derived from phosphorus is reacted with hydrogen fluoride gas to produce a mixture of dichlor and difluor, which is then combined with isopropyl alcohol to produce sarin. The process is complex and highly dangerous as the Aum Shinrikyo cult discovered. Breathing air containing 1 part per million of sarin for ten minutes causes death. The manufacturing process also involves a high risk of explosion. Soman (GD in the series) substitutes a more complex alcohol for isopropyl, which doubles sarin's potency. See generally Tucker, *War of Nerves*, supra 24–41, 105–106, 122–123, 130–139.

28. Tucker, *War of Nerves*, supra 368; Coll, *Ghost Wars*, supra 487–88.

29. The Matsumoto attack resulted in 7 deaths and more than 200 injuries. The attack on the Tokyo subway caused 12 deaths and several thousand injuries. Despite the construction of a sophisticated laboratory staffed by highly motivated scientists, it took Aum Shinrikyo some two years to prepare for the Tokyo attack. The subway death toll would, however, have been far greater had not the cult leader, Shoko Asahara, rushed the distillation and deployment of the cult's stock of sarin in fear of an imminent police raid. Tucker, *War of Nerves*, supra 333–49.

30. One useful way of putting the lethality of biological weapons in perspective is by considering the following formula. The assured killing of 50 percent of the population in an area of 120 square kilometers would require 1 million tons of TNT, 160 metric tons of sarin gas, 1 megaton of uranium-235, but only 6.5 kilograms of anthrax.

31. As with the manufacture of chemical weapons, the fabrication of a biological weapon requires a sophisticated and controlled laboratory setting that is difficult to envision along the northwest frontier of Pakistan where bin Laden and the remnants of his entourage are hiding. The only documented instance of a bacterial attack by nonstate terrorists occurred in 1984 in a small town in Oregon. A transplanted Indian religious cult poisoned salad bars in local restaurants with Salmonella in an unsuccessful effort to influence the outcome of a municipal election. Some 750 people were infected, although none fatally. See Judith Miller, Stephen Engleberg, and

William Broad, *Germs: Biological Weapons and America's Secret War* (New York: Simon & Schuster 2001), 15–33.

32. The known living specimens of variola are in the possession of the Centers for Disease Control and the Russian Vector Institute.

33. Evidence collected in Afghanistan points to al Qaeda attempts to cultivate bubonic plague and botulinum toxin. Traces of anthrax experimentation were also discovered at several al Qaeda sites, including a partially constructed laboratory designed as a production facility near Khandahar. The mailings in 2001 to the Senate office buildings in Washington, D.C., is the only known instance in which a private individual or group has attacked a general civilian population with (possibly) weaponized anthrax.

34. There is reliable evidence that bin Laden attempted to buy a Russian nuclear warhead on the black market in the early 1990s. Scheuer, *Through Our Enemies' Eyes,* supra 133–34, 200–202; Graham Allison, *Nuclear Terrorism: The Ultimate Preventable Catastrophe* (New York: Times Books, 2004), 27.

35. Lebed's missing weapons claim appears to have been the product of misinformation, although Graham Allison corroborates Lebed's assertion that many Soviet nuclear devices were built without permissive action links. See Allison, *Nuclear Terrorism,* supra 90.

36. Delivery is a relatively easy problem to solve as only a small percentage of international container traffic is inspected on departure or entry to American and European ports.

37. Materials found in abandoned al Qaeda safe houses in Afghanistan discuss the making of nuclear weapons, although in crude terms. Allison, *Nuclear Terrorism,* supra 26.

38. In its natural form uranium consists of two principal isotopes, uranium-238 and a minute quantity, roughly 0.7 percent, of uranium-235. Uranium-238 is not a fissile material, but it is a fertile isotope from which plutonium-239 can be bred or uranium-235 extracted. Uranium-235 is one of only two fissile isotopes that occur naturally on earth (the other being tritium, a gaseous isotope of hydrogen that is used in the production of thermonuclear weapons). Enrichment is accomplished by gasifying uranium-238, spinning it in a high-speed centrifuge, and siphoning off the infinitesimally lighter weight uranium-235. Because the difference in the two elements involves only a minute number of particles, the process is slow. Fifteen hundred centrifuges working in tandem on a twenty-four hour basis would require a year to produce a sufficient quantity of uranium-235 to build a single bomb. Even for States willing to make the enormous investment required, there is no guarantee of success, as Saddam Hussein proved despite a fruitless expenditure of a billion dollars or more. Plutonium-239 is a synthetic element typically extracted as a waste product from a nuclear reactor's spent fuel rods. Reprocessing spent fuel rods is a more complex task than refining uranium-235, although India, which has only a small supply of natural uranium, successfully produced a sufficient quantity of plutonium-239 to build a significant nuclear arsenal. The North Korean nuclear program is also plutonium based.

39. Much of what is accurately described as enriched uranium is not weapons-grade material. Reactor grade fuel, which can be purchased commercially, is typically 2 to 5 percent enriched, a level insufficient for the construction of a detonable

device. While it might be possible to build an explodable device with fissile material as little as 20 percent pure, a 90- to 93-percent enrichment rate is the preferred military grade.

40. Chechen secessionists planted a dirty bomb made up of dynamite and Cesium-137 in Moscow's Ismailovsky Park in 1995, but alerted a Russian television station to its location before exploding it. Allison, *Nuclear Terrorism,* supra 31.

41. Why al Qaeda has not yet attempted to detonate a dirty bomb is something of a mystery. Still, from a counterterrorism perspective, it makes more sense to focus resources on plausible threats from conventional weapons like dirty bombs and on the securing of high-value targets like nuclear stations and chemical plants than on the averting of implausible scenarios involving nuclear weapons or attacks on the food chain.

42. While some 25 separate crimes are considered criminal offenses under international law, the development and acquisition of weapons of mass destruction is not among them. Barry Kellman, "WMD Proliferation: An International Crime?," *The Nonproliferation Review* (Summer 2001): 93.

43. The 1977 Geneva Protocols I and II sought to extend Geneva Convention protections to "armed conflicts in which peoples are fighting against colonial domination and alien occupation and against racist regimes in the exercise of their right of self-determination," as well as to civilians caught up in internal civil conflicts. The Protocols have been rejected by the United States and many other Western countries for fear that their broad definition of the right to self-determination might be used as a justification for terrorist acts.

44. The Biological Weapons Convention prohibits the development, production, or stockpiling of biological agents and delivery systems that have no peaceful purpose. States are also required to destroy all weaponized biological agents. Article IV of the Convention requires State parties to prohibit the development of biological weapons by persons within their territorial jurisdiction. The Convention, however, has no enforcement protocol.

45. The Chemical Weapons Convention expands on the Geneva Protocol by imposing a complete ban on the development, production, and stockpiling of chemical weapons. It also requires signatory States to destroy existing stockpiles of chemical weapons over time and to dismantle production facilities or convert them to peaceful uses.

46. India, Pakistan, Israel, and North Korea, among others, are not signatories to the Nuclear Nonproliferation Treaty.

47. In a similar vein, many of the chemicals scheduled under the Chemical Weapons Convention are of a dual-use nature.

48. Bosco, "An Indefinable Problem," supra 47.

49. Ibid., 45. The United States Code, 18 U.S.C. § 2331, similarly defines international terrorism to mean "activities that—(A) involve violent acts or acts dangerous to human life that are a violation of the criminal laws of the United States or of any State, or that would be a criminal violation if committed within the jurisdiction of the United States or of any State; (B) appear to be intended—(i) to intimidate or coerce a civilian population; (ii) to influence the policy of a government by intimidation or coercion; or (iii) to affect the conduct of a government by mass destruction,

assassination, or kidnapping; and (C) occur primarily outside the territorial jurisdiction of the United States."

50. The Security Council on October 8, 2004, adopted Resolution 1566 "recalling" that "criminal acts, including against civilians, committed with the intent to cause death or serious bodily injury, or taking of hostages, with the purpose to provoke a state of terror in the general public or in a group of persons or particular persons, intimidate a population or compel a government or an international organization to do or to abstain from doing any act, which constitute offences within the scope of and as defined in the international conventions and protocols relating to terrorism, are under no circumstances justifiable by considerations of a political, philosophical, ideological, racial, ethnic, religious or other similar nature." By limiting the definition to terrorist crimes defined under international conventions and protocols, the Security Council in effect gutted the more expansive Russian proposal.

51. Adam Roberts, "The 'War on Terror' in Historical Perspective," *Survival* 47, no. 2 (Summer 2005): 103.

52. See Bosco, "An Indefinable Problem," supra 48.

53. Only three prosecutions were brought under these statutes from the time they were enacted through the 1980s. The author of this chapter brought two of the three prosecutions.

54. In some cases the executive will simply act unilaterally as President Bush did in early 2002 by issuing a secret Presidential order authorizing the National Security Agency (NSA) to conduct surveillance of communications inside the United States without a warrant. The Administration insists that NSA surveillance is limited to calls originating from or placed to a party overseas and to international transit traffic. (A substantial portion of international telephone traffic, whether or not originating from or directed to the United States, passes through U.S.–based switching stations, as does most of the world's e-mail.) After the NSA initiative was exposed, Attorney General Alberto Gonzalez presented a brief to Congress attempting to provide legal justification for the spying program. See U.S. Department of Justice, *Legal Authorities Supporting the Activities of the National Security Agency Described by the President,* January 19, 2006. Gonzalez's principal argument is that as Commander in Chief of the Armed Forces, the President has an inherent Article II power to conduct warrantless surveillance of enemy forces for intelligence purposes, a grant of authority allegedly affirmed by Congress in the Authorization for Use of Military Force (AUMF) enacted in the wake of 9/11. As explained by Justice Jackson in his concurring opinion in *Youngstown Sheet & Tube Co. v. Sawyer,* 343 U.S. 579 (1952), the President's authority is at its zenith when he is acting in accordance with Congressional authorization, at its intermediate strength when he acts on his own authority in the absence of a denial or grant of power by Congress, and at its lowest ebb when he acts in a manner incompatible with laws enacted by Congress. While Gonzalez contended that the NSA authorization falls into the first category (citing Franklin Roosevelt's authorization of the warrantless surveillance of persons suspected of subversive activity during World War II), the argument is difficult to square with the intervening enactment by Congress in 1978 of the Foreign Intelligence Surveillance Act (FISA), which was intended to restrict and regulate intelligence-related domestic surveillance. Gonzalez also cited several expansive references to the AUMF in *Hamdi v. Rumsfeld,* 542 U.S. 507 (2004), as supporting the detention of U.S.

citizens as enemy combatants, although with only an oblique reference to Justice O'Connor's cautions that "[w]e have long since made clear that a state of war is not a blank check for the President when it comes to the rights of the Nation's citizens," and that in times of conflict the Constitution "most assuredly envisions a role for all three branches when individual liberties are at stake." Ibid., 536.

55. The legal responses of France, Spain, and the United Kingdom, as well as that of the European community in general, to post–World War II terrorism are sketched in Jeremie J. Wattellier, "Comparative Legal Responses to Terrorism: Lessons from Europe," 27 *Hastings International and Comparative Law Review* (Winter 2004): 397–408.

56. The Oklahoma City bombing and Aum Shinrikyo attack on the Tokyo subway system in 1995 raised the profile of the threat of terrorism and led Congress the following year to enact the Antiterrorism and Effective Death Penalty Act, which as its names implies, was a hotchpotch piece of legislation. Among other measures, the Act restricts habeas corpus, streamlines the deportation of alien criminals, and enhances and broadens the penalties for terrorist crimes. The Defense Against Weapons of Mass Destruction Act of 1996, although less noticed, for the first time attempted to address in a legal context the threat posed by chemical, biological, and nuclear weapons. Within six weeks of September 11, Congress rushed into law the USA Patriot Act of 2001, adopting a number of measures, some constructive and long overdue, others superfluous or of questionable utility. The principal provisions of the Patriot Act eliminated legal barriers, including grand jury secrecy rules, that restricted the sharing of information between law enforcement and intelligence agencies; granted permission to domestic law enforcement to make broader use of evidence gathered under FISA surveillance warrants; authorized court-approved roving wiretaps and the monitoring of e-mail and Internet usage; stiffened regulations involving money laundering while granting law enforcement agencies greater access to private bank records; and permitted the seven-day detention without formal charges of noncitizen aliens suspected of having terrorist ties. Its most controversial provisions expanded the definition of "terrorist group" to include any group that engages in violence or the destruction of property (a definition that covers any number of groups that have no connection to foreign terrorism) and broadened the authority of law enforcement agencies to obtain business and other private records of citizens without any showing of cause or prior judicial approval. To be fair, as Ackerman notes, legislation enacted in Britain after the September 11 attacks on the United States and the July 2005 London bombings "makes the Patriot Act seem mild by comparison." *Before the Next Attack,* supra 69.

57. Walter Laqueur, "The Terrorism to Come," *Policy Review* (August/ September 2004): 59.

58. See Philip B. Heymann, *Terrorism, Freedom and Security: Winning Without War* (Cambridge, MA: The MIT Press, 2003).

59. The metaphor of war, as Bruce Ackerman points out, also creates a particular complication in the legal context because unlike classic wars, a war on terrorism has no defined end. Unlike the prisoner of war who under the Geneva Conventions is to be repatriated at the conclusion of hostilities, a terrorist "enemy combatant" could conceivably be detained indefinitely. Ackerman, *Before the Next Attack,* supra 6.

60. The traditional IRA arguably fell in this category. In the author's experience as a terrorism prosecutor, an active service member of the IRA could on the assurances of the leadership be put at liberty pending trial without concern that the member would engage in further violations of the law or fail to appear for trial and (if convicted) sentencing. There was, in other words, an acceptance on the part of the IRA of the rules of the game.

61. The arrest of Shoko Asahara, the charismatic leader of Aum Shinrikyo, effectively extinguished the cult. The same fate befell the Branch Davidians when David Koresh was killed during the FBI siege of his Waco, Texas, compound.

62. Shortly after being sentenced, Moussaoui filed a motion with the court seeking to withdraw his guilty plea, stating that he had lied in claiming to have been a part of the September 11 conspiracy.

63. The post–September 11 record of the Department of Justice in prosecuting terrorism cases in the civil courts is not strong. Although there have been some convictions of genuine significance, many have involved relatively minor offenses involving immigration violations and the possession of fraudulent documents. Several high-profile cases, such as the one brought against José Padilla, who was initially alleged to have plotted with al Qaeda to detonate a dirty bomb, have either resulted in acquittals, or in the case of Padilla, in a marked downward ratcheting of the charges.

64. R. F. Foster, *Modern Ireland 1600–1972* (London: Penguin Press, 1988). The story of the rise of the Provisional IRA as the heir to Irish republican fundamentalism is more colorfully told in Patrick Bishop and Eamonn Mallie, *The Provisional IRA* (London: Corgi Books, 1987).

65. The name is associated with that of Lord Diplock, the Law Lord who chaired a specially created "Commission to consider legal procedures to deal with terrorist activities in Northern Ireland." The Diplock Commission's recommendations were adopted in their entirety by the British government as part of the Northern Ireland (Emergency Provisions) Act of 1973.

66. See Ackerman, *Before the Next Attack,* supra 77–100.

67. While less exciting than an emergency constitution, there is some assurance to be taken from Justice O'Connor's plurality opinion in *Hamdi v. Rumsfeld,* 542 U.S. 507 (2004), that a mixed federal court-military tribunal solution would comport with the existing Constitution. Ibid., 533–34, 538. In *Hamdan v. Rumsfeld,* 126 S. Ct. 2749 (2006), the Supreme Court strongly indicated that it would find a tribunal system based on the Uniform Code of Military Justice and the Geneva Conventions constitutional.

68. See *Terminiello v. City of Chicago,* 337 U.S. 1, 37 (1949) (Jackson, J., dissenting).

CHAPTER 8

1. I should like to thank the Leverhulme Trust for the award of a Research Fellowship in support of this work.

2. Franz Kafka, *The Trial* [1925], in *The Collected Novels of Franz Kafka,* trans. Willa and Edwin Muir (London: Penguin, 1988), 9. This is the celebrated opening sentence.

3. Kafka, *The Trial,* 117.

4. In Agamben's recent work the measures passed in the United States in the wake of 9/11 are explicitly used to illustrate these propositions. Giorgio Agamben, *Homo Sacer,* trans. Daniel Heller-Roazen (Stanford, CA: Stanford University Press, 1998), 168–69; *State of Exception,* trans. Kevin Athill (Stanford, CA: Stanford University Press, 2005), 3–4. See also the sympathetic discussion in Judith Butler, *Precarious Life* (London: Verso, 2004), 60ff.

5. The gulag analogy was made by Irene Khan, Secretary General of Amnesty International, in a speech at the Foreign Press Association introducing a damning report on the United States, *Guantánamo and Beyond: The Continuing Pursuit of Unchecked Executive Power* (2005): "Guantánamo has become the gulag of our times, entrenching the notion that people can be detained without any recourse to the law." The speech is available at http://t2web.amnesty.r3h.net/library/print/ ENGPOL100142005 (accessed July 5, 2005). It was widely reported, and bitterly resented, in Washington.

6. Franz Kafka, "In the Penal Settlement" [1919], in *Metamorphosis and Other Stories,* trans. Willa & Edwin Muir (Harmondsworth, Middlesex, United Kingdom: Penguin, 1961), 169–99.

7. On the "alliance of values" in this context, see Alex Danchev, "'I'm With You.' Tony Blair and the Obligations of Alliance: Anglo-American Relations in Historical Perspective," in *Iraq and the Vietnam Syndrome,* ed. Lloyd Gardner and Marilyn Young (New York: New Press, forthcoming).

8. Kafka to Felice, 25 March 1914 and 3 March 1915, in Franz Kafka, *Letters to Felice,* trans. James Stern and Elizabeth Duckworth (Harmondsworth, Middlesex, United Kingdom: Penguin, 1978), 507, 574.

9. Kafka, "Penal Settlement," 169. Perhaps self-servingly, both Lynndie England and Charles Graner, who passed her the leash, are at pains to emphasize the docility of the detainee. See "The Abu Ghraib Files" on *Salon.com,* incorporating new documentary evidence from the U.S. Army's Criminal Investigation Command (CID) investigations in 2004–2005 at http://www.salon.com/news/abu_ghraib/2006/03/ 14/ (accessed March 24, 2006).

10. Adam Zagorin and Michael Duffy, "Inside the Interrogation of Detainee 063," *Time,* June 20, 2005. The full interrogation log for the period November 23, 2002 to January 11, 2003, is at http://www.time.com/time/2006/log/log.pdf (accessed April 3, 2006).

11. "AR 15-6 Investigation into FBI Allegations of Detainee Abuse at Guantánamo Bay, Cuba, Detention Facility," April 1, 2005 (amended June 9, 2005), http://www.humanrightsfirst.org (accessed March 24, 2006) [hereafter Schmidt Report].

12. Interrogators' professional taste in music is best described as eclectic. Al-Qahtani was also treated to "Enter Sandman" by the heavy-metal band Metallica (said to have reduced him to tears because he thought he was hearing the sound of Satan). The rap artist Eminem is another favorite (*Slim Shady,* Interscope, 1999). Christina Aguilera for her part turns out to be peculiarly appropriate. "I won't let you break me, think what you want/To all my dreamers out there I'm with you/All my underdogs I feel you/Lift your head high and stay strong keep pushin' on" (*Stripped,* RCA, 2002).

13. Zagorin and Duffy, quoted in "Detainee 063." As the Schmidt Report recounts, in the wake of the Abu Ghraib scandal, the FBI began an internal investigation to determine whether its agents had observed "aggressive treatment" of detainees at Guantánamo during the period September 2001 to July 2004. A total of 493 agents were contacted by e-mail, and 434 responded; 26 of these stated that they had. The allegations were disclosed in December 2004 as a result of releases under the Freedom of Information Act. Typically, it was the disclosure, rather than the allegations (or the activities themselves), that prompted the inquiry.

14. George Bush, "Humane Treatment of al Qaeda and Taliban detainees," February 7, 2002, in *The Torture Papers,* ed. Karen J. Greenberg and Joshua Dratel (New York: Cambridge University Press, 2005), 134–35. The Third Geneva Convention flatly prohibits "any form of coercion" of POWs in interrogation—the most protective standard of treatment found in international law.

15. "AR 15-6 Investigation of the 800th Military Police Brigade" [hereafter Taguba Report], March 2004, *Torture Papers,* 405–556.

16. Conversation with Seymour Hersh, October 20, 2005; "Abu Ghraib Files." Hersh was instrumental in the Taguba Report being made public—like most of the others, it was intended to be an internal inquiry—and the first to underline its severity. See Seymour Hersh, *Chain of Command* (London: Penguin, 2005), 22ff.

17. "It was a kind of 'Animal House' on the night shift," a remark by the former Secretary of Defense James Schlesinger, chairman of the so-called Independent Panel on DoD detention operations, was made at the news conference on the release of their report. *Guardian,* August 25, 2004. "Specific intent" is one of the most egregious arguments in the notorious "torture memo" from the Assistant Attorney General, Jay S. Bybee, to Alberto R. Gonzales, then Counsel to the President, August 1, 2002, "Standards of Conduct for Interrogation under 18 USC 2340-2340A," *Torture Papers,* 172–217, esp. 174–75, a memo written "as an immunity, a blank check," as one insider has said. Jane Mayer, "A Deadly Interrogation," *New Yorker,* November 14, 2005. The torture memo was silently rescinded and replaced by the Office of Legal Counsel in December 2004, shortly before Gonzales's confirmation hearings as Attorney General. The replacement memo has been described as "the minimum possible retraction" by David Luban, "Liberalism, Torture, and the Ticking Bomb," in *The Torture Debate in America,* ed. Karen J. Greenberg (New York: Cambridge University Press, 2006), 59–62, 72.

18. Schmidt Report, p. 20. The report also notes that the Commander's testimony that he was unaware of the creative approaches taken in the interrogation was inconsistent with his assurance to superiors that the interrogation plan had been approved and was being followed "relentlessly" by his command.

19. The report on DoD interrogation operations by the Naval Inspector General, Vice Admiral Albert Church, states that such issues were addressed by the Independent Panel. In fact, they were specifically excluded from the Panel's terms of reference: "Issues of personal accountability will be resolved through established military justice and administrative procedures, although any information you may develop will be welcome." Secretary of Defense memo, May 12, 2004, *Torture Papers,* 961–62. Only the Executive Summary of the Church Report has been made public, http://www.defenselink.mil/news (accessed March 24, 2006); the Schlesinger Report is in *Torture Papers,* 08–75.

20. These are the "AR 15-6" investigations, governed by "Procedure for Investigating Officers and Boards of Officers," September 30, 1996, http://www.usma.edu/EO/regspubs/r15_6.pdf (accessed March 24, 2006). In at least two contentious cases, the investigating officer himself advised the need for a more senior appointment: Furlow begat Schmidt, Fay begat Jones. See "AR 15-6 Investigation of the Abu Ghraib Prison and 205th Military Intelligence Brigade" [hereafter Fay-Jones Report], August 2004, *Torture Papers*, 987–1131. On the problematic nature of the investigations in general, see Human Rights First, "Command's Responsibility: Detainee Deaths in US Custody in Iraq and Afghanistan," February 2006, http://www.humanrightsfirst.org (accessed March 24, 2006).

21. See Alex Danchev, "The Reckoning: Official Inquiries and the Iraq War," *Intelligence and National Security* 19 (2004): 436–66. Mark Danner makes a similar point about the torture inquiries. *Torture and Truth* (London: Granta, 2004), 40.

22. Agamben, *State of Exception*, 4.

23. The official discourse of the war on terror is hot on nonpersons of various stripes. "In addition to EPWs [Enemy Prisoners of War] and compliant, non-hostile CIs [civilian internees], units...were confronted with capturing...other classifications of detainees, such as non-state combatants and non-compliant CIs." Quoted in Human Rights First, "Command's Responsibility," 104.

24. Human Rights First, "Leadership Failure: Firsthand Accounts of Torture of Iraqi Detainees by the US Army's 82nd Airborne Division," September 2005, http://www.hrw.org (accessed March 24, 2006); excerpted in "Torture in Iraq," *New York Review of Books*, November 3, 2005.

25. See Fay-Jones Report, *Torture Papers*, 1030. The 1987 version of FM 34-52 is available at http://www.globalsecurity.org; the 1992 version at http://www.fas.org/irp/doddir/army/fm34-52.pdf (accessed April 3, 2006). The UCMJ applies to U.S. Forces on active duty, at all times and in all places. Article 93 addresses "Cruelty, Oppression or Maltreatment."

26. The techniques and the rationales are summarized and evaluated in the "Working Group Report on Detainee Interrogations in the Global War on Terrorism," April 6, 2003, *Torture Papers*, 340–59.

27. Abdul Rahim Muslim Dost, a poet, has written an account of his incarceration, *The Broken Chains* (forthcoming). *Guardian*, April 3, 2006. Moazzam Begg's account of a similar experience, *Enemy Combatant* (London: Free Press, 2006), is very wise on mutual incomprehension.

28. Church Report, 10; Schmidt Report, 20; JTF-GTMO, "Information from Guantánamo Detainees," March 4, 2005, http://www.jtfgtmo.southcom.mil/; Heather MacDonald, "How to Interrogate Terrorists," *Torture Debate*, 92.

29. "Person of the Week: Jose Padilla," *Time*, June 14, 2002. The Padilla case has been scrupulously examined by Human Rights First (HRF), http://www.humanrightsfirst.org/us_law/inthecourts/supreme_court_padilla.htm (accessed April 3, 2006). Those variously identified as "UBL bodyguards" would make a small army.

30. Anonymous MI officer, in Jane Mayer, "The Experiment," *New Yorker*, July 11 and 18, 2005.

31. Hersh, *Chain of Command*, 4; Jane Mayer, "Lost in the Jihad," *New Yorker*, March 10, 2003.

32. Rohan Gunaratna, in Mayer, "Lost in the Jihad."

33. Zagorin and Duffy, "Detainee 063." One of the claims made for the intelligence obtained from the interrogation of detainees is that *The 9/11 Commission Report* (New York: Norton, 2004) would have been impossible to compile without it; and that, by extension, it forms the basis for our understanding of that event, and the wider phenomenon of al Qaeda. This seems at once exaggerated and misleading—better understanding calls for patient detective work of a rather unassuming kind—though it is true that the Commission's reconstruction of the plot is underpinned in part by "intelligence reports on interrogations," notably the loquacious KSM. See, e.g., notes to chap. 7, 525–26.

34. The precepts are set out in Major General Geoffrey Miller, "Assessment of DoD Counterterrorism Interrogation and Detention Operations in Iraq" [hereafter Miller Report], September 2003, *Torture Papers*, 451–59.

35. Statement of Cofer Black, Joint Investigation into September 11, September 26, 2002, at http://www.fas.org/irp/congress/2002_hr/092602black.html (accessed April 6, 2006). He was discussing "choices made for us" in the area of "operational flexibility." Black was Director of the CIA's Counterterrorist Center (1999–2002). He is described by Richard Clarke as "a hard-charging, get-it-done kind of CIA officer who had proved himself in the back alleys of unsavoury places." *Against All Enemies* (New York: Free Press, 2004), 205.

36. John Reid, "20th Century Rules, 21st Century Conflict," April 3, 2006, http://www.mod.uk (accessed April 5, 2006). Reid felt the need to publish a clarification, emphasizing that he was not in favor of "legal exceptionalism." *Guardian*, April 5, 2006.

37. Christine Brooke-Rose, *Life, End Of* (Manchester, United Kingdom: Carcanet, 2006), 26.

38. These are the names used by prison personnel for the detainees who appear in the iconic photographs, available at http://www.guardian.co.uk/gall/0,8542,1211872,00.html, and exhibited at the International Centre of Photography in New York later in 2004, at http://www.icp.org/exhibitions/abu_ghraib/ (accessed January 4, 2005).

39. Eliot Weinberger, "What I Heard about Iraq," *London Review of Books*, February 3, 2005. Todd Brown was a Company Commander with the 4th Infantry Division. The account of a pseudonymous interrogator in Afghanistan verges on the same conclusion: Chris Mackey, with Greg Miller, *The Interrogator's War* (London: Murray, 2004). An unusually frank assessment by a senior British officer serving with the Coalition forces in Baghdad found that the U.S. Army's "cultural insensitivity, almost certainly inadvertent, arguably amounted to institutional racism." Brigadier Nigel Aylwin-Foster, "Changing the Army for Counterinsurgency Operations," *Military Review* 6 (2005): 3. The Director of the U.S. Army's School of Advanced Military Studies, who told the *Washington Post* that the Brigadier was "an insufferable British snob," said his remark had been made in the heat of the moment. *Guardian*, January 12, 2006.

40. JTF-J2 memo, "Request for approval of Counter-Resistance Strategies," October 1, 2002, *Torture Papers*, 227–28.

41. General Counsel memo, "Counter-Resistance Techniques," November 27, 2002 (approved December 2, 2002), *Torture Papers*, 236.

42. Jane Mayer, "The Memo," *New Yorker,* February 27, 2006. The reference is to a killing spree by U.S. Army soldiers in the Vietnamese hamlet of My Lai, in 1968, during a search-and-destroy mission in a Vietcong stronghold known as "Pinkville." The story was broken by the young Seymour Hersh.

43. Danner, *Torture and Truth,* 33. The author of the e-mail was Captain William Ponce. Colonel Steven Boltz was the Deputy Chief of Staff for Intelligence at Coalition headquarters in Baghdad. Ironically, he had been brought up on intelligence shortcomings in Vietnam, emphasized to him by his father. The plaintive call for effective interrogation techniques echoes the JIC's "last call" for any scraps of intelligence on WMD, for the famous British government dossier of September 2002.

44. Miller Report, *Torture Papers,* 451.

45. Detainee statement to CID, on the night of January 20, 2004, "Abu Ghraib Files," chap. 6.

46. Fay-Jones Report, *Torture Papers,* 1086; "Abu Ghraib Files," chap. 8. Sergeant Michael J. Smith and Sergeant Santos A. Cardona were eventually brought to trial (separately) in 2006. Smith came first; he was found guilty on most counts, but given a light sentence of six months. The proceedings were followed in detail by HRF, in an illuminating blog, at http://www.humanrightsfirst.org/blog/index. htm (accessed March 24, 2006).

47. Fay-Jones Report, *Torture Papers,* 1088.

48. Christopher Browning's classic study of Reserve Police Battalion 101, *Ordinary Men* (New York: Harper Perennial, 1992), asks why so many of those men became killers. There is no comparison in the enormity of the crimes; but there is a similar need to explore situation and motivation, conformity, and resistance. At Abu Ghraib and elsewhere, of course, there were ordinary women, too.

49. Fay-Jones Report, *Torture Papers,* 989.

50. Brian Ross and Richard Esposito, "CIA's Harsh Interrogation Techniques Described," November 18, 2005, http://abcnews.go.com/WNT/Investigation/story? id=1322866 (accessed April 5, 2006).

51. "Abu Ghraib Files," chap. 5. The story is told, anonymized, in the Fay-Jones Report, *Torture Papers,* 1056–58; and more fully in Mayer, "Deadly Interrogation." The homicide ruling was made by the Armed Forces Institute of Pathology.

52. This was Corporal Charles Graner, one of the ringleaders in the torture and abuse at Abu Ghraib, and Specialist Sabrina Harman. The images are in the "Abu Ghraib Files," chap. 5.

53. Lieutenant Colonel Steven Jordan, AR 15-6 investigation interview with Taguba, p. 133, at http://www.aclu.org/torturefoia/released/a53.pdf (accessed March 24, 2006). Jordan himself was one of those chiefly responsible for the lethal anarchy at Abu Ghraib; his testimony is often misleading and self-serving, as Taguba pointed out, but this particular exchange has the ring of truth. Cf. Taguba Report, *Torture Papers,* 440; Fay-Jones Report, *Torture Papers,* 1047–49.

54. Fay-Jones Report, *Torture Papers,* 1085–86. Kimbro's exemplary professionalism is recognized by both Fay-Jones and Taguba. He provided a number of statements to investigators and appeared as a witness at the trial of the Army dog-handler Michael J. Smith. For more of his testimony, see *Washington Post,* June 11, 2004.

55. Taguba Report, *Torture Papers*, 444.

56. The issue is aired more fully in the torture inquiries than in the WMD inquiries, though searching analysis is still lacking. See, e.g., Church Report, 11; Fay-Jones Report, *Torture Papers*, 1046, 1049, 1107; Schlesinger Report, *Torture Papers*, 940.

57. Cf. David Omand, "The Ethics of Using Secret Intelligence for Public Security," speech at Chatham House, March 28, 2006; and Paul R. Pillar, "Intelligence, Policy and the War in Iraq," *Foreign Affairs* (March/April 2006), http://www.foreignaffairs.org (accessed February 11, 2006).

58. Schmidt Report, 13; Working Group Report, *Torture Papers*, 357. Sleep deprivation, "physical training," and face or stomach slap were thought to pose similar problems.

59. The Church Report begins with a brief disquisition on interrogation and a potted history of policy development.

60. Samuel Beckett, *Eh, Joe* [1966], in *I Can't Go On, I'll Go On* (New York: Grove, 1976), 584.

61. Georg Christoph Lichtenberg, *The Waste Books,* trans. R.J. Hollingdale, (New York: NYRB, 2000), 204. From Notebook K, 1793–96.

62. Human Rights First, "Command's Responsibility," 1.

63. As appears to be the case with the rescue operation to free the British and Canadian peace activists, Norman Kember, James Loney, and Harmeet Singh Sooden, in Baghdad in March 2006.

64. Donald Rumsfeld, "The Unknown," *Pieces of Intelligence* (London: Simon & Schuster, 2003), 2.

65. Albert Camus, "Preface to Algerian Reports" [1958], *Resistance, Rebellion and Death,* trans. Justin O'Brien (London: Hamish Hamilton, 1961), 83.

66. *The Trial,* 147.

67. Walt Whitman, "Song of Myself," *Leaves of Grass* [1892] (Oxford: World's Classics, 1998), 48.

68. Walter Benjamin, "Franz Kafka" [1934], in *Selected Writings,* ed. Michael W. Jennings *et al.,* trans. Harry Zohn, vol. II, pt. 2 (Cambridge, MA: Harvard University Press, 2005), 808. See also Elias Canetti, *Kafka's Other Trial* [1969], in *Letters to Felice,* trans. Christopher Middleton, 64–66.

69. *The Trial,* 172.

CHAPTER 9

1. "The most important failure was one of imagination...Al Qaeda's new brand of terrorism presented challenges to US Governmental institutions that they were not well designed to meet." *The 9/11 Commission—Final Report of the National Commission on Terrorist Attacks Upon the United States,* July 2004, 9 (Executive Summary).

2. "Reports that say that something has not happened are always interesting to me, because as we know, there are known knowns; there are things we know we know. We also know there are known unknowns; that is to say we know there are some things we don't know. But there are also unknown unknowns, the ones we don't know we don't know. And if one looks throughout the history of our country and other free countries, it is the latter categories that tend to be the difficult ones."

U.S. Secretary of Defense Donald Rumsfeld, "US Department of Defense Press Briefing," February 12, 2002.

3. "The United States has a long history of defining internal threats as either foreign or domestic and assigning responsibility to the intelligence and law enforcement agencies accordingly. This division reflects a fundamental policy choice and is codified in law. For example, the National Security Act of 1947 precludes CIA from exercising any internal security or law enforcement powers. The Congressional investigations of the 1970s into the activities of the intelligence agencies, including their efforts to collect information regarding anti-Vietnam War activists and other 'radicals', reinforced the importance of this division in the minds of the Congress, the American public, and the agencies. The emergence in the 1990s of a threat posed by international terrorists who operate across national borders demanded huge changes in focus and approach from intelligence agencies traditionally organized and trained to operate primarily in either the United States or abroad. The legal authorities, operational policies and cultures that had molded agencies like CIA, NSA and the FBI for years had not responded to the 'globalization' of terrorism that culminated in the September 11 attacks in the United States." *Report Of The Joint Inquiry Into The Terrorist Attacks Of September 11, 2001—By The House Permanent Select Committee On Intelligence And The Senate Select Committee On Intelligence,* December 2002.

4. For example, R. Betts, "Surprise, Scholasticism and Strategy: A Review of Ariel Levite's Intelligence and Strategic Surprises," *International Studies Quarterly* 33, no. 3; and R. Betts and T. Mahnken, eds., *Paradoxes of Strategic Intelligence: Essays in Honor of Michael I. Handel* (Frank Cass: London, 2003).

5. The classic case being the failure of superefficient, successful IBM to realize the value of software and counter the rise of Microsoft

6. C. Christensen, *The Innovator's Dilemma* (London: Harper Business, 2003).

7. The management scientist Gary Hamel has commented that business innovations almost always happen "despite the system, not because of it."

8. Onora O'Neill, *A Question of Trust* (Cambridge: Cambridge University Press, 2002), 47.

9. Ibid.

10. Norman Dixon, *On the Psychology of Military Incompetence* (London: Pimlico, 1994).

CHAPTER 10

1. For a great assessment of the topic, see Ephraim Kam, *Surprise Attack. The Victim Perspective,* 2nd ed. (Cambridge: MA: Harvard University Press, 2004).

2. George Tsebelis, *Veto Players. How Political Institutions Work* (Princeton: Princeton University Press, 2002).

3. For the classical approach on intelligence as a bureaucratic process, see Graham Allison and Philip Zelikow, *Essence of Decision. Explaining the Cuban Missile Crisis,* 2nd ed. (New York: Longman, 1999), 199.

4. Christopher Coker, *Waging War Without Warriors: The Changing Culture of Military Conflict* (Boulder & London: Lynne Rienner Publishers, 2002), 5, 11.

5. Robert Cooper, *Breaking of Nations: Order and Chaos in Twentieth Century* (London: Atlantic Books, 2003).

6. See Adrian (Zeke) Wolfberg, "Investing in Social Capital of Knowledge," paper presented at the International Conference on Intelligence Analysis, McLean, Virginia, May 2–4, 2005, https://analysis.mitre.org/proceedings/Final_Papers_Files/20_Camera_Ready_Paper.pdf.

7. Gregory F. Treverton, *The Next Steps in Reshaping Intelligence* (Santa Monica, CA: RAND Corporation, 2005), 17.

8. Walter Laqueur, "The Question of Judgement: Intelligence and Medicine," *Journal of Contemporary History*, 18 (1983): 533–548.

9. Stephen Marrin, "Improving Intelligence Analysis and Its Incorporation into Policymaking: Lessons from the Medical Community." Paper presented at the Annual Convention of the International Studies Association, Montreal, Canada. March 17–20, 2004.

10. See, for instance, Gerard Alexander, "Institutions, Path Dependence, and Democratic Consolidation," *Journal of Theoretical Politics* 13, no. 3 (2001): 249–70.

11. Treverton, *The Next Steps in Reshaping Intelligence,* 19.

12. Simon Caulkin, "The New Avengers," *Management Today,* London, November 1995, 44.

13. K.R. Brousseau, and M.J. Driver, "Enhancing Informed Choice: A Career-Concepts Approach to Carreer Advisement," *Selections* 10, no. 3 (Spring 1994): 24–34.

14. George Maior and Sebastian Huluban, "From *Hardware* to *Software* Reforms in Romania's Civil Military Relations: The Policies of Personnel Management," *Baltic Defence Review* 2, no. 8 (2002): 103–23.

15. See, for instance, Colin S. Gray, "How Has War Changed Since the End of the Cold War?," *Parameters* XXXV, no. 1 (Spring 2005).

16. Hew Strachan, "The Lost Meaning of Strategy," *Survival* 47, no. 3 (Autumn 2005).

CHAPTER 11

1. Actually the number of previous exercises was somewhat less than 40 since some of the planned exercises were not carried out.

2. See I. Ben-Israel, "Philosophy and Methodology of Intelligence: The Logic of Estimate Process," *Intelligence and National Security* 4, no. 4 (October 1989): 660–718; and Isaac Ben-Israël, *Philosophie du Renseignement* (Paris-Tel Aviv: editions de l'eclat, 2004).

3. Roberta Wohlstetter in her classic book, *Pearl Harbor: Warning and Decision* (Stanford, CA: Stanford University Press, 1962), attributes the failure to the fact that the American intelligence was attracted by "noise" (that is, unimportant reports) that covered the real "signals." However, it is clear that there was a problem there of selection and interpretation, and not lack of sufficient information.

4. For an excellent treatment of these psychological factors, see R.J. Heuer, Jr., *Psychology of Intelligence Analysis* (Washington, DC: Center for the Study of Intelligence, Central Intelligence Agency, 1999).

5. But then one must add "groupthink" to the list of psychological pitfalls of which one should be aware.

6. See *Report of the Select Committee on Intelligence on the United States Intelligence Community's Prewar Intelligence Assessments on Iraq* (Washington, DC: U.S. Senate, July 9, 2004).

7. See, for example, "The 9-11 Commission Report," *Final Report of the National Commission on Terrorist Attacks upon the United States* (Washington, DC: Official Government Edition, 2004).

8. This follows the late philosopher Sir Karl Popper, especially in his books *Logic of Scientific Discovery* (London: Hutchinson and Co., 1959); and *Conjectures and Refutation—The Growth of Scientific Knowledge* (London: Routledge & Kegan Paul, 1962).

9. There is a certain analogy of this logic with what happens in biological evolution: first, mutations are created randomly, and then, only those mutations that are compatible with the environment survive.

10. Elsewhere I have called this the "Amended Critical Methodology." See Ben-Israel, "Philosophy and Methodology of Intelligence."

11. To put it shortly, to estimate is to create and falsify competing alternative hypotheses.

12. In real life, it is seldom the case that we have only two potential explanations (that is, conjectures, hypotheses, and alternatives) for a certain observed phenomenon. Full analysis should take all these options into consideration. The analysis is more simplistic and was used only to demonstrate the power of the proposed methodology. A fuller and more accurate analysis of the Yom-Kippur case can be found in Ben-Israel, "Philosophy and Methodology of Intelligence."

13. For a fuller treatment of deception using my proposed method, see Ben-Israël, *Philosophie du Renseignement.*

14. See, for example, the Duelfer Report, *Comprehensive Report of the Special Advisor to the DCI on Iraq's WMD,* September 30, 2004), http://www.cia.gov/cia/reports/iraq_wmd_2004/; and the Senate *Report of the Select Committee on Intelligence* ; and the Butler Report, *Review of Intelligence on Weapons of Mass Destruction—Report of a Committee of Privy Counsellors* (London, The Stationary Office: July 14, 2004).

15. In the words of the Carnegie Report, "In the Iraqi case, the world's three best intelligence services—those of the United States, Great Britain, and Israel—proved unable to provide the accurate information necessary for acting in the absence of imminent threat." See J. Crincione, J. Tuchman Mathews, G. Perkovich, with Alexix Orton, *WMD in Iraq: Evidence and Implications* (Washington, DC: Carnegie Endowment Report for International Peace, January 2004), 61.

16. This is not a hypothetical statement. It was my actual assessment, suggested to Israel Air Force Intelligence, in February 2003, prior to the war in Iraq, after being briefed on the situation and the current analysis in Iraq.

17. Operation "Defence Shield" in April 2002.

18. The introduction of precision-guided munitions technology into modern warfare, and the need to supply "targeting intelligence" to operating forces, has a similar effect on the relationship between commanders and intelligence officers in classic

war (between armies) as well. For that matter, see I. Ben-Israel, "The Revolution in Military Affairs and the Operation in Iraq," in *After the War in Iraq: Defining the New Strategic Order,* ed. S. Feldman (Brighton, UK: Sussex Academic Press, 2003), 55–74.

19. See Paul Feyerabend, *Against Method* (London: Verso, 1975).

20. This appears in a letter to the author. See I. Ben Israel, "Philosophy and Methodology of Military Intelligence—Correspondence with Paul Feyerabend," *Philosophia* 28, nos. 1–4 (June 2001): 71–102.

21. Francis Crick worked under R.V. Jones in the British Air-Force Intelligence during WW II and later on discovered the structure of DNA with James Watson.

CHAPTER 12

1. By "intelligence and security community" I am referring here not just to the secret and semisecret agencies, but also the police and the Special Branch of the police. The focus here, however, is on the former. By "systems" I mean the way they organize themselves and their relationship with each other as well as their relationship with other communities who are engaged in the same fight for freedom.

2. *Inquiry into Intelligence, Assessment and Advice prior to the Terrorist Bombings on Bali 12 October 2002,* Cm 5724, December 2002, paras. 20–35.

3. *The Butler Report,* especially 141–48.

4. *The Butler Report,* 142.

5. Security source, March 16, 2006.

6. Dame Eliza Manningham-Buller, "The International Terrorist Threat and the Dilemmas in Countering It," www.mi5.gov.uk/output/Page387.html.

7. See *The Times Higher Education Supplement,* September 23, 2005 and October 14, 2005; *The Financial Times,* September 27, 2005.

8. See Glees et al., *The Open Side of Secrecy.*

9. Sir David Veness and Dame Eliza Manningham-Buller, speaking at Demos, February 22, 2005 and June 20, 2005, respectively.

10. This comment was made in the media on November 18, 2005.

11. This point was made at Oxford Intelligence Group, Nuffield College, December 5, 2005.

12. *The Sunday Times,* November 13, 2005; and security source, November 29, 2005.

13. This speech was given February 13, 2006.

14. http://thescotsman.scotsman.com/index.cfm?id=2104522005.

15. Security source, November 29, 2005.

16. I was the commentator in question. *The Scotsman,* October 18, 2005, http://thescotsman.scotsman.com/index.cfm?id=2104522005.

17. Interviewed on BBC Radio Four's *Today* program on November 9, 2005.

18. *The Guardian,* July 10, 2004.

19. *Butler Report.*

20. Sir David Omand was interviewed for the record in London on September 14, 2005.

21. Security source, December 1, 2005.

22. Security source, November 29, 2005.

23. Confidential information, December 7, 2005.

24. Glees et. al., *The Open Side of Secrecy*, 91.

25. *New Frontiers of Intelligence Analysis*, papers presented at the conference on "New Frontiers of Intelligence Analysis: Shared Threats, Diverse Perspectives, New Communities," Rome, Italy, March 31—April 2, 2004, published by Global Futures Partnership of the Sherman Kent School for Intelligence Analysis, the Link Campus University of Malta, Gino Germani Center for Comparative Studies of Modernization and Development, pp. 81–82. I am indebted to Hans-Josef Beth of the German Embassy, London, for alerting me to this important report.

26. Glees et al., *The Open Side of Secrecy*, 82, 85.

27. Ibid., 83.

28. Ibid., 85.

29. Confidential information from a security source, November 29, 2005.

30. Confidential information from a former Austrian Government Minister, Lisbon, September 2005.

31. The EU, it points out, agrees upon legislation and facilitates practical co-operation between Member States' police forces and judicial systems in order to disrupt the activities of criminal gangs, bring criminals to justice, and build an effective, fair, and managed asylum and immigration system. In the civil law field it brings in measures to make access to justice across borders easier and more economical, giving people confidence in the ability of courts throughout the EU to deliver justice.

32. *The Times*, October 7, 2005.

33. *The Butler Report*, 102–3; also Philip H.J. Davies, "Collection and Analysis on Iraq: A Critical Look at Britain's Spy Machinery," *Studies in Intelligence* 49, no. 4 (December 2005): 41–54.

34. *The Butler Report*, 9, 112, 114.

35. Ibid., 114.

36. "Ministers are not helped by assessments which are expressed in language of 'on the one hand' and 'on the other' and which thus leave the reader with no conclusion...We conclude that the JIC has been right not to reach a judgement when the evidence is insubstantial. We believe that the JIC should, where there are significant limitations in the intelligence, state these clearly alongside its Key Judgements."

37. *The Butler Report*, 145.

CHAPTER 13

1. The research for this chapter was supported by awards from the Leverhulme Trust and the British Academy which are gratefully acknowledged. It has benefited from conversations with officials in Europe and the United States. The author would also like to thank Matthew Aid, Paul Lashmar, Martin Rudner, and Cees Wiebes for information and suggestions. All errors remain the responsibility of the author.

2. Sheila Kerr, "The Debate on US Post–Cold War Intelligence: One More New Botched Beginning?," *Defense Analysis* 10, no. 3 (1994): 323–50.

3. The literature on open-source intelligence is large and cannot be surveyed within this short chapter, but see, in particular, Stevyn Gibson's important essay, "In the Eye of the Perfect Storm: Re-imagining, Reforming and Refocusing

Intelligence for Risk, Globalisation and Changing Societal Expectation," *Risk Management* 7, no. 4 (2005): 23–41. The leading advocate of open source is Robert Steele; see, for example, R.D. Steele, *On Intelligence: Spies and Secrecy in an Open World* (Oakland, CA: OSS International Press, 2001).

4. David Leppard, "MI5 Wants 800 More Spies to Take on Islamic Threat," *Sunday Times,* November 13, 2005.

5. Scott Shane, "Official Reveals Budget for US Intelligence," *New York Times,* November 8, 2005.

6. Azar Gat, *The Development of Military Thought: The Nineteenth Century* (Oxford: Clarendon Press, 2001), 236–37; see also Hans Morgenthau, *Politics Among Nations: The Struggle for Power and Peace* (New York: Knopf, 1948; 6th ed., 1985), 379; J.F.C. Fuller made similar observations in *Armament and History* (New York: Scribner's, 1945).

7. Robert Fox, "GWOT is History. Now for SAVE," *New Statesman,* August 8, 2005.

8. One of the most elaborate exercises in medium-term future prediction using nonofficials has been the U.S. National Intelligence Council's *Mapping the Global Future: Report of the National Intelligence Council's 2020 Project* (Honolulu, HI: University Press of the Pacific, 2005).

9. Robert Jervis, "An Interim Assessment of 9/11: What Has Changed and What Has Not?," *Political Science Quarterly* 117, no. 1 (2002): 37–54.

10. Thomas Copeland, "Is the New Terrorism Really New? An Analysis of the New Paradigm for Terrorism," *Journal of Conflict Studies* XXI, no. 2 (2001): 91–105; Alexander Spencer, *Questioning the Concept of "New Terrorism,"* Peace Conflict & Development, no. 8 (January 2006): 1–33, www.peacestudiesjournal.org.uk.

11. A. Cronin, "Behind the Curve: Globalization and International Terrorism," *International Security* 27, no. 3 (2002/03): 30–58.

12. Martin Wolf, *Why Globalization Works* (New Haven, CT: Yale, 2004).

13. M. Pugh and Neil Cooper, *War Economies in a Regional Context: Challenges of Transformation* (Boulder, CO: Lynne Rienner, 2004).

14. John Brennan, "Is This Intelligence? We Added Players, but Lost Control of the Ball," *Washington Post,* November 20, 2005. On crime and war, see J.A. Scholte, *Globalization: A Critical Introduction* (London: Palgrave, 2006), 284–85.

15. Jennifer Brower and Peter Chalk, *The Global Threat of New and Reemerging Infectious Diseases: Reconciling U.S. National Security and Public Health Policy* (RAND Science and Technology, 2003); George Armelagos, "The Viral Superhighway," *The Sciences* 38, no. 1 (1998): 24–29.

16. Ian Forbes, "Making a Crisis out of a Drama: The Political Analysis of BSE Policy-Making in the UK," *Political Studies* 52, no. 2 (2004): 342–57.

17. Although extensive plans were drawn up for the possibility of a SARS outbreak in the United Kingdom in 2003, the intelligence aspect was not developed. See Health Protection Agency, "Interim Contingency Plan For Severe Acute Respiratory Syndrome (SARS)," Interim—December 2003, http://www.hpa.org.uk/infections/topics_az/SARS/pdfs/SARSContingencyDec03.pdf.

18. Donald H. Henderson, "Public Health Preparedness," discussed in American Association for the Advancement of Science press release, "Report Considers Role of

Science in a World Made Vulnerable by Terrorism," http://www.aaas.org/news/releases/2002/0624terrorism.shtml.

19. D.P. Fidler, "The Globalization of Public Health: The First 100 Years of International Health Diplomacy," *Bulletin of the World Health Organisation* 79, no. 9 (2001): 842–49.

20. Christopher Lee, "Secrecy Is Infectious: Bill Would Shield Biomedical Research," *Washington Post,* November 14, 2005.

21. National Intelligence Council NIE 99-17D, *The Global Infectious Disease Threat and Its Implications for the United States* (Washington, DC: NIE Publication, 2000).

22. Institute of Medicine, *America's Vital Interest in Global Health* (Washington, DC: National Academy Press, 1997).

23. At present WHO coordinates a Global Outbreak Alert and Response network, but its range of intelligence partners is limited and its resources are thin.

24. See Laurie Garrett, *The Coming Plague* (New York: Penguin Books, 1994).

25. For a review of current intelligence sharing, see Stephen Lander, "International Intelligence Co-operation: An Inside Perspective," *Cambridge Review of International Affairs* 17, no. 3 (2004): 481–93.

26. During the Bosnian conflict the British dominated ACE Rapid Reaction Corps headquarters at Iliza hosted NICs belonging to the United States, United Kingdom, Canada, France, Germany, Belgium, Italy, Greece, Denmark, Norway, and Sweden. Larry K. Wentz, ed., *Lessons From Bosnia: The IFOR Experience* (Washington, DC: NDU Press, 1997), chap. 4.

27. On agencies and Whitehall, see Oliver James, *The Executive Agency Revolution in Whitehall: Public Interest versus Bureau-shaping Perspectives* (London: Palgrave-Macmillan, 2002).

28. Bruce D. Berkowitz and Allan E. Goodman, *Best Truth: Intelligence in the Information Age* (New Haven, CT: Yale University Press, 2000).

29. Robert Baer, *See No Evil: The True Story of a Ground Soldier in the CIA's War on Terrorism* (New York: Random House, 2002).

30. In 2005 many academics were recruited to undertake a "lessons learned" review of how information warfare experiences from the Cold War might be applied to current challenges.

31. The author is a member of the World University Network Group on Terrorism.

32. Scott Shane, "A T-Shirt-and-Dagger Operation," *New York Times,* November 13, 2005.

33. "ODNI Announces Establishment of Open Source Center," ODNI News Release No. 6-05, November 8, 2005, http://www.dni.gov/press_releases/20051108_release.htm (accessed August 25, 2006).

34. The National Intelligence Center's work on 2020 Future Vision suggests that the latent American ability to harness the possibilities of nonofficial engagement is impressive; see note 8.

35. Robin Winks, *Cloak and Gown: Scholars in America's Secret War* (London: Collins Harvill, 1987).

36. Bruce Hoffman, "Responding to Terrorism Across the Technological Spectrum," RAND P7874, 1994.

37. The CIA sees it differently and published a study claiming to "reject the idea that the Intelligence Community ignored the impending collapse of communism and break-up of the Soviet Union." Benjamin B. Fischer, ed., *At Cold War's End: US Intelligence on the Soviet Union and Eastern Europe, 1989–1991* (Washington, DC: CIA History Staff, 1999).

38. Robert M. Gates, *From the Shadows: The Ultimate Insider's Story of Five President's and How They Won the Cold War* (New York; Simon and Schuster, 1996), 449.

39. Timothy Garton Ash, *The Polish Revolution: Solidarity* (London: Penguin, 1983, 1989).

40. While the track record of academics and journalists was better, it was still patchy. See Michael Cox, "The End of the Cold War and Why We Failed to Predict It, in *Rethinking the Cold War,* ed. A. Hunter (Philadelphia: Temple University Press, 1998), 157–74.

41. Apparently, Dutch intelligence in The Hague was among the most sceptical.

42. Glen Rangwala's material is archived at http://middleeastreference.org.uk/iraqweapons.html#about.

43. Richard J. Aldrich, "Whitehall and the Iraq War: The UK's Four Intelligence Enquiries," *Irish Studies in International Affairs* 16, no. 1 (2005), 73–88; Alex Danchev, "Story Development or Walter Mitty the Undefeated,' in *The Iraq War and Democratic Politics,* ed. Alex Danchev and John Macmillan (London: Routledge, 2005), 238–59.

44. HC 898, Lord Butler, *Review of Intelligence on Weapons of Mass Destruction* (London: TSO, 2004) 73; Ian Davis and Andreas Persbo, "After the Butler Report: Time to Take on the Group Think in Washington and London," *BASIC Papers: Occasional Papers in International Security* no. 46 (July 2004), http://www.basicint.org/pubs/Papers/BP46.htm.

45. Space does not permit the exploration of management issues here; however, one attractive model is the U.S. Defense Science Board, which has performed impressively over the last three years and consists mostly of "outsiders."

Index

Note on Arabic names: The prefixes "al-" and "el-" have been retained but ignored when the entry is alphabetized, so that al-Zarqawi is listed under Z. "Bin" is treated as a primary element and appears under B.

About the Contributors

RICHARD J. ALDRICH is Head of the School of Politics and International Relations at the University of Nottingham and also Deputy Director (South Asia) of the Institute of Asia-Pacific Studies. His most recent publications include *Witness to War* (2004) and *The Faraway War* (2005). During 2005 he was a Leverhulme Research Fellow, and his current work includes projects on globalization, on communications security, and on the role of intelligence in state formation.

ISAAC BEN-ISRAEL is a Professor at the Cohen Institute for the History and Philosophy of Sciences and Ideas and at the School of Government and Policy at Tel-Aviv University. He is Head of the Program for Security Studies and Head of Tel-Aviv Workshop for Science Technology and Security. He is also Chairman of the Israel Space Agency. In 2003 he founded RAY-TOP Ltd., which advises the defense industry on technological and strategic issues. Before pursuing an academic career, he was a Major General and Director of Defence R&D Directorate in the Israeli Ministry of Defence. He previously headed the Israeli Air Force Intelligence Analysis and Assessment Division and Operations Research Branch. He has received several awards for developing weapon systems. His book *Dialogues on Science and Military Intelligence* (Tel Aviv: 1989) won the Itzhak-Sade Award for Military Literature.

JACK CARAVELLI is a Senior Visiting Fellow at the U.K. Defence Academy and Visiting Professor at Cranfield University. He was Deputy Assistant Secretary at the U.S. Department of Energy (2000–2003) where he directed the department's largest threat reduction program. From 1996 to 2000 he served on the White House National Security Council where he was the President's principal adviser for nonproliferation policies and programs involving Russia and the Middle East. He began his governmental career in 1982 at the Central Intelligence Agency, where he served in various managerial, analytic, and staff positions.

ALEX DANCHEV is Professor of International Relations at the University of Nottingham. He has held Fellowships at St Antony's College, Oxford; King's College, London; and the Woodrow Wilson Center for Scholars in Washington, D.C. His most recent books are *Georges Braque,* a biography, and *The Iraq War and Democratic Politics,* an edited collection.

ANTHONY GLEES is Professor of Politics at Brunel University and Director of the Centre for Intelligence and Security Studies. He has a long-standing concern with intelligence and policy making and also with political subversion and has published widely on these topics. His most recent books are *The Stasi Files,* on East Germany's U.K. intelligence operations (2003) and *Spinning the Spies,* written together with Philip H.J. Davies (2004), on Tony Blair's management of intelligence and security issues in the run-up to the invasion of Iraq. His report on U.K. campus extremism, *When Students Turn to Terror,* written together with Chris Pope, was published by the Social Affairs Unit in October 2005. He is currently completing a study of the British Parliamentary Intelligence and Security Committee with John Morrison and Philip H.J. Davies.

CHRISTIAN HEYER is Deputy Head of the Secretariat of the Parliamentary Control Panel for the Oversight of the Intelligence Services of the German Bundestag and a lecturer on Constitutional Law and Political Science at the University of Applied Science for Economics and Technology in Berlin. He is a lawyer by training. He conducted research at the Institute for Criminology of the University of Bonn and worked for a Member of the Bundestag before joining the Bundestag administration in 1996. He has extensive experience dealing with parliamentary oversight of intelligence work in a major European country.

SEBASTIAN HULUBAN is a doctoral candidate in Modern History at the University of Bucharest with a dissertation on the construction of multinational military loyalties. He was educated at the Eastern Illinois University and the Central European University at Budapest. He has also served as an Advisor on Strategic Affairs and International Security to the State Secretary for Defence Policy, Romanian Ministry of Defence (2004–2005).

LOCH K. JOHNSON is Regents Professor of Political Science at the University of Georgia. He is editor of the journal *Intelligence and National Security* and has written and edited numerous books. His best-known books on U.S. intelligence include *Bombs, Bugs, Drugs, and Thugs: Intelligence and America's Quest for Security* (2000), *Secret Agencies: US Intelligence in a Hostile*

World (1996), *America's Secret Power: The CIA in a Democratic Society* (1989), and *Season of Inquiry* (1985). He had previously served as Special Assistant to the Chair of the Senate Select Committee House Subcommittee on Intelligence Oversight from 1975 to 1976, Staff Director of the House Subcommittee on Intelligence Oversight from 1977 to 1979, and Assistant to Chairman Les Aspin, Aspin-Brown Commission on Intelligence (1995–1996).

GEORGE MAIOR is a member of the Romanian Senate and President of its Defence Committee. He was Deputy Minister for Defence from 2000 to 2004, following seven years of service at the Ministry for Foreign Affairs. He took his LL.M. in International and Comparative Law at George Washington University in 1992, and his Ph.D. in International Relations in Romania in 1997.

JOHN N.L. MORRISON is a Senior Fellow at the Centre for Intelligence and Security Studies, Brunel University. Before joining academia he had a distinguished career with British Intelligence. He joined the British Defence Intelligence Staff (DIS) in 1967 as a desk analyst. His DIS career culminated with his appointment as its senior civilian intelligence professional (2-star equivalent), serving four years as Deputy Chief of Defence Intelligence and Head of the Defence Intelligence Analysis Staff. During this period he represented the Ministry of Defence (MoD) and DIS as a member of the Joint Intelligence Committee, U.K. representative to the NATO Intelligence Board and Head of Profession for MoD Intelligence Analyst classes. On electing to take early retirement in 1999 he was selected by the parliamentary Intelligence and Security Committee to be its first Investigator, a position he held until 2004.

RICHARD G. STEARNS is a United States District Court Judge for the District of Massachusetts. He was educated at Stanford University, Balliol College at Oxford University, and Harvard University. He had served as an Assistant U.S. Attorney and as Associate Justice, Superior Court of Massachusetts before assuming his current position upon nomination by President Clinton in 1994. In addition to his judicial duties, he serves as a rule of advisor to the Department of Defense's international counterproliferation program, which is presently active in 27 countries in eastern and southern Europe and central Asia. He has extensive experience dealing with cases involving terrorism and espionage and is the author of *Massachusetts Criminal Law: A Prosecutor's Guide* (25th ed., 2005).

STEVE TSANG is Louis Cha Fellow and University Reader in Politics at St Antony's College, University of Oxford, where he is also Director of the Pluscarden Programme for the Study of Global Terrorism and Intelligence.

He had previously served as Dean of St Antony's College and as Director of the Asian Studies Centre. His main publications include 11 books, of which four are single-authored scholarly works. His two most recent books are the monograph *The Cold War's Odd Couple: The Unintended Partnership between the United Kingdom and the Republic of China, 1950–1958* (London: I.B. Tauris, 2006) and the edited volume *If China Attacks Taiwan: Military Strategy, Politics and Economics* (London & New York: Routledge, 2006).

MARK URBAN is the Diplomatic Editor of the BBC's flagship news analysis program *Newsnight* and a former defense correspondent for the *Independent,* a leading British newspaper. He is the author of several books, including *Generals: Ten British Commanders Who Shaped the World* (London: Faber and Faber, 2005), *The Man Who Broke Napoleon's Codes* (London: Faber & Faber, 2001), *Big Boys' Rules: SAS and the Secret Struggle Against the IRA* (London: Faber & Faber, 2001), and *UK Eyes Alpha: The Inside Story of British Intelligence* (London: Faber and Faber, 1997).

PETER WILSON is a director of Libra Advisory Group Ltd., which specializes in security strategy and reform for governments, donors, and multinational corporations. His clients include the British Government's Security Sector Development Advisory Team, where he is Intelligence & Security Adviser. He has worked on reform of intelligence and national security structures in a range of developing and postconflict countries including Ethiopia, Indonesia, Kosovo, and Sierra Leone. He was educated at Oxford University and INSEAD and is the co-author (with Craig Wilson) of *Make Poverty Business* (London: Greenleaf, 2006).